"*True Betrayal* is one of the best guides I've encountered on navigating betrayal's pain. It offers down-to-earth strategies for seeking answers from the person who hurt you, clarifies how much to trust a spouse going forward, and presents the often-overlooked options you have after being betrayed. *True Betrayal* is an indispensable resource for clarity, answers, healing, and renewed strength."

Sam Hodges IV, President, DivorceCare

"When a person is betrayed by their spouse, they incur overwhelming hardship. They need attainable, practical guidance to navigate the complexities of their suffering. Brad Hambrick facilitates the healing process with insight, wisdom, concision, and compassion. The G4 model gives individuals flexibility to process their pain with a group or through individual counseling. These options will serve a variety of needs!"

Jenny Solomon, Cofounder, Solomon Soul Care and the Sentinel Institute; author of *Reclaim Your Marriage*

"You never asked for unfaithfulness to be the darkest valley in your marriage. But this is where you find yourself. You will face a myriad of weighty emotions and difficult decisions. Hambrick deftly pastors you through these emotions and decisions while honoring you. Slowly ponder his counsel. Take it to heart at each step in this arduous journey."

Aaron Sironi, Faculty and Counselor, Christian Counseling & Educational Foundation (CCEF)

"I know of no other resource that offers the kind of compassion and wisdom so desperately needed by a betrayed spouse. Going through the process outlined in *True Betrayal* will help you find your footing as you look to honor God with your decisions. Here is real help that can bring the healing your soul is longing to experience."

Bob Lepine, Pastor, Redeemer Community Church of Little Rock; author of *Build A Stronger Marriage*

"I have had the honor of walking through this curriculum countless times one-on-one with ladies for eleven years and have been leading in group settings weekly for the past seven years. Brad puts words to the feelings we have all had during the healing process. This curriculum would be beneficial for anyone needing help working through the deep wounds caused by their spouse's sexual sin."

Andrea Silvey, G4 leader, The Summit Church,
Raleigh-Durham, NC

"In *True Betrayal,* Brad Hambrick provides wisdom and pastoral insight to help you care for the suffering while also carefully addressing the sin of marital infidelity. This guide offers practical, Scripture-based steps to encourage hope and healing for marriages experiencing the pain of sexual betrayal. I highly recommend it!"

Shauna Van Dyke, Executive Director, The Association
of Biblical Counselors (ABC); founder & biblical counselor,
Truth Renewed Ministries

"We found the *False Love* and *True Betrayal* group curriculum to be extremely beneficial for both the betrayed and the betrayer. Brad Hambrick's unique approach takes both spouses on an individual journey to self-awareness and healing. If you're wondering, *How did we get here?* and *What do we do next?*, this may be just what God has in mind for you. Healing is possible and worth every effort it takes."

Gary and Mona Shriver, Cofounders, Hope & Healing
Ministries, Inc.; coauthors of *Unfaithful: Hope & Healing
after Infidelity*

TRUE BETRAYAL

9 STEPS FOR PROCESSING YOUR SPOUSE'S INFIDELITY

Brad Hambrick

New
Growth
Press

newgrowthpress.com

New Growth Press, Greensboro, NC 27401
newgrowthpress.com
Copyright © 2025 by Brad Hambrick

Cover Design: Faceout Books, faceoutstudio.com
Interior Typesetting and Ebook: Lisa Parnell, lparnellbookservices.com

ISBN: 978-1-64507-505-9 (paperback)
ISBN: 978-1-64507-506-6 (ebook)

Library of Congress Cataloging-in-Publication Data on file

Printed in the United States of America

29 28 27 26 25   1 2 3 4 5

Contents

What Is G4?

G4 is a peer support and recovery group ministry (e.g., like AA or Celebrate Recovery) built on two 9-step models that allow individuals to invest a season of their life to overcoming a life-dominating struggle of sin or suffering. G4 provides a safe environment where members learn insights and skills that will allow them to engage in biblical community more fully.

WHY THE NAME "G4"?

"G" is for gospel-centered groups. Rather than making an issue, struggle, or sin the centerpiece of our groups, we strive to make the gospel of Christ the core of all our groups. *Our identity is not found in an issue but in an individual—the person of Christ.*

"4" designates the four types of groups that will be featured:

1. **Recovery:** Groups for those struggling with a life-dominating sin, addiction, or traumatic life event
2. **Support:** Groups for those needing encouragement and support during a period of suffering or hardship
3. **Therapeutic Educational:** Groups for those needing information or resources about a specific life issue
4. **Process:** Groups for those needing help processing problematic emotions or multiple life stressors

SEVEN CORE VALUES OF A G4 GROUP

G4 seeks to uphold seven core values that help the ministry—both leaders and participants—care for and honor one another as they seek wholeness and holiness in their area of life struggle.

1. Bible-based and gospel-centered
2. Recognize the difference between sin and suffering
3. Built on honesty and transparency
4. Uphold confidentiality
5. Avoid struggle-based identity
6. Blend discipleship, accountability, and a guided process
7. Transitions into larger small group ministry

SUBJECT-SPECIFIC CURRICULUM AVAILABLE

G4 has ten subject-specific curricula available. Each uses one of the 9-step models, either sin or suffering, to walk through a process for finding wholeness and holiness for that life struggle.

Sin/Responsibility-Based Curriculum

1. *False Love* (sexual addiction and adultery)—bradhambrick.com/falselove
2. *Gaining a Healthy Relationship with Food*—bradhambrick.com/healthy
3. *Overcoming Anger*—bradhambrick.com/anger
4. *Substance Abuse*—bradhambrick.com/addiction
5. *Anxiety/Depression**—bradhambrick.com/anxiety

Suffering-Based Curriculum

1. *Anxiety/Depression*—bradhambrick.com/depression
2. *Navigating Destructive Relationships*—bradhambrick.com/destructive
3. *Taking the Journey of Grief with Hope*—bradhambrick.com/grief
4. *Trauma*—bradhambrick.com/trauma
5. *True Betraya*l (processing a spouse's sexual addiction or adultery)—bradhambrick.com/truebetrayal

---

* Anxiety/Depression are dealt with together so that each can be addressed from both a responsibility and suffering paradigm.

The 9 Steps of G4

G4 does not believe there is a one-size-fits-all solution to the struggles of life. Neither do we believe there is any magic in these sets of 9 steps. However, *we do believe that these steps capture the major movements of the gospel in the life of an individual.* We also believe that God transforms lives through the gospel as he gives us a new heart.

In G4 groups, we attempt to walk through the gospel in slow motion with a concentrated focus upon particular life-dominating struggles. *We do this in a setting of transparent community because we believe God changes people in relationships.*

We believe that the gospel speaks to both **sin**—*things we do wrong—and* **suffering**—*painful experiences for which we are not responsible—to bring forgiveness, comfort, and hope.* We also believe that every person is both a sinner and a sufferer. However, we believe the gospel is best understood and applied when we consider how the gospel relates to the nature of our struggle. The nine steps below are those used by G4 groups to address struggles of sin and suffering.

SIN-BASED GROUPS	SUFFERING-BASED GROUPS
STEP 1. ADMIT I have a struggle I cannot overcome without God.	STEP 1. PREPARE yourself physically, emotionally, and spiritually to face your suffering.
STEP 2. ACKNOWLEDGE the breadth and impact of my sin.	STEP 2. ACKNOWLEDGE the specific history and realness of my suffering.
STEP 3. UNDERSTAND the origin, motive, and history of my sin.	STEP 3. UNDERSTAND the impact of my suffering.

SIN-BASED GROUPS	SUFFERING-BASED GROUPS
STEP 4. REPENT TO GOD for how my sin replaced and misrepresented him.	STEP 4. LEARN MY SUFFERING STORY which I use to make sense of my experience.
STEP 5. CONFESS TO THOSE AFFECTED for harm done and seek to make amends.	STEP 5. MOURN the wrongness of what happened and receive God's comfort.
STEP 6. RESTRUCTURE MY LIFE to rely on God's grace and Word to transform my life.	STEP 6. LEARN MY GOSPEL STORY by which God gives meaning to my experience.
STEP 7. IMPLEMENT the new structure pervasively with humility and flexibility.	STEP 7. IDENTIFY GOALS that allow me to combat the impact of my suffering.
STEP 8. PERSEVERE in the new life and identity to which God has called me.	STEP 8. PERSEVERE in the new life and identity to which God has called me.
STEP 9. STEWARD all of my life for God's glory.	STEP 9. STEWARD all of my life for God's glory.

How to Use a G4 Series Book

Thank you for picking up a G4 resource. Books in the G4 series are a bit different from most books. Most books seek to *educate you on a subject*. By contrast, books in the G4 series seek to help you *navigate a journey through a life struggle*. With most books, if you understand the content, you are ready to move to the next chapter. But in the G4 series, the goal is implementation more than education. You need to have "completed" a step, not just have "understood" its content.

For this reason, it is recommended that you work through this material with the help of others. The most common way that people work through this material is in G4 group, a lay-led counseling group hosted at a local church. You could also work through this material with a counselor or friend who is serving as a mentor. But because G4 materials take you through some of the hardest challenges in life, we strongly encourage you to enlist support as you traverse these pages.

G4 series books are the kind of literature you want to read with a pen, notebook, and Bible close at hand. This book will ask you many questions—the kind of questions that only you know the answer to, and the kind of questions that require reflection to answer. Take your time. The more honest you are, the more this book will benefit you.

This book also contains frequent devotionals that invite you to reflect on passages of Scripture. As you work through this book, we want you to cultivate the habit of daily Bible study to find hope, direction, and meaning. Keep this book with your Bible, and expect to move back and forth between the two as you read.

Often our hardships tempt us to rush, both mentally and emotionally. That means you may initially get anxious or frustrated as you work through this material. That's normal. Slowing down to reflect is difficult when life is messy. But it's worth it. Be honest about any impatience that emerges on this journey. Outside of the Bible, the best tool for change is simple honesty with people who care about you.

If you are not familiar with the 9 steps of G4, it is recommended that you review all the steps before you begin. Get the big picture of why this journey is laid out the way it is before you start working through the details of your struggle. You can find a 15-minute video that overviews these 9 steps at the following websites:

- bradhambrick.com/g4sin for our sin/responsibility-based curriculum. These steps are used when a life struggle emerges from our choices, beliefs, and values.
- bradhambrick.com/g4suffering for our suffering-based curriculum. These steps are used when a life struggle emerges from something we have little or no control over. This *True Betrayal* book is built around the 9 steps for suffering struggles.

The *True Betrayal* book is built around the 9 steps for suffering-based struggles. Too often we engage material like this through the lens of our fears and failures. As we read, we process each paragraph hearing our own self-doubt, the rejection of those we've failed, or the tone of those who have berated us for failing. This is especially true when life is hard. For this reason, we provide a free video teaching for each part of each step at **bradhambrick.com/truebetrayal**. Watching these videos before you begin each step will help you engage this material in the redemptive tone in which it was written. Allow these videos to offset the tendency to see things through the lens of your fears or failures and to enhance your learning experience as you take this journey.

With G4 resources, we encourage you to use a consistent cycle to maximize your growth:

1. WATCH the video—use your phone's camera to scan the QR code to find each video and hear the step in a redemptive tone.
2. READ the step—read the material to gain a clearer understanding of what you need to achieve in this step.
3. WORK the step—do the exercises and Bible studies to make and reinforce the desired progress.
4. DISCUSS the step—share what you're learning and how you're growing with a G4 group. Learn from their experiences and how they navigated challenges like your own.

5. CELEBRATE progress—celebrate the progress you made and receive encouragement when progress is slow or you experience setback.

6. ADVANCE to the next step—move forward *after* you complete each step and surrender more of your life to God.

The graphic below is meant to provide a visual for this cycle. Most steps are broken into parts, so it is easier (not easy) to make consistent progress on your G4 journey. It is recommended that you use this cycle for each part of each step.

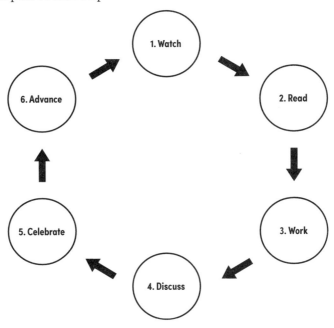

Figure 1. The Process of Working Through a G4 Curriculum

G4 series workbooks take the pace of Aesop's tortoise rather than the rabbit. Keep this in mind: Be content with progress and don't get impatient with your pace. Your goal is to finish the race. Consistent progress is the best way to ensure this happens and that the change you achieve is lasting. A journey this important is worth the time you invest to ensure you complete it well.

STEP 1
PREPARE yourself physically, emotionally, and spiritually to face your suffering.

At the end of this step, I want to be able to say . . .

"Living in denial about my spouse's sin would be more costly than anything God would take me through in the restoration process. It is good of God to help me accurately see what is happening in my life, even if seeing it is painful. Therefore, I will put myself in the best possible physical, emotional, relational, and spiritual position to face my suffering."

STEP 1

PART ONE

DON'T HURRY; DON'T GIVE UP

The video for this part of Step 1 can be found at: bradhambrick.com/truebetrayal1p1.

This was never a subject you wanted to study. It was never a challenge you thought you'd face. The idea of starting this journey may feel suffocating. Chances are, you've recently heard yourself think or say things like this:

- "I can't believe I'm reading this. I want to vomit . . . throw this book across the room . . . scream!"
- "But sometimes I don't feel anything. I just sit there. I'm waiting for the pain to return."
- "This can't be true. There must be another explanation. My spouse wouldn't . . .'"
- "I hate you [spouse] because I loved you and that's what let you hurt me like this. I was a fool!"
- "We'll never be like we were before. I'll never have innocent trust again."
- "What else don't I know? Who else knows? It could happen again."
- "I don't want to share. Don't want to be 'one of many.' Thinking of you with someone else makes me feel desperate, furious, stupid, expendable, etc."
- "Where are you? What are you doing? Who are you with?"
- "This would've been preventable if we'd never married, but then I'd lose all our memories together."
- "Finally, something explains all the weirdness and distance that was going on."

- "I imagine every person I see knows. I feel exposed."
- "Days feel like weeks; weeks feel like months. When will this agony ever be over?"
- "How many times can I replay events, both real and imagined, in my mind?"
- "How do I know when I know the truth?"
- "I feel like last year's model spouse. You had me and wanted more/better?"
- "Every statement gets met with a question now. Nothing 'just is' anymore."
- "I am beginning to realize that no matter what I do or ask, it won't unwrite history."

One wife whose husband had been unfaithful described her experience like this:

> I heard Gary come in, and I heard the boys greet their father. Normal sounds. But this wasn't a normal household. Nothing was normal anymore. I wasn't normal. All I could do was cry and ask questions. I was obsessed. Everyone would be fine if I could just move on. They could all just live their normal little lives with all the other normal people . . . Nothing surprised me anymore. Except me—I surprised me all the time. —Gary and Mona Shriver[1]

If the statements above sound like you, you're starting the right journey. As much as it may feel like it, these thoughts aren't a reason to give up. As a secular researcher on sexual addiction reminds us, ending your marriage won't remove the pain and might create more.

> To abandon the relationship at this point, however, is akin to having a broken bone and not setting it. Broken relationships require attention as well. Failure to attend to this self-care can be crippling to future relationships. And if there are children involved, problems are inevitable. Whether you go or stay, it makes no difference. Mending will be required. And as painful as it is, there will be less pain and more effective healing when the fracture is dealt with as soon as possible. . . . The great irony of using divorce as a way to escape the inevitable

grief is that it creates more. . . . You'll likely feel pressure from others to end your relationship as though that would end the emotional turmoil you're in. . . . Most therapists suggest you make no significant life changes during the first year of recovery. —Stefanie Carnes[2]

Note: In several places in *True Betrayal* we will reference literature that addresses sexual addiction. This does not assume that your spouse is a sex addict. But many of the books cited in *True Betrayal* come from counselors who have extensive experience working with marriages impacted by habitual sin and those authors sometimes use the term *sexual addiction.*

> Please don't mistake for guilt the sense of regret or angst you feel over making difficult choices.

You are processing a lot in these early pages. As you do, here are a few things to help you get your bearings on this journey:

1. **You will make every decision.** You are facing many decisions that were forced upon you by your spouse's actions. As Dr. Carnes indicated, many people will have opinions about what you should or shouldn't do. *True Betrayal* won't try to tell you what to do. It will try to equip you to make informed decisions that honor your faith, represent your values, and prioritize the key relationships in your life.

2. **Work at your own pace.** In G4 groups, each participant works at their own pace. If you get overwhelmed and need to take a break, please do so. G4 is not a race. You're not competing with anyone. Unless your safety is threatened, please take the time you need.

3. **Good choices won't be easy choices.** Getting good advice (content of this curriculum) and social support (G4 group) won't make healthy choices easy choices. You will likely still feel torn. Please don't mistake for guilt the sense of regret or angst you feel over making difficult choices. Just because the best available choice is sometimes hard doesn't make it a bad or wrong choice.

▶ **Reflection:*** How do you feel reading these three guiding principles? This is an important and often neglected question. Allow yourself to be human on this journey. Don't expect yourself to be a superhero. You are not just a spouse, parent, or decision-maker. You are a person, and this journey is hard.

With those foundational principles in place, we are ready to explore the first part of Step 1. We'll try to avoid the twin pitfalls of the early stage of this journey: (a) rushing ourselves into making important decisions, and (b) surrendering to the idea that nothing we do matters.

DON'T HURRY; DON'T GIVE UP

The news of your spouse's sexual sin can feel like a siren calling for intense, immediate action. When something BIG happens, it is natural to think we should have a big and immediate response. That instinct is common and understandable, but we quickly realize we don't have enough information to make big, decisive decisions. At this point in our journey, we don't know what we know; meaning that we don't know if the information we currently have is the truth, the whole truth, and nothing but the truth. We don't know (i.e., have certainty about) what we think we know (i.e., the pieces of information we discovered or have been told).

With that in mind, let's consider three recommendations to help you pace yourself as you make decisions and interact with your spouse.

1. **Avoid threats.** It is very easy to get caught up in saying "what I ought to do" or "what I have every right to do." Anger is an appropriate response to betrayal. At its core, anger says two things: (a) this is wrong, and (b) it matters. Your anger toward your spouse's sin is right on both claims.

    However, in this caution against making threats, we are offering practical guidance rather than moral guidance. Statements like, "I ought to tell your whole family what you did," or "I have

---

* It is recommended that you keep a notebook or journal with this book. *True Betrayal* is not a book you just read. To be effective, you will need to study, reflect, journal, and discuss what you are learning. Give this journey the time it needs. Allow your journal to become a memoir of how God led you to arrive at important decisions. Writing out answers to the reflections and Bible studies will also help you participate more effectively in your G4 group meetings.

every right to divorce you and fleece you in the alimony," further destabilize an already precarious situation. Because of this, these statements do more harm than good to you. Whatever cathartic relief they provide, the net effect of these kinds of statements is that they make the uncertain path in front of you murkier rather than clearer.

It is better to say, "I am angry . . . I feel hurt . . . I don't feel safe with you . . . I don't believe anything you say . . . I don't know if I am willing to remain married," than to say, "What if I sleep with your best friend? Maybe I should send them some pictures . . . Don't think I haven't had chances to cheat. Maybe next time I'll take my chance . . . You were willing to risk our family for a sexual thrill, so don't think I'll let you see the kids if we divorce."

> At this point in our journey, we don't know what we know.

While simple truth doesn't seem to communicate all that you are experiencing, threats muddle rather than clarify what you are trying to communicate. The ensuing conversations become about who propositioned you, divorce details, or child visitation schedules rather than the impact of your spouse's sexual sin on you and the marriage. You walk away more convinced your spouse doesn't "get it," and your spouse walks away thinking about the content of the threats more than their own sin.

▶ **Read James 3:1–12.** Please don't read this passage as a rebuke or an admonition to keep quiet about your pain. It is neither. But James is telling us that our words matter because our words—like a rudder—impact the direction of our life. This devotion is merely a caution to remember that rash words in hard times can be like a match near gasoline. Yes, your spouse's sin spilled and spread the gasoline. But being careless with our words hurts everyone involved. Weighing your words is a way to reduce your own pain and, if you have children, the impact this season has on them. Your spouse has no right at this time to say, "Talk nicer," but your heavenly Father—out of concern for limiting the pain you experience—would encourage you to avoid temptation toward careless speech only meant to return pain to your spouse.

▶ **Note:** For guidance and talking with your children, please see Appendix B.

2. **Be patient making changes.** The revelation of sexual sin drops like a bomb. If we don't make significant decisions quickly, it can feel like we are condoning or ignoring the explosion. But as we've alluded to, it is likely that you currently have incomplete and inaccurate information. That should impact how you make decisions more than the alarms going off in your soul.

   When a child is lost in a public place, the first thing we tell them to do is "Stay put. Don't run and, thereby, get more confused. Instead, look for someone who can help; perhaps a police officer or employee." Similar advice applies after the discovery of sexual sin. We don't want to add to the disorientation. We want to find people who can help.

   Ill-informed, bold changes can add to the confusion in your life and marriage. If you later realize these initial changes were not a good fit, you may feel like you are "going back on your word" or are "being weak" if you reverse or alter them. The most important thing you can do as the dust settles is begin getting the information you need to make important decisions and find a support network. More will be said about this later in Step 1. The best initial action is to go from isolated to guided, rather than unaware to running alone in the darkness of partial or inaccurate information.

   Separation is one of the more difficult decisions. In the following situations, immediate separation is advisable:

   - If the sexual sin is against a child. In this case, your spouse's actions are criminal, not just immoral. Contacting Child Protective Services or law enforcement and taking the steps necessary to ensure the safety of children is your responsibility as a citizen. This responsibility supersedes any obligations you may feel as a spouse.
   - If your spouse has a history of being abusive and the affair is what has prompted you to look for help, it is likely that *Navigating Destructive Relationships* in the G4 series is the better resource for you and that it is wise for you to seek additional guidance on how to ensure your safety. If you

need someone to talk to about making this kind of plan, the National Domestic Violence Hotline is 1–800–799–7233 and has experienced helpers available 24/7.[3]

In Step 1, Part Two, we will provide guidance, realistic expectation, and wise nonnegotiables.

It is easy for separation to become a distraction (e.g., finding an apartment, deciding who pays what bills, setting time with kids, determining how often to talk on the phone). It introduces many changes that must be managed. Where criminal behavior or violence is involved, that distraction is more than warranted. When nonnegotiables are resisted, separation may be wise. However, using separation simply as a statement of the seriousness of the sin can be counterproductive.

The goal for decision-making in this early phase is to keep the main thing the main thing. Premature separation, verbally attacking the adultery partner, punitively telling your spouse's parents or friends, or having a revenge affair all accomplish one thing—replacing the original sexual sin as the focal point of change.

3. **Don't excuse or deny sin.** If the prior two points were about "don't hurry," this one is about "not giving up." Surrender can come in two varieties: denial or excuse. We want to avoid both.

Some of us are tempted to try to live in denial as if our spouse's sin never happened. Maybe we just don't think we can handle knowing the truth. Maybe we think that ignoring sin is the same thing as forgiveness. But we need to realize that to make the best quality choices we'll need to face the reality of what has happened.

▶ **Read John 8:32.** It is easy to doubt this passage after the revelation of your spouse's sexual sin. It is easy to think, *I know the truth now, but I don't feel free. I feel weighed down and trapped. Knowledge isn't power. It sapped my strength.* That may be accurate in the short-term. If it is, that isn't a sign of weakness on your part. It is a sign that you're human and you care deeply about your marriage. However, we need to realize ignorance is not freedom. Ignorance is fiction. Part of preparing yourself to face your suffering is realizing that knowing the truth is better than living in ignorance, even if the truth is more painful.

A second variety of surrender is explaining away your spouse's sin in amoral, blame-shifting, or fatalistic categories. There are many versions of this kind of thinking.

- *This is just what men/women do.*
- *I must not have met their needs, so this is my fault.*
- *Maybe if I had been willing to have more sex or if I were more romantic, this wouldn't have happened.*
- *Maybe I don't deserve to have a faithful spouse. After all, I'm not perfect either.*

▶ **Reflection:** What is your version of these kind of statements?

▶ **Read Galatians 5:14 and James 2:8.** In our current circumstance, it can be easy to read these verses defensively. We might ask, "Does loving my neighbor as myself mean I'm supposed to be prematurely forgiving or overlook this offense?" No. We need to see how loving my neighbor as myself is the antithesis of sexual sin. In sexual sin, people use their neighbor to love themselves so they can feel like a god—highly praised and affirmed. Your spouse's sexual sin was an affront to God and the foundational command to love one another. That is one reason it hurts so bad. Nothing about avoiding threats or being patient with change diminishes this. The reason that these advisements are given is to help ensure that the main thing causing the pain gets the full attention it merits.

Finishing Step 1, Part One

While it has only been a few pages, this first part of Step 1 can be exhausting. Your mind is doubtlessly swirling with *what if* and *what about* questions. That is normal. If we could resolve those questions in these few pages, your situation wouldn't warrant a study of this length and depth. Hopefully, you feel a bit of relief that we won't try to oversimplify your situation.

With that said, there is one final subject before we conclude Part One of Step 1. Our goal for this G4 study is to understand the entire process. Life may surprise you. But we want this study to be as predictable as possible. As we take this nine-step journey, it will unfold in three phases. The outline below helps you see the forest (three clusters) and the trees (nine steps):

- **Phase One: Steps 1–3**
  - » Establish an environment of stability as you understand how your spouse's sin has impacted you.
- **Phase Two: Steps 4–6**
  - » Articulate, grieve, and counter the destructive beliefs we often embrace during times of intense suffering.
- **Phase Three: Steps 7–9**
  - » Identify healthy ways to reengage with life, your spouse, and other relationships that counter the impact your spouse's sin has had on you.

Thank you for demonstrating courage and humility in your willingness to begin this journey.

G4 GROUP DISCUSSION: STEP 1, PART ONE

As you discuss this material in G4 group, these questions are meant to facilitate a more honest and beneficial dialogue about this material. Anyone is free to respond to whichever questions they choose.

Experienced Members

- What was most frustrating about this curriculum when you started your G4 journey?
- When did you wish you had adhered to the counsel of James 3 in the early stages of learning about your spouse's sexual sin?

New Members

- What brings you to G4? How much of your story are you willing to share?
- Is it more reassuring or intimidating to hear that you'll make every decision on this journey?
- How can we pray for you?

Everyone

- When life is hard, are you more prone to give up or hurry?

- What would (or did) it look like for you to adhere to the advice of Stefanie Carnes's quote early in your journey?
- Do we need to discuss any safety-level concerns from the past week?

STEP 1
PART TWO

REALISTIC EXPECTATIONS AND NONNEGOTIABLES

The video for this part of Step 1 can be
found at: bradhambrick.com/truebetrayal1p2.

I n a relational crisis, determining realistic expectations and identifying wise nonnegotiables is difficult. It can feel like trying to corral
a bag of spilled marbles on a ship during a tropical storm. With every
new piece of information, with every conversation that goes poorly or
well, with each memory you're trying to recontextualize, it feels like
the marbles (i.e., expectations) move all over the place.

It's normal to feel this way given what you're facing. "Normal"
doesn't mean easy. Knowing that something is common doesn't always
bring comfort. But it does help you realize that your response isn't
because of something you're doing wrong, as if most people in your
situation corral their marbles easily.

In this part of Step 1, we want to help you identify realistic expectations for you and your spouse. We also want to help you narrow down
what the most important nonnegotiables should be, from within the
seeming thousands of realistic expectations you might have.

REALISTIC EXPECTATIONS

What am I allowed to expect? Is it too much to ask her to change cell
phones? Is it unrealistic to expect him to never masturbate again?
Can I expect him to fully invest in his recovery while at the same time
pursue me? Is it selfish to want to be pursued like that at a time like
this? The questions can go on and on.

At this stage in the process, it is enough to recognize that you and
your spouse are not on the same timetable. Your spouse has known

about the sexual sin much longer than you have. What is "breaking news" to you is history for them. These factors greatly impact expectations.

In Step 2, you will begin the process of learning the history your spouse has been living. In Step 3, you will learn more about how these separate timetables affect you and your marriage. Having realistic expectations begins with recognizing that the two of you are not on the same page. You are just now realizing why you have been on separate pages.

1. **Realistic expectations for you.** You can expect yourself to be all over the place. Angry at the sin. Hurt by the betrayal. Sometimes eager to forgive so you can move on. Sad for your loss. Overwhelmed to the point of being nauseous. Ready to divorce. Yearning for when things were good. Fearful that your whole marriage has been a lie. Questioning your judgment about everything, because if you missed this, what else did you miss? Wondering if your racing thoughts will ever stop. Depressed because you don't think things will ever be the same. Insecure and wanting to be held. Disgusted at the thought of being touched or intimate again. Then you get angry again as you prepare for another ride on the emotional merry-go-round.

    ▶ **Read Psalm 55.** You might underline every emotion in this psalm. If you gave each emotion its own color, the page would look like a rainbow of dark, unsettled emotions. Oddly, this psalm doesn't end resolved. The final phrase is, "But I will trust in you" (v. 23). As the psalm ends, David does not believe the person who betrayed him will change, so he is entrusting that person to God's judgment. If your emotions vacillate like David's in this psalm, know you are not alone and that God inspired this psalm to help you put words to your experience and invite you to talk with him about what's going on in your life.

    If we tried to take the emotional chaos of the previous paragraph and articulate six common experiences that are reasonable expectations of yourself in the coming days and weeks, those would be the following:

- *Your emotions will fluctuate, but a recurrence of unpleasant emotions is not a "setback."* Avoid calling a day with unpleasant emotions a "bad day" and reserving the title of "good day" for days with only pleasant emotions. That is unfair toward yourself. In this season, a good day is one where your unpleasant emotions do not overwhelm you to the point that you're unable to fulfill your basic responsibilities.

- *As you learn new information about your spouse's sexual sin, the progress you made previously will be disrupted.* If you recently learned of your spouse's sexual sin, it is highly unlikely you know everything you need to know. More information is likely to come to light and, when it does, your unpleasant emotions will be more intense again.

- *The common themes of sexuality or betrayal in television, movies, and books will be upsetting.* It may be wise to cut back on your media intake for a while. This represents the kind of self-care decisions we'll explore frequently in the early steps of *True Betrayal*. It is wise to think through how to be a good steward of your emotional capacities when you're facing a challenge of this magnitude.

- *"Petty" conflicts of others will be hard to tolerate, find interesting, or feel compassion toward—for a time.* This isn't because you're becoming a cold, hard person. It does mean your capacity for empathy and compassion is saturated with your own challenges during this season. These capacities will return as you process your current marital crisis in a healthy way.

- *Sleep and eating habits will be a truer reflection of your progress than your emotions.* To evaluate how you're doing, gauge your body more than your emotions. It is likely your appetite and sleep cycle will stabilize before your emotions. You have more direct influence over your diet and sleep patterns, and these help regulate your emotions. Don't hesitate to consult your physician for a sleep aid if your sleep is disrupted for an extended period.

- *You may excessively cling to those things or people that you view as dependable or that you have control over.* In chaos, we desperately want order. Your workplace, your day-to-day routine with your children, or the orderliness of your home may feel more important to you than ever. That doesn't mean your priorities are out of whack. It is an indication that you long for predictability and the ability to influence outcomes.

This list is not exhaustive. It is meant to be representative of common responses.

▶ **Reflection:** Which of these responses has been prominent for you since you've learned of your spouse's sin? How did it feel to read about these responses? What self-care steps seem wise in light of these responses?

2. **Realistic expectations for your spouse.** Change is not a straight line. That hurts to say. There are few instances where this statement hurts more than when we're discussing betrayal within a marriage. But this does not mean that recurrence of sin is acceptable just because it's normal. In a moment, we will discuss what to set as nonnegotiables. But before we get there, we will discuss unrealistic expectations during the messiness of change.

"If you love me" or "if you were really sorry" phrases are common ways for unrealistic expectations to get expressed. Consider the examples below. How would you articulate what is unrealistic about them?

- "If you loved me, you wouldn't struggle with lust. I would just be enough for you."
- "If you loved me, you would never think fondly of your adultery partner again."
- "If you loved me, you would be the husband/wife you promised to be."
- "If you loved me, you would be improving on [blank] responsibilities while pursuing purity and integrity."

The content of these expectations is not unrealistic. Purity, fidelity, and integrity are reasonable expectations. What often makes these kinds of statements unrealistic is their pace. They lack a sense of process. They are destinations without a journey. They are like a diet commercial with a "Then" (obese; unfaithful) and "Now" (fit; faithful) picture that lacks an exercise or meal plan in between.

The need for a process is the reason it is recommended that your expectation for your spouse be to complete *False Love* with a mutually trusted counselor, pastor, mentor, friend, or G4 group. This concise statement of expectation accomplishes several things.

1. *False Love* puts the plethora of expectations you will have in an orderly process that is choreographed with your journey through *True Betrayal*.
2. This expectation moves your spouse toward at least one more mutually trusted person for accountability.
3. It prevents the tyranny of the moment from making your expectations seem unending and overwhelming.

This expectation helps you and your spouse navigate the inevitable fluctuation of emotions. When your spouse is tempted to be defensive or fatalistic, they can remember, The one thing being asked of me is that I go through a structured process with a mutually trusted source of accountability. That is more than fair. When you are tempted to give up because you're weary, you can gauge, Is my spouse putting a good-faith effort into a thorough process of change? In the ups and downs of the journey ahead of you, you will both need this kind of simple, clear expectation statement.

▶ **Read 2 Corinthians 7:10–13.** Notice Paul does not ask us to put confidence in worldly grief (mere remorse) to overcome sin. One of the trademarks of godly grief over sin is earnestness; that is, persistence in one's effort to change. Notice why Paul wrote this passage (v. 12), not for the sinner, nor even for the person sinned against. But instead, Paul wrote this for those around these two people, that they would have a way to discern the genuineness of repentance and faith. This is one of the primary reasons it is recommended that your summative request be, "Go through *False Love* with the accountability of someone we mutually trust." *False Love* operationally defines the types of actions earnestness would entail, and having mutually trusted accountability removes the burden of you having to interpret the genuineness of repentance in the ebb-and-flow of change.

3. **Realistic expectations for your sexual relationship.** This too is likely to fluctuate. You may be disgusted by sex and not want your spouse to touch you, kiss you, or even be in the room when you change clothes. You may become hypersexual, trying to use sex to recreate the lost security and oneness. You may vacillate between these two responses.

The biggest disruption either reaction brings to the marriage is the way it is viewed later. The hypersexual response is often looked back upon with shame—"My spouse cheats or looks at porn and I shamelessly throw myself at them like I was lucky to be part of their harem." The desire for security through marital sex is viewed as weakness. Or the hypersexual response can be looked back on as successful—"When I did everything my spouse wanted sexually, they didn't stray, so I should keep doing it." But this grounds security in our performance, which is exhausting and leads to imbalanced relationships.

False Love puts the plethora of expectations you will have in an orderly process that is choreographed with your journey through *True Betrayal*.

The disgusted-by-sex response is often looked back upon as a source of security—"Avoiding sex kept me safe. I couldn't be hurt again—at least not in the same way." But this grounds security in isolation and self-protection rather than trust, which can lead to creating distance in all relationships.

At this early stage, realize that sex will not be normal for a while. Give yourself and your spouse grace when sex is awkward, absent, or intensely emotional. Try to avoid generalizing the current experience of sex as the future normal for your marriage. Nothing is normal right now. Sex is the celebration of intimacy. There is work to be done before intimacy is restored. Until that time, sex will not be what it was designed to be. Allow your expectations of sex to recognize that.

A period of abstinence may be wise, especially when your spouse's engagement with sexual sin has reached an addicted level where they believe that sex is ultimate. Sex is good and important, but it's not ultimate. When your spouse views sex as ultimate, more sex or better sex will not be a blessing to your marriage or contribute to their purity. Instead, it may be advisable to agree to a time of sexual fasting. Ninety days is a common time frame for this.

The goal of this kind of sexual fasting is not punitive. The intent is not to withhold sex. Rather, the goal is to establish a proportional role for sex in your spouse's emotions and your marriage. Sex should not be an antidote to a mutant craving in your spouse. Sex should be a mutual celebration of a mutually valued relationship. Taking a time when you and your spouse demonstrate your commitment to the marriage during a season of abstinence allows sex to be reengaged with a sense that sex is a way to celebrate a good marriage rather than preventing one spouse from being bad.

ESTABLISH NONNEGOTIABLES

What should I ask for? is a common question. But a better one is, What should I not compromise on? In Step 1, we're assuming you just recently learned of your spouse's sexual sin, at least a recurrence of it. In this phase, it can feel like whether "things get better" depends on you knowing what to ask for in the minutes and hours after learning of your spouse's sin.

A primary goal for *True Betrayal* is to relieve that burden. What you do or do not ask of your spouse at this time will not be the determining factor in whether they change. There are many choices your spouse and you will make between now and that outcome (whatever it may be). The burden that your immediate choices determine the future of your marriage is not yours to carry.

Your ultimate request is that your spouse takes the necessary steps to forsake their sin and restore the marriage. But that is not what is referred to here as nonnegotiables. *Nonnegotiables*, as the word is used here, means the immediate steps that are necessary to limit further damage and display the initial fruits of repentance. Until these nonnegotiables are met, the process of restoration has not begun because the actions of destruction continue. Your spouse cannot claim to be rebuilding something they are still actively tearing down.

Here are three nonnegotiables that we encourage you to establish:

1. **If your spouse's sexual sin involves any direct interaction with a real person, they should break off all contact**. This applies to emotional affairs and physical adultery. In Step 2, Part Three of *False Love*, your spouse will receive this advice:

    - **Cut off all contact.** Clearly state that you are requesting no future contact for any reason. Document this request. If your adultery partner continues to pursue you and stalking behaviors emerge, a restraining order may be needed. The main point is to clearly request no future contact.
    - **Disclose all forms of contact.** Any means of contact should be disclosed to your spouse (e.g., secret cell phone, secret email address, rendezvous times in your schedule, etc.). When you end the relationship, you should tell your adultery partner that all these forms of contact have been disclosed to your spouse.

      Also, disclose all *attempted* contact. Ending an adulterous relationship requires more than doing the right thing one time. If your adultery occurred in an ongoing relationship, the other person will likely not want the relationship to end. Your adultery partner will likely fight for the relationship they thought they had.

      It is vital that you disclose any contact or attempted contact by your adultery partner to your spouse. Even if you get a phone call from an unknown number, choose not to answer it. If they leave no voice mail, tell your spouse. If a friend of the adultery partner gives you a note, refuse to read it and tell your spouse.

      You may think this sounds harsh. It is not mean; it is definitive. It is choosing to honor your marriage and relinquish your sin. This doesn't mean you won't grieve. It does mean there is a clear path for honoring God in this situation.
    - **Open communication.** "Open" should mean that your spouse or someone your spouse trusts to represent them is copied on any email or present for any meeting. One way we reveal who we love most is by who we talk to about another. That means when you talked about your spouse to your adultery partner, it revealed that your primary allegiance was to

your adultery partner. Now you are reversing this allegiance by insisting that your spouse is aware of all communication.

- **Avoid the "Closure Trap."** There is no such thing as closure after adultery. *Closure* is a word that gives the impression of a settled, happy ending. One of the two romantic relationships in your life will die an awkward, painful death. More uncomfortable still, you are going to decide which relationship ends (your marriage or your adultery relationship).

  You might ask, "Why are you being so graphic and harsh?" The reason is simple: "closure" is the lie most people believe that leads them back into adultery multiple times even while they claim they are trying to restore their marriage. *Closure* is an innocent word that masks its devastating consequences.[1]

  > The burden that your immediate choices determine the future of your marriage is not yours to carry.

  Until this step is taken, you should not attempt to take any of the other restoration steps in *True Betrayal*.

Your spouse needs to know that, for your marriage to get better, the adulterous relationship must be cut off. Indecision in this matter is a decision against your marriage. Until your spouse has made a real commitment to end communication with the other person, the uncertainty of your marriage should be reflected in the home. —Winston Smith[2]

2. **If there was any sexual contact with another person, your spouse should get tested for sexually transmitted diseases.** This nonnegotiable serves two purposes. First, it is a protective measure for your physical health. Until this is done, it is unwise for there to be sexual intimacy between you and your spouse. You should know any health risk you are exposing yourself to when being intimate with your spouse. You will not have the information necessary to assess that risk unless or until your spouse is tested for STDs.

   Second, this nonnegotiable requires your spouse to face the physical risk their sin introduced for them and you. It is easy, especially in the early stages of their sin being known, to only focus on the emotional and relational betrayal of their sin. Their sin was immensely hurtful. But it was also dangerous. Getting tested for STDs is not punitive but intended to be sobering toward the impact of their sin; it is part of genuine repentance.

3. **If your spouse's sexual sin involved online activity, accountability software should be installed on each of your spouse's devices with internet access.** There are many options for this type of software. Some are free; others come with a monthly subscription fee. The primary function of these forms of software is to provide a report of any questionable websites visited on that device. Accountability software also sends a report if the program is turned off while the device is active.

   To utilize accountability software in a way that fosters growth, here are several principles to keep in mind:

   - Accountability software is beneficial when someone *wants* to change, but privacy (being alone with their technology) is a significant point of temptation. Accountability software does not create an impenetrable force field from sin.
   - To be effective, accountability software needs to be installed on any device with Wi-Fi or internet access.
   - Initially you, as the spouse, will likely want to receive the report. Later we will advise that an accountability partner receive these reports to protect you from taking on a parental role with your spouse and to facilitate the restoration of trust.
   - When trust is thin, accountability software provides a form of verification that your spouse has abstained from problematic sites. This provides more assurance than your spouse saying, "I've been good. I promise."

As you reflect on these principles, you should realize the goals for accountability software are modest. This software is merely a tool that removes counterproductive privacy and provides tangible evidence of change (or lack thereof). But these modest benefits are still significant benefits. In the early stages of pursuing purity and, thereby, restoring trust, they are significant enough that it is recommended to be on your list of nonnegotiables.

CONCLUSION

As you work through Step 1, it is common to feel both exhausted because you've done so much and discouraged because you wish more progress had already been made. If that is where you are, it is not a sign that you have done something wrong; it is an indication that you are in the early stages of a hard journey.

In Steps 2 and 3, you will learn more about your spouse's sin that will be hard to hear, and you will identify ways their sin has impacted you that you wish weren't true. Those are heavy steps. The weight of that journey is why we'll take time to create a thorough self-care plan in the next two parts of Step 1. This journey is not a race, even though you will feel sped up many times. Be sure to take this journey at a sustainable pace and allow yourself to rest or take a break when you need to.

G4 GROUP DISCUSSION: STEP 1, PART TWO

As you discuss this material in G4 group, these questions are meant to facilitate a more honest and beneficial dialogue about this material. Anyone is free to respond to whichever questions they choose.

Experienced Members

- Which realistic expectation was most important for you to remember early in your journey?
- What was your experience like in the early stages of articulating your nonnegotiables?

New Members

- Which realistic expectation is hardest for you to embrace at this point in your journey?
- What parts of Psalm 55 most resonated with where you are currently?
- How can we pray for you?

Everyone

- How are you balancing the role of others to more objectively assess the earnestness of your spouse (2 Corinthians 7) without surrendering your voice as the primary decision-maker?
- How are you navigating the tension between being exhausted over how much you've done and discouraged that more progress has not already been made?
- Do we need to discuss any safety-level concerns from the past week?

STEP 1
PART THREE

FINDING THE RIGHT KIND OF COMMUNITY

The video for this part of Step 1 can be found at: bradhambrick.com/truebetrayal1p3.

As hard as it is to face the reality of what your spouse has done, facing it alone is even harder. Yet, there may be nothing more frightful than the thought of talking to someone about it. This feels like the ultimate lose–lose scenario. Isolation adds to the pain of betrayal, but conversation adds to the humiliation.

For a season, your G4 group may provide all the community you can handle. Managing things at home and having one other social setting to process your experience may reach your capacity to talk about this hardship. In time, more social support is likely to be needed. We want to examine that in this part of Step 1.

EIGHT CRITERIA FOR FINDING COMMUNITY

If we're not careful, we only talk when our emotions overwhelm us and inadvertently spill out into the conversation. The less intentional we are about identifying community, the more likely this informational leakage is to be random and disruptive to our progress.

The question becomes, Who do I talk to? The criteria below are meant to help you identify the best people. As you initially read through the list, realize it is probably unwise to think that you would identify one person for each criterion. Instead, after you've read through the list, you'll be encouraged to list two to three people who best fit the balance of these criteria.

1. **Consider telling those who are charged with your spiritual care.** In general, we feel fake where we have not been honest. This may

be felt most acutely at church. The longer we go without confiding in anyone at church, the more we feel like we are only going through the motions or that sermons and shepherding care from our church are irrelevant or hurtful.

Who do you trust most at your church? Is it a pastor, an elder, or your small group leader? The criteria below will also help you determine who would be the best person to invite to support you and your family on this journey.

> As hard as it is to face the reality of what your spouse has done, facing it alone is even harder.

2. **As much as possible, seek agreement with your spouse on those with whom you share.** If your spouse is cooperating with the request to work through *False Love*, this is likely a decision the two of you can make together. That would be ideal. If your spouse is currently uncooperative, it is still recommended that you inform your spouse of the person(s) to whom you are speaking. If your spouse is against talking to anyone, it is wise to begin with a counselor who has obligations of confidentiality to allow time for your spouse's defensiveness to subside.

You are not seeking your spouse's permission to talk about what has impacted your marriage. Your spouse does not have the right or authority to control who you speak with. But these matters are part of your shared story, not just your individual story, so as much as possible, you want to honor your spouse by letting them know who you are informing about the challenges your marriage is facing.

3. **Tell those you are willing to include in the full journey.** This may be the most significant criterion. Understanding the principle behind this recommendation allows you to avoid many of the unintended disruptions that come from confiding in people about your hardships. It is far better to have three people you trust to walk this full journey with you than a dozen people who only know part of your story because you shared a snippet with them in a moment of distress.

The more people who get snippets of the story, the harder it will be to navigate your social life during and after restoration (if that is the outcome). When people, even very nice people, only know part of your story, they will relate more to you and your spouse as if the part of your story they know is still the present reality. This means even as you make progress, social interactions with these people will take you back to ground you've already traversed.

You can't keep a dozen people updated on your life. That would be a full-time job. As you are seeking to garner support for this journey—which is wise and good— you should be thinking of a few people that you trust enough that you would want them to be encouragers for you throughout this process.

> It is far better to have three people you trust to walk this full journey with you than a dozen people who only know part of your story.

4. **Do not tell those who would quickly tell you what you "should" do.** Your marital difficulties are not a subject on which it is useful for people to have strong, preconceived opinions. It is fine for people to have strong opinions about marriage, adultery, sexuality, separation, divorce, and restoration. But as you look for support, you are not looking for someone to educate you on these topics. You are looking for someone to support you as you navigate these realities and possibilities.

Similarly, your life is not a social cause. It is fine for people to have strong opinions about how churches and Christian ministries have mishandled advice given to spouses in your situation. But you are not looking for someone trying to "balance the scales of history" via your hardship. You are looking for someone to support you as you weigh difficult decisions based on the information and cooperation (or lack thereof) you receive in the steps ahead.

Your emotions will fluctuate dramatically in the coming days and weeks. You want those you confide in to be a source of stability and perspective, rather than people who are emotionally reacting to your spouse's sin as if they were personally offended or pressuring you to conform to their theological ideals.

5. **Make sure your motivation is to seek comfort, not revenge.**
   When your spouse hurts you, it is natural to want your spouse to
   hurt too. One way we can hurt people is to damage their reputation. We have all heard a "prayer request" that was a thinly veiled
   excuse to share unnecessary information. We don't want to do
   that in the name of gathering social support. When revenge is our
   motive for who we tell and what we say, it creates more mess than
   relief.

   This is where the other criteria on this list serve us well. By
   pursuing the principles of these other criteria, we are avoiding the
   temptation toward revenge. Our sharing is purposeful and within
   the appropriate parameters. By refraining from revenge, you are
   not prioritizing the protection of your spouse's reputation. Unless
   there is change, in time it will become known and it's not your
   responsibility to prevent that. Instead, you are expressing faith in
   God's ways as your source of protection over you (Proverbs 3:5–8)
   and your marriage.

   ▶ **Read Romans 12:18–13:6.** If we're not careful, we can read the
   end of Romans 12 and take it to mean that we should be passive
   when others hurt us. This passage does not say that any proactive response to the sin of others is supplanting God's role. If that
   were the case, Paul would not have written Romans 13 the way he
   did. After Paul said, "Don't take revenge" (paraphrasing Romans
   12:19), he said, "Call the police if you need to" (paraphrasing
   Romans 13:1–6). In your case, this is more likely the equivalent
   of church leadership, a trusted counselor, or wise friend, unless
   your spouse's sin is also illegal in addition to being immoral. We
   do want to guard our heart against bitterness and the desire for
   revenge. Those things harm our soul. But taking steps to limit or
   mitigate the damage of our spouse's sin is not vengeful; it is wise.
   Even taking the time to weigh these criteria is one way you are
   protecting your heart from these temptations.

6. **Have a prepared statement for those who ask questions but do
   not need to know.** It will likely be obvious to some people around
   you that something is wrong. There are two principles to keep
   in tension: (a) you can always tell more; you cannot tell less, and

(b) truth stops speculation and, thereby, reduces gossip. In most cases you can acknowledge your pain and appreciate their concern with a succinct statement like:

"I am facing some hard things right now and would appreciate your prayers. At this point, I am keeping it as a personal matter."

If it is obvious to others that the stress is coming from your marriage, you might say:

> When revenge is our motive for who we tell and what we say, it creates more mess than relief.

"We are facing some challenges right now and are working through them. We would appreciate your prayers, but we have as many people in a supportive role as can be helpful."

If said with warmth, a simple statement like this allows you not to be fake while not giving snippets of information to dozens of people who see you upset.

7. **Allow parents and other family to be told as part of confession, if possible.** Confession is an important part of restoration. In some of your spouse's closest relationships, it is better if your spouse initiates the disclosure of their sin. It is part of their ownership of their sin and gets them out of the cycle of waiting for their sin to be discovered before they acknowledge it. In *False Love*, confiding about their sin is done incrementally until Step 5.

   If your spouse's sin results in job changes, separation, or other obvious life alterations, then waiting to talk to parents and family will likely not be an option. It is better if your spouse is the one to inform their parents and family. However, there should be agreement about what is shared, so there is not minimization of their actions that would vilify your decisions. In that case, if your spouse refuses to do so, there is nothing wrong with you taking that step.

8. **Talk to your children.** Appendix B provides age-appropriate and situation-appropriate guidelines for these conversations. It is better

to have intentional conversations when you have prepared what you will say rather than avoiding the topic until circumstances spark the conversation, making your words and emotions much less predictable.

▶ **Exercise:** After reading these criteria, make a list of people you think would be wise to invite on this journey with you. After you've made your list, take time to pray about who you decide to share with. If one or two people are obvious fits, reach out to them. If the others are less clear, wait until you are confident that sharing with them is a good decision.

- _____
- _____
- _____

CONCLUSION

Here are the two realities you are keeping in balance: (1) it is not good to be alone with your pain, and (2) you want companions on this journey who are helpful. The first reality shouldn't rush us to include people who conflict with the second reality. The second reality reminds us why we took the time to carefully consider these eight criteria.

As we'll say many times on this journey, don't rush. The content of _True Betrayal_ gives you guidance to weigh and use to assess your life and marriage. But you are the decision-maker. Make decisions when you are ready to make them, not just because you got to a certain page in this book where we discuss that decision.

G4 GROUP DISCUSSION: STEP 1, PART THREE

As you discuss this material in G4 group, these questions are meant to facilitate a more honest and beneficial dialogue about this material. Anyone is free to respond to whichever questions they choose.

Experienced Members
- Looking back, what do you wish you had done differently in this part of your journey?

- What were the biggest obstacles—emotional, relational, or logistical—for you implementing this material?

New Members

- Outside of our G4 group, who is supporting you in this journey?
- How are you doing with the "I can tell you're upset" conversations that pop up?
- How can we pray for you?

Everyone

- How did the Romans 12–13 devotion help you see that passivity is not the only alternative to revenge?
- Which of these eight criteria is most difficult for you to properly assess right now?
- Do we need to discuss any safety-level concerns from the past week?

STEP 1
PART FOUR

COMPLETING YOUR SELF-CARE PLAN

The video for this part of Step 1 can be found at: bradhambrick.com/truebetrayal1p4.

Whether or not you would have used the term "self-care plan" to describe your early work on this G4 journey, we've spent most of Step 1 working on elements of self-care; that is, preparing ourselves for the difficult journey ahead. But in the first three parts of Step 1, we've examined parts of a self-care plan that are highly relational—between you and your spouse or you and supportive friends. In this final part of Step 1, we're going to complete our plan by looking at elements of self-care that focus more on caring for your body as you ensure a season of intense suffering.

SELF-CARE AND PHYSICAL ENDURANCE

Christians are often concerned that self-care is selfish, a version of pride. If you have resisted prioritizing self-care for this reason, we want to affirm your desire to have a character that is above reproach. However, it is important for you to be able to differentiate healthy self-care from selfish self-love.

Do you recall the presentation at the beginning of every airplane flight? What do you do if you're traveling with a child and oxygen masks are needed? You put one on yourself first and then help the child. Why? If you pass out, the child is alone and in greater danger. Putting on your mask, a form of self-care, ensures your capacity to do other things that are needed. The practices we'll discuss below have a comparable impact. Self-care practices increase your stamina and resilience to see this journey through to completion.

During times of great difficulty, it's common for people to neglect their own self-care. . . . Feelings of shame or embarrassment often prevent a partner from turning to resources that could normally be a source of comfort. —Stefanie Carnes[1]

Breathe

We can often miss how disrupted simple things, like our breathing, get when life feels chaotic. When our breathing becomes short and choppy, it activates a stress response in our body, making our anxiety worse. This stress response activates our adrenal system and speeds up our thinking.

Even now, as you read, practice taking a long deep breath in through your nose and then out through your mouth. Be slow and rhythmic. Focus your mind on your breathing. Cooling the nasal cavity this way has the additional benefit of deactivating the stress response. Intentionality with your breathing also reminds you that you have control over important parts of your life.

> ▶ **Breathing Practice:** In the days ahead, there will inevitably be times of intense stress. When you realize your stress response is activating, remind yourself to take a few deep breaths before engaging in a conversation or making a significant decision.

Sleep

When life gets hectic, sleep gets interrupted, scarce, or of poor quality. Living with a sleep debt negatively impacts our quality of decision-making and emotional regulation. If you are having trouble regularly getting six to eight hours of continuous sleep, consider the following suggestions.

- Believe that sleep is intended to be a good gift from God and do not feel guilty for resting.
- If your bedroom is a trigger to significant stress and poor sleep, consider sleeping in a guest room for a season.
- Play soft music or nature sounds to help prevent your mind from ruminating while trying to sleep.

- Reduce the level of caffeine and sugar in your diet, especially after the noon hour.
- Avoid daytime naps so that your sleep is in concentrated blocks if you have trouble sleeping through the night.
- Establish a bedtime routine to help habituate your body toward sleep.
- Establish a deep, slow breathing pattern that simulates breathing during sleep.
- Talk with a medical professional about the possibility of a sleep aid.
- Memorize a Scripture passage about God's care for you, and repeat it slowly as you lie down.

▶ **Assessment:** How consistently are you getting adequate sleep? Which of the suggestions above would best serve to enhance how you are stewarding your body through sleep?

Eat Healthy

Our diet impacts more than our physical health. It has a major influence on our cognitive health (i.e., focus and clarity) and emotional regulation. Where does our body get the component parts that comprise balanced brain chemistry? From our diet. If we recognize how much our diet influences our cholesterol, blood pressure, and energy levels, why don't we equally appreciate its role in our brain chemistry and subsequent emotional health?

Beyond these physiological influences of a healthy diet, what we eat often reveals how much we believe our day-to-day choices matter. When we stop paying attention to what we put in our body or when we begin to just eat to survive, it can reveal an "it doesn't matter what I do" attitude that negatively impacts how we make decisions and interact with people.

Consider the following suggestions to help with your diet:

- Eat a fruit or vegetable at each meal. The more color in the foods you eat, the more likely you're giving your body the full spectrum of nutrients it needs.

- Drink plenty of water throughout the day. Inadequate hydration adds to your sense of fatigue and makes it harder for your body to filter itself adequately.
- Make sure you're eating adequate protein. When we don't have adequate protein, it impairs our immune system and, with the added stress of unhealthy relationships, that means we get sick more often.
- If you haven't been to the doctor in a year or more, consider getting a checkup to determine other ways you can wisely care for your body.

> Self-care practices increase your stamina and resilience to see this journey through to completion.

▶ **Reflection:** How much do you believe your day-to-day choices—like what you eat—can positively impact your life? Have you fallen into the trap of thinking, *If this won't make the big thing better (i.e., my marriage difficulties), then I shouldn't worry about it*? This is one way we drift into allowing our life to further deteriorate. How would your life be better if you regained a sense that choices like these made an impact on your quality of life?

Exercise

Exercising as part of your self-care plan isn't about getting in better shape or trying to be more attractive. Relational crises, like the betrayal of a spouse, are extremely stressful and can leave us prone to both depression and anxiety. Cardiovascular exercise is one of the most effective counters to stress, depression, and anxiety. Exercise cleanses the body of chemicals generated by stress, boosts energy levels, improves sleep quality, and facilitates a more proactive attitude toward life. If possible, consider twenty to thirty minutes of cardiovascular exercise at least three days per week.

YOU CAN DO THIS

Completing Step 1 is a significant achievement. It is easy to dismiss the importance of this early work you've done. Because the road in front of us is hard and so much is uncertain, we can pull back in fear and wonder if it's worth the effort.

> ▶ **Read Psalm 91.** This psalm calls out to God as refuge and fortress. Notice how the psalmist prays through the various times of day in verses 5 and 6 (day, night, noon). The psalmist takes comfort that sin will be punished in verse 8. The psalmist reminds himself of God's unseen protection in verses 11 and 12 but acknowledges the dangerous setting in which that protection is given in verse 13. Finally, in the last three verses, the psalmist reminds himself that his responsibility is to cling to God amid trouble. Read verses 14 to 16 as God's words directly to you (replace the pronoun *he* or *him* with your name). Allow this psalm to be a reminder that you are not alone, that God is with and for you on this journey, and that he invites you to be completely honest about what you're facing as you cry out to him.

You may wonder, *Is there any hope? Is it worth putting in the kind of effort that will be asked of me on this* True Betrayal *journey?* Those are fair questions. At the personal level, the answer is yes. Taking this journey helps you get to a healthier place. Not facing these painful realities leaves them unprocessed and allows them to have undue influence on your emotions and future relationships.

At the marital level, if "worth it" means "reconciled," the answer is no one can know at this point. The choices you and your spouse make in the days, weeks, and months ahead will determine that. However, if "worth it" means finding the answer to the question: Could our marriage ever be healthy and restored again after something so painful? the answer is yes—yes it is worth it and yes your marriage can be restored. Counselors, like Doug Rosenau, who work with many couples in this situation arrive at the same conclusion.

> Most marriages in which both partners are committed to making the partnership work and go through the confession and repentance process usually survive and often become even more intimate. —Doug Rosenau[2]

G4 GROUP DISCUSSION: STEP 1, PART FOUR

As you discuss this material in G4 group, these questions are meant to facilitate a more honest and beneficial dialogue about this material. Anyone is free to respond to whichever questions they choose.

Experienced Members

- What part of basic self-care was most beneficial to you early in your journey?
- What aspects of your self-care plan do you still implement today because you found them beneficial and enjoyable?

New Members

- What self-care practice do you think would make the biggest difference in your life?
- How are your current sleep patterns?
- How can we pray for you?

Everyone

- Have you avoided self-care practices because you think they're selfish?
- What part of the Psalm 91 devotion ministered to you most?
- Do we need to discuss any safety-level concerns from the past week?

What I Already Know
Feels Like It Could Crush Me

STEP 2

ACKNOWLEDGE the specific history and realness of my suffering.

At the end of this step, I want to be able to say . . .

"I will look at my life and acknowledge what has
happened. I will not try to move forward out of a false
history [based on lies] or with no history [denial].
I trust that God can and will redeem the real events
of my life. Acknowledging the real history of my
marriage is an act of faith in God's care for me.
Even though doing so may create fear [describe],
I trust it will produce hope [describe]."

STEP 2

PART ONE

RECEIVING A FULL DISCLOSURE

The video for this part of Step 2 can be found at: bradhambrick.com/truebetrayal2p1.

Chances are your imagination has been running wild. When we don't know the facts about a bad situation, we tend to fill in the blank with the worst possibilities. More painful still, our imagination has the capacity to create more scenarios than could have really happened. But because we don't know the truth, we emotionally react as if every hypothetical could be true.

In Step 2, as we work to acknowledge the specific history and realness of your suffering, you will begin to gather as many facts as you can. This will likely begin to make sense of things that felt "off" in your marriage for a long time. As this happens, remain humble toward your interpretations. You still have partial, incomplete information and our pain always intensifies our interpretations. For much longer than we like, things will become "clearer" without yet being "clear."

> The one cheated on often knows something is not quite right but can't put a finger on it. The one in the affair is often oblivious to the changes taking place: the different behavior patterns, the irritability or indifference towards the mate and the marriage, and distorted thinking along these lines: the partner is becoming less attractive, the tension is somehow the mate's fault, the partner is no longer understanding, and the marriage was never that good anyway. —Doug Rosenau[1]

A temptation emerges as you get more information—it leads you to think more information gives you more control. As you learn more about the what, when, and how of your spouse's sin, it is natural to think this information can be used self-protectively to somehow make your spouse stop sinning.

> If you are in a relationship with an addict, please know it is the addict's responsibility to identify and avoid pornographic materials. It is not your responsibility to protect the addict from all things you think are pornographic. —Mark Laaser[2]

We might wonder, *What's the point in trying to learn the truth? What kind of freedom does knowing the truth bring (John 8:32)?* Knowing the truth frees us from entertaining an infinite number of hypotheticals frees us from taking responsibility for your spouse's sin, and frees us from ignorance. In Step 2, you will go through the process of learning the extent of your spouse's sexual sin (at least as much as they will disclose at this time), and you will receive some initial guidance on what to do with that information.

Step 2 is built around answering three questions:

1. What is helpful for me to know?
2. What are the benefits of a full disclosure?
3. When do I start evaluating the health of my marriage before the betrayal?

In this part of Step 2, we will explore the first of these questions. The primary place we'll gain information is from our spouse. For that reason, we'll start by considering how to engage your spouse (to the degree he or she is cooperative).

WHAT SHOULD I ASK MY SPOUSE?

In Step 2 of *False Love*, we ask your spouse to begin compiling a full disclosure; that is, a detailed factual account of their sin. The purpose of a full disclosure is to end the I-have-to-ask-the-right-questions-in-order-to-get-the-full-answer game (not a fun or fair game). The pressure to ask the right questions, in the right way, to get accurate information is unfair and makes it harder for you to process what you're learning. The structure of the full disclosure is meant to remove the burden of knowing all the questions you want or need to ask as you are just learning what happened.

If your spouse is unwilling or procrastinates in completing this exercise, then there is no magic way to compel or accelerate their cooperation. In such cases, your options could include abstaining from sexual involvement, sleeping in a separate bedroom, requesting a higher degree of counseling involvement, or contacting your church leaders for an additional level of disciplinary involvement.

> No matter how many details you know about your partner's acting out, the ultimate choice to change his behavior lies with him or her, not with you. Having more information won't give you more control. On the contrary, sometimes too much information can cause you additional problems. You may end up obsessing even more about your partner's behavior. . . . The formal disclosure may take up to two hours or more. . . . Many couples consider this session to be a turning point in their relationship, an opportunity to establish a healthier marriage.
> —Stefanie Carnes[3]

While completing the full disclosure exercise is a good and necessary step for your spouse, it will likely be very difficult to hear. Acknowledging the good-but-hard reality of the full disclosure will help both of you during this exercise.

> [Spouse Testimony] It was the best and worst day of my life. I knew for once that he told the truth at the risk of great personal cost. It gave me hope that he could grow up and face life's responsibilities. It was the first time his words and his actions were congruent. I felt outraged and sick, yet I also felt respected and relieved. It gave me hope for our relationship.
> —Stefanie Carnes[4]

> Adultery is like a funeral, and you need to view the body. Mates need a thorough, honest confession (viewing the body) to validate that a real loss has taken place. Then they can slowly grieve and reclaim the marriage. If confession comes out in dribbles, then trust continues to be broken. —Doug Rosenau[5]

▶ **Read Job 1:13–22.** Hearing reports of evil invading your life is incredibly hard. In these verses, we watch Job receiving devastating news. Notice that as you read Job's intensely emotional response (v. 20) you admire Job rather than view him as weak. Even when his words border on despair (v. 21a), you naturally read them as filled with faith because they are still addressing God and looking to God for hope (v. 21b). Use Job's initial response as an example for your initial response to your spouse's disclosure—emotionally honest, physically expressive, and directed Godward. It is wise to discuss your spouse's disclosure with God in prayer before you try to discuss it with your spouse.

Discussing the disclosure with God before your spouse does not replace bringing your questions to your spouse. It would be tempting for both of you to believe that one intense, honest conversation should "put this subject to rest." Repent and forgive in one lengthy talk, right? Wrong. In *False Love*, your spouse has been taught that disclosure and confession are two separate actions. Rarely does the shame, deception, recidivism, and defensiveness of sexual sin allow these actions to occur simultaneously, although most people giving their disclosure would (at that time) consider it fully confessional.

> Whether your marriage survives or not, you will have to forgive and let go of bitterness. But you can't forgive a wound you haven't acknowledged—you won't even know what you have to forgive. You are laying a foundation for forgiveness by being honest about how you've been wounded. . . . For your marriage to become better, you have to talk about what happened and why. —Winston Smith[6]

If we think full disclosure and forgiveness should be done in one, intense conversation, we are prone to believe that asking additional questions is wrong or makes the situation worse. There does come a time when additional questions are counterproductive, but that is when either (1) the questions are being asked as a form of punishment to force the offending spouse to relive their shame, or (2) you already know the answers to the questions and are holding on to false hope that eventually the answers will become untrue. Otherwise, questions are a healthy part of coming to grips with what happened and gathering the information necessary to know what future decisions are wise.

Full Disclosure Follow-Up

After your spouse's full disclosure, you will have a myriad of questions—maybe more questions than you had before hearing their full disclosure. That is a natural response to pain and uncertainty. However, if we ask randomized questions (i.e., as they pop into our mind), we will receive randomized answers. This makes the primary benefit of the full disclosure harder to obtain.

For this reason, it is recommended that you write out your questions as they come to you ("popcorn" style) and then organize them. Having your questions grouped together will help your spouse's answers fit into a cohesive history and, thereby, help you assimilate the answers. Now that your spouse has put the effort into writing out their full disclosure, this reciprocated effort is warranted. There are several ways that you can organize your questions.

> It is wise to discuss your spouse's disclosure with God in prayer before you try to discuss it with your spouse.

- *Based upon the full disclosure outline*—The recommended outline for the full disclosure is organized around different expressions of sexual sin. This structure can be helpful when your spouse's sin fits the description of sexual addiction and has a variety of behavioral expressions.
- *Based upon the history of your marriage*—In this approach, the questions are organized around the chronological history of your dating relationship and marriage. This structure can be helpful when the double life and lies associated with your spouse's sexual sin makes it difficult for you to have confidence that you know your marital history accurately.
- *Based upon spheres of life*—In some cases, the most natural way to organize your questions are around different domains of your spouse's life: work life, work trips, time allegedly engaged in hobbies, guys'/girls' nights out, phone calls you needed to step away for, etc. This structure can be helpful when you still

have a high degree of uncertainty about which life events were legitimate and which were cover-ups.

- *Based upon the dominant emotions you are feeling*—When the other structures prove ineffective, you can arrange questions based upon the dominant emotions that prompt the questions (e.g., anger, fear, confusion, sadness, etc.). This structure is helpful when you believe your spouse has been honest with you, but you do not think they "get" their sin's impact on you.

The "Why" Question

The "why" question is the most common question with the least satisfying answer. Most of the time the "why" question creates a catch-22 scenario: Either the answer comes across as blame-shifting (e.g., "Because you/we weren't . . .") or pleading ignorance (e.g., "I don't know. It just kind of happened"). One is insulting, and the other infuriating.

To get anywhere productive with this legitimate question, we must grapple with the nature of sin. Sin is ultimately foolish, and foolishness will never be explained rationally. When we try to explain sin rationally it always results in some form of blame-shifting.

> All sin is ultimately irrational. . . . Though people persuade themselves that they have good reasons for sinning, when examined in the cold light of truth on the last day, it will be seen in every case that sin ultimately just does not make sense.
> —Wayne Grudem[7]

As you ask the why question, you need to recognize that the best answer that you are going to get is either an expression of *repentant dissatisfaction* (e.g., "I was upset with you for not appreciating me and, wrongly, I found someone who would . . . ," or "I was under pressure and I used porn as a form of escape") or *acknowledged foolishness* (e.g., "It doesn't make any sense now, but I wanted to learn about different sexual experiences, and porn was a fun way to do it," or "Once I started getting attention, I liked it and never did anything to stop it from escalating").

No answer to the why question will be satisfying. Ultimately, when asking the why question, you are looking for the idolatry at the root of the sin—what did your spouse want so badly that they were willing to sin to get it? Your spouse may not be able to see their desire as an idol at this stage. In Step 3 of *False Love*, your spouse will explore the motives behind their sin. This is when you can anticipate more productive conversations about why to begin to emerge.

▶ **Read Deuteronomy 29:29.** This verse reminds us that there are some things we will not know or understand in this life. Often, the answer to the why question for our suffering is one of those "secret things." This verse also reminds us that God has revealed many things about who he is, how he responds to sin, and how he responds to suffering that helps us even when we don't know the secret things.

> Ultimately, when asking the "why" question, you are looking for the idolatry at the root of the sin.

In a time when secrets have been so painful, this can be a hard truth for us to accept. But we can trust that God's secrets are not the secrets of an unfaithful spouse, but of a good parent. On your *True Betrayal* journey, we will ask your spouse to be fully forthcoming so that the only secrets you have to grapple with are things like motives behind sin, which are often hard to determine.

Playing the Detective?

You might ask, "What if I don't think my spouse is telling me the whole truth? How far do I go to get the truth? Should I check their computer, phone, bank records, etc.?" Ideally, you would be honest with your spouse and say, "I am having a hard time believing you and would like for you to live transparently enough to settle my fears." Throughout *False Love*, your spouse will learn that transparency in marriage is normal and healthy, not a punitive response to their sin.

If your spouse responds with resistance or negligence to your direct request, then you may choose to pursue verifying your concerns. If you seek to verify your concerns by checking on your spouse's activity without their awareness, then you should adhere to the following principles:

- You should not do anything illegal in the pursuit of information. Your spouse's immoral actions do not warrant you taking illegal actions, no matter how hurt you feel.
- If your spouse is actively engaged in *False Love* with a counselor, mentor, or G4 group, it is recommended that you allow time for new information to come forward via disclosure rather than discovery.
- If you are considering taking an investigative step, it is recommended that you engage in personal counseling. The distress that would warrant this step is more than you should process on your own.
- You should resolve to tell your spouse what you have done, what you found, and why you deemed this step necessary. More secrets will not make your marriage better and will not make your emotions more settled.
- You should not make this your regular practice. Investigation, even when it finds nothing, does not build trust. If your search finds problematic information and your spouse will not acknowledge clear facts of sin, this would be reason to bring that information to your pastoral leaders for church discipline and the possibility of separation. If your search proves empty, then you should inform your spouse of your search, your concern, and trust that God will expose your spouse's sexual sin (if ongoing). God was faithful to do this already. That is what prompted your *True Betrayal* journey.

CONCLUSION

Arghh!?! When we didn't know the extent of our spouse's sin it hurt. Now that we know more about the extent of our spouse's sin it hurts. Often, we're not sure which one hurts more. There is no need to try to put the two types of pain on a scale.

But there is a significant difference between the pain of a broken bone and the pain of surgery. The most significant difference is not the intensity of the pain, however much that may vary. The important difference is that one is the pain of destruction (i.e., a broken bone), and the other is the pain of healing (i.e., surgery).

The work we are doing in Step 2 is the latter. No doubt, it is painful. But it is pain that can lead to healing. That healing may be the restoration of your marriage. That healing may only be a healthier personal recovery from the impact of your spouse's sin. Time will tell. But you can take some comfort in knowing the type of pain you're experiencing in Step 2.

G4 GROUP DISCUSSION: STEP 2, PART ONE

As you discuss this material in G4 group, these questions are meant to facilitate a more honest and beneficial dialogue about this material. Anyone is free to respond to whichever questions they choose.

Experienced Members

- What was it like for you to receive your spouse's full disclosure?
- Which of the methods of organizing your follow-up questions did you use, or wish you had used?

New Members

- What parts of the Job 1 devotional were most relatable for you?
- Have you been able to find relief from the pressure to "ask the right question" to get accurate information?
- How can we pray for you?

Everyone

- How are you managing the inevitable dissatisfaction with the why question?
- How was the destructive-versus-healing-pain distinction helpful as you continue in your G4 journey?
- Do we need to discuss any safety-level concerns from the past week?

STEP 2
PART TWO

THE BENEFITS OF A FULL DISCLOSURE

The video for this part of Step 2 can be found at: bradhambrick.com/truebetrayal2p2.

In Part One of Step 2, we defined a full disclosure and talked about how to receive one. In that discussion, we acknowledged that receiving a full disclosure is an emotionally weighty exercise. That begs the question, Is it worth it? And, if so, What are the benefits? Those aren't defensive questions. They are important questions.

In this part of Step 2, we will explore two questions to help us understand why the hard work of a full disclosure is worth it.

1. What are the benefits of a full disclosure for you?
2. What are the benefits of a full disclosure for your spouse?

SEVEN BENEFITS FOR YOU

You have major decisions in front of you. Big decisions are intimidating and unsettling. Big decisions with inadequate or inaccurate information are even more scary. Below are seven ways that receiving a full disclosure will help you be in a better position to make the important decisions you're facing.

1. **You gain clarity about the situation**. Working on a marriage with undefined sexual sin is like buying a house without having an inspection. Even if the house needs repairs, you might still buy it. But to buy the house not knowing its condition is foolish. Similarly, you may choose to not only forgive your spouse, but also to restore the marriage. Even despite the damage created by your spouse's sin, many spouses choose this option. But to forgive something that has not been properly acknowledged is unwise. When the sin

is inadequately disclosed, there is no way to know if your spouse has ended their sin or if they are taking adequate steps to be free from their sin.

Some people try to call forgiving without knowing the extent of the sin "giving the benefit of the doubt." That is not an accurate description. When we "give the benefit of the doubt," we are assuming the other person is a good-faith actor. We don't consider it wise to give the benefit of the doubt to a con man or thief. Why? Not because these sins are unforgivable or irredeemable, but because until these individuals are honest about their pattern of behavior and methods of deceit, they cannot be considered good-faith actors. This is the same reason that you are asking for a full disclosure to gain clarity about your situation.

2. **You validate that you're not crazy.** The lies that cover sexual sin create an alternative (i.e., false) history. The longer you try to live in that false history—because it is the only marital history your spouse would invite you into—the less your home, emotions, and marital conversations make sense. You start to feel crazy. You start to doubt your ability to read situations and make decisions.

[Testimony of a Counselee] One of the most helpful things about the disclosure for me was that it confirmed my reality. My husband had repeatedly told me how crazy and jealous I was. Over time I started believing him. Finding out I had not misread the situation helped me to begin trusting myself, that I wasn't crazy as he had said or as I had thought. —Stefanie Carnes[1]

▶ **Read Jeremiah 6:14–17.** God is confronting his people because their explanation for their actions did not match the situation. They were saying "Peace, peace" (i.e., "Everything is fine. Nothing is going on. You've got nothing to worry about") when they should have been confessing their sin (vv. 14–15). God confronts their lies. But God doesn't stop there. God calls on his people to look at their lives and examine them by his standards (vv. 16–17). That is the equivalent of a full disclosure. God is modeling the response he would have you give to that voice in your mind that questions, Do I really want to know the truth? Wouldn't it be easier to live in blissful ignorance again? For the sake of your sanity and your spouse's integrity, it is worth it.

3. **You assess when to trust (and not trust) your suspicions**. This benefit is less about the past and more about the future. You likely had a history teacher who said, "Those who fail to study history [past] are doomed to repeat it [future]." That is the principle we're applying here. Undoubtedly, you asked your spouse many times, "Is everything okay? You seem off . . . Is something wrong? You feel distant . . . Is something going on? I feel like I'm on the outside of our relationship."

   These questions were likely met with denial (e.g., "Nothing is wrong, I'm just tired and stressed"); anger (e.g., "Why do you keep accusing me of stuff?"); or false sympathy (e.g., "It hurts me to see you worry about stuff like this"). Regardless of the approach, your true instincts were deemed false. This negatively impacts your confidence in your ability to read the moment and anticipate the future.

   A full disclosure should include statements of "You were right to question me when [describe situations when your questions were valid]." As you respond to the full disclosure, it is appropriate for you to ask, "Was I right to be concerned when I questioned you about [situation you felt like something was off]?" This process is important to help you not overgeneralize your suspicions and thereby begin to believe that every suspicion you have is necessarily true.

4. **You regain a reasonable sense of control.** When your spouse deceptively controlled your access to information, they had undue influence over the marriage. This does not necessarily mean they are a "controlling spouse" as that term is most often used regarding an abusive marriage. As we will see later in Step 2, if a destructive pattern of control existed prior to or in addition to your spouse's sexual sin, that is more serious to the viability of the marriage than their infidelity.

   Even so, when information is withheld, control is not balanced in the marriage. When one spouse has complete and accurate information, but the other spouse has incomplete or inaccurate information, the more informed spouse has more ability to make choices that can contribute to their desired outcome. The full disclosure creates balance in the quantity and quality of information both spouses have.

5. **You gauge your spouse's commitment to the marriage.** *Honesty is the best indicator of your spouse's level of commitment to the marriage.* In sexual sin, deceit is as much of a problem as lust. Honesty is a better gauge of commitment than tears, gifts, promises to change, or significant acts of kindness. If your spouse is unwilling to be honest, they are more committed to keeping their sin hidden than to the restoration of the marriage.

   This is important for you and your spouse to keep in mind. It is easy for your spouse to think that because a full disclosure hurts you (hearing hard truth does sting), it is not a sign of commitment. It may be easy for you to think along the same lines. A full disclosure and nondefensive response during the follow-up allow your spouse to relearn, through experience, what commitment to the marriage looks, sounds, and feels like.

   ▶ **Read Matthew 15:1–20.** Jesus said it was vain to try and worship God and seek to honor our covenant relationship with him if we are being dishonest (vv. 8–9). Jesus picked apart the games that the Pharisees and scribes would play to say that they were technically honoring the covenant expectations (vv. 3–7). Jesus was responding to a question where the Pharisees and scribes were trying to turn the whole subject back on him (vv. 1–2). What Jesus wanted from them was honesty. Why? Because dishonesty (i.e., when our words, actions, and motives are not aligned) reveals that we are not prioritizing the relationship with the person we are deceiving (vv. 10–20). Honesty reveals which relationships are primary in our life.

6. **You measure the realistic hope about the future of the marriage.** A common question is, How much hope for the future of the marriage should I have? Sometimes we hyper-spiritualize the question: You should have as much hope as God is powerful. The sentiment

of this statement may be sincere. But it is not an effective gauge. God is all powerful, yet not all marriages will be (or should be) restored.

The better gauge would be your spouse's honesty. You should have as much hope as your spouse is honest. Think of the honesty between you and your spouse as a map. In effect, we're asking, How confident should I be that we will arrive at our desired destination?

> Honesty is the best indicator of your spouse's level of commitment to the marriage.

The answer would be, As confident as your map is accurate. Even if the journey is hard, in God's strength, you can make it. But if the map is inaccurate, you won't arrive at your destination.

7. **You identify the information necessary for future decisions**. Often the unfaithful spouse will say or think something like, If I told my spouse [the worst thing I did], I know there would be no future for our marriage. That logic is evidence of trying to control the outcome. The statement may or may not be true. But a restored marriage is not the primary point of the full disclosure. The full disclosure is about having accurate information to help you make the choices in front of you and your spouse while living with integrity.

Admittedly, these are bittersweet benefits. They are benefits which require courage from you and your spouse to be realized. As you learn the truth, it is important to make decisions rather than have reactions. Yes, you will be emotional about what you've learned. That is healthy and normal. But let your actions be guided by thought and reflection rather than a mere reflex against the pain of what you're learning.

FIVE BENEFITS FOR YOUR SPOUSE

Asking for a full disclosure is not a means of punishing your spouse. Giving a full disclosure is not an exercise in penance by your spouse. Disclosure is an opportunity to participate in God's redemption by choosing to live in the light of truth. Viewing disclosure as penance or punishment should be avoided. These views place you in a parental role over your spouse and exacerbate shame in your spouse.

To help you approach the disclosure as an opportunity for you and your spouse to participate in an act of God's grace, consider the following five points that describe the benefits of disclosure for your spouse.

1. **They end their denial**. This may be the most painful part of the full disclosure for your spouse. For months or years, your spouse lived in a way that denied the severity of their sin—living as if you would never find out (i.e., that they would never face the consequences of their actions). When you found out, this denial began collapsing. As they go through the process of a full disclosure, this false reality completely implodes.

   During the full disclosure, your spouse not only stops lying to you, but also quits lying to themselves. To lie well, you must begin to "buy" (i.e., believe) what you're "selling" (i.e., lying about). The full disclosure is when the reality of "what I've done" and that "I am the one who did it" comes crashing in on your spouse.

   Hopefully, realizing this will increase your compassion for the difficulty of the exercise for your spouse. But that compassion should not tempt you to rescue them for the difficulty of disclosure. It is a good and necessary pain.

2. **They are freed from putting up a false front**. Honesty is a simpler way of life than deceit. As Mark Twain famously said, "If you tell the truth, you don't have to remember anything." While this aspect of the full disclosure may be the most embarrassing part for your spouse, it is likely to also be the most liberating. As your spouse completes the full disclosure, they get to be a real person in the real world for the first time since their sexual sin began.

   ▶ **Read I John 1:8.** When we deny our sin, we deceive ourselves. Put another way, when your spouse refused to repent, they were not who they thought they were. Blame-shifting and excuse-making created a false self-perception. Without repentance, we all redefine things to excuse what should be blamed on our own selfish, foolish choices. The longer we resist repentance, the more false our sense of self and interpretation of others becomes. Acknowledging sin is the first step to living in reality. Your spouse will never interpret themselves, you, or your marriage accurately until they repent.

> When your spouse refused to repent, they were not who they thought they were.

The end of the false front is one of the reasons for hope we've alluded to in this *True Betrayal* journey. Earlier we noted that when a couple does the hard work of marital recovery, they often become closer than they were before the infidelity damaged their marriage. Your spouse being more authentic—hiding less because they are not putting up a false front—is one of the primary reasons for this increased closeness.

3. **They gain hope that their actions could matter**. Before the full disclosure, the thought, *If my spouse really knew me, our marriage would be over*, saps any real hope for the future of the marriage. Your spouse lived as if there were only two options: lie or divorce. This made the choice to lie seem like the lesser of two evils.

   The full disclosure liberates your spouse from this false dichotomy. While the future of the marriage may still be uncertain, it becomes clear that lying is no longer an option your spouse can excuse as legitimate. Before the full disclosure, a "good day" between you and your spouse was like the illusion of an oasis in the desert. It gave false hope because it wasn't grounded in reality. Now, on this side of the full disclosure, generated hope can be trusted as solid.

4. **They have a chance to be truly known.** Pornography and adultery are artificial realities. Pornography is a fake world set to a soundtrack enacted by actors. Adultery is a relationship that isn't required to bear the weight of real-life responsibilities and is artificially infused with an us-against-the-world mentality. As exciting as either may be, ultimately, we know both are false and empty. For this reason, pornography and adultery foster loneliness. They're fake, and we know we're fake as we live in them.

Honesty allows us to be truly known. When we're honest, we're no longer haunted by "if my spouse knew . . ." Before full disclosure, that thought is frightening. After the full disclosure and the initial pain of our sin being exposed to the light subsides, the opportunity for real relationship emerges. That is a significant benefit your spouse can begin to experience if they cooperate with this process.

5. **They get a new start.** A new start is not a do-over, getting to live as if nothing happened. That is an exaggerated view of forgiveness and restoration. A new start does mean that the reference point of life changes. Before disclosure, each day was lived bracing against the day when sin would be revealed. Each day was lived waiting for when your spouse would have to "start over." It is like playing a board game knowing the board is about to be flipped over.

   After disclosure, your spouse is free to fully engage life and your marriage. While there is still work to do to restore trust and show themselves to be a person of integrity, that work matters now. When the board was about to be flipped by their secret being exposed, "progress" didn't matter. Now it does. A full disclosure provides a substantive foundation for your spouse to engage in the process of marital restoration.

CONCLUSION

The harder a task is, the clearer we need to understand the reasons the task is "worth it." Sharing and receiving a full disclosure is exceedingly hard for both you and your spouse. That is why we devoted this much time to exploring the benefits to make it worth it.

It is not your responsibility to compel your spouse to cooperate with this process. That is not why we shared the benefits that exist for your spouse. But we wanted to help you see that this is a gracious expectation—one that has benefits for your spouse as much as for you and your marriage.

It is appropriate to remind you again to take the time you need to recover after each step. If you feel emotionally exhausted or threadbare after this part of your journey, take time to rest. Review your self-care plan. It is better for you and your marriage if you do not push yourself so hard that fatigue begins to further disrupt how you relate to one another in this already difficult time.

G4 GROUP DISCUSSION: STEP 2, PART TWO

As you discuss this material in G4 group, these questions are meant to facilitate a more honest and beneficial dialogue about this material. Anyone is free to respond to whichever questions they choose.

Experienced Members

- What was (or could have been) the most beneficial thing you did after receiving your spouse's full disclosure?
- How long after the full disclosure conversation(s) did it start to feel worth it?

New Members

- What fears or concerns do you have as you anticipate your spouse's full disclosure?
- What parts of your self-care plan would be wise to implement after hearing the full disclosure?
- How can we pray for you?

Everyone

- How did the devotional on Matthew 15 help you see the process of giving and receiving a full disclosure differently, hopefully more redemptively than punitively?
- How would you answer if someone asked you, How does a full disclosure benefit both spouses individually and the marriage?
- Do we need to discuss any safety-level concerns from the past week?

STEP 2
PART THREE

EVALUATING YOUR PRE-BETRAYAL MARRIAGE

The video for this part of Step 2 can be found at: bradhambrick.com/truebetrayal2p3.

W hen you're going in one direction and things get hard, you may assume that if you simply turn around and go in the other direction, things will get better. That is a reasonable, but not necessarily accurate, assumption.

Why do we articulate that human tendency? Some of us on this *True Betrayal* journey are thinking that if we can just get back to how things were "before," then things would be "better." That may or may not be true. Sometimes, it is very true. Sometimes sexual sin disrupts good marriages marked by honor and care. Other times, it is false. The pain of betrayal by sexual sin can blind us to more severe problems that existed in our marriage. In that case, getting back to the way things were before would be a curse, not a blessing.

That is what we want to assess in this part of Step 2—*How healthy was your marriage before the betrayal of your spouse's sexual sin?* To keep things simple, we'll say there are three options.

First, you may find that your pre-betrayal marriage was good. In that case, you are doing the hard work of marital restoration in hopes of getting back to and fostering the closeness that previously existed. For marriages that were previously good, there is every reason to believe that removing the sin will produce a good, healthy, and thriving marriage again.

Second, you may find that your pre-betrayal marriage was adequate. In that case, it is likely that you are doing the hard work of marital restoration and wanting a commitment to work on things that should have been addressed earlier. For marriages that were adequate, it may be that both you and your spouse need to commit to better marital practices to have a thriving marriage.

Third, you may find that your pre-betrayal marriage was problematic. In that case, you are not trying to get back to where you were before. If patterns like abuse, control, addiction, or comparable problems were present, sexual sin is likely not the biggest problem facing your marriage. It is only the most recent and, perhaps, the most emotionally taxing problem. For problematic marriages, it is fair to ask for a commitment to work on the more severe problems, not just sexual integrity.

> The pain of betrayal by sexual sin can blind us to more severe problems that existed in our marriage.

PRE-BETRAYAL MARRIAGE SURVEY

Evaluating the pre-betrayal marriage requires objectivity during a time of highly fluctuating emotions. It is important to keep in mind *why* you are doing this assessment. You are trying to identify if there are concerns about the marriage that are more severe than your spouse's sexual sin. If there are, you don't want addressing the sexual sin to take priority over more important issues (e.g., something on the level of abuse or major, unknown debts).

It would be unwise to allow this evaluation to shift your focus from marital restoration to marital enrichment.

- *Marital restoration* (the focus of *True Betrayal*) involves addressing challenges that threaten the viability of the marriage. If marriage were a vehicle, this would be a transmission overhaul.
- *Marital enrichment* involves identifying ways to enhance mutual enjoyment in a healthy marriage. If marriage were a vehicle, this would be the oil changes and tire rotations.
- Marital enrichment solidifies marital restoration; it is not a replacement for marital restoration. Undoubtedly, you will find marital enrichment areas you want to improve in this assessment. Those elements are things that can be a focus of attention in Step 7, Step 8, and after you complete your G4 journey.

Use the survey below to evaluate your pre-betrayal marriage. Instructions: Read the following statements. Consider how well each describes your marriage *before your spouse's sexual sin*. This exercise should be completed after the full disclosure to ensure that you know when "before" began.

Note: This instrument is only a survey. Unlike most G4 tools formatted like this, there is not a scoring key. The benefit of this tool is that it prompts you to assess key areas of your pre-betrayal marriage. The more CD or SD responses, the less healthy your pre-betrayal marriage would have been.

(CD) Completely Disagree, (SD) Somewhat Disagree, (NS) Not Sure, (SA) Somewhat Agree, or (CA) Completely Agree

1. I knew the important life events that shaped my spouse's character and beliefs.	CD	SD	NS	SA	CA
2. Our marriage was free from the use of illegal drugs.	CD	SD	NS	SA	CA
3. Our marriage was free from the abuse or excessive use of alcohol.	CD	SD	NS	SA	CA
4. Our marriage was free from gambling.	CD	SD	NS	SA	CA
5. Our marriage was free from lying to cover up painful or embarrassing events.	CD	SD	NS	SA	CA
6. We showed the ability to love and support one another in good times and bad.	CD	SD	NS	SA	CA
7. I allowed my spouse to see my weaknesses without defensiveness or fear.	CD	SD	NS	SA	CA
8. My spouse allowed me to see their weaknesses without defensiveness or fear.	CD	SD	NS	SA	CA
9. I was not jealous or controlling with my spouse.	CD	SD	NS	SA	CA
10. My spouse was not jealous or controlling with me.	CD	SD	NS	SA	CA
11. I agreed with how we divided the responsibilities of managing our home.	CD	SD	NS	SA	CA
12. We were able to talk about new responsibilities when they emerged.	CD	SD	NS	SA	CA

13. I believed my spouse's friends were a positive influence on our marriage.   CD SD NS SA CA

14. My spouse believed my friends were a positive influence on our marriage.   CD SD NS SA CA

15. We had couple friends who modeled a healthy marriage.   CD SD NS SA CA

16. I voluntarily abstained from actions that made my spouse fearful or upset.   CD SD NS SA CA

17. My spouse voluntarily abstained from actions that made me fearful or upset.   CD SD NS SA CA

18. My sense of humor did not put my spouse down or highlight their weaknesses.   CD SD NS SA CA

19. My spouse's humor did not put me down or highlight my weaknesses.   CD SD NS SA CA

20. I felt safe expressing my thoughts and opinions with my spouse.   CD SD NS SA CA

21. My spouse felt safe expressing their thoughts and opinions with me.   CD SD NS SA CA

22. I was willing to be interrupted to hear what my spouse had to say.   CD SD NS SA CA

23. My spouse was willing to be interrupted to hear what I had to say.   CD SD NS SA CA

24. I honored my spouse even when we disagreed.   CD SD NS SA CA

25. My spouse honored me even when we disagreed.   CD SD NS SA CA

26. I did not use "being honest" as an excuse to be harsh or dogmatic.   CD SD NS SA CA

27. My spouse did not use "being honest" as an excuse to be harsh or dogmatic.   CD SD NS SA CA

28. I did not allow my personal or marital goals to take precedence over our marriage.   CD SD NS SA CA

29. My spouse did not allow personal or marital goals to take precedence over our marriage.   CD SD NS SA CA

30. I felt safe when my spouse expressed their anger or hurt.   CD SD NS SA CA

31. I recognized that my spouse should not be expected to meet all my emotional needs.　　**CD SD NS SA CA**

32. My spouse recognized that I should not be expected to meet all their emotional needs.　　**CD SD NS SA CA**

33. We were able to talk about our family finances without defensiveness or arguing.　　**CD SD NS SA CA**

34. I felt free to make spending decisions within our family budget.　　**CD SD NS SA CA**

35. I did not hide expenses or debt from my spouse.　　**CD SD NS SA CA**

36. My spouse did not hide expenses or debt from me.　　**CD SD NS SA CA**

37. I regularly put intentional time and effort into romancing my spouse.　　**CD SD NS SA CA**

38. My spouse regularly put intentional time and effort into romancing me.　　**CD SD NS SA CA**

39. We were balanced in who initiated sex.　　**CD SD NS SA CA**

40. I was satisfied with the frequency and quality of sex in our marriage.　　**CD SD NS SA CA**

41. My spouse was satisfied with the frequency and quality of sex in our marriage.　　**CD SD NS SA CA**

42. I felt like I could meet my spouse's sexual expectations and desires.　　**CD SD NS SA CA**

43. The language my spouse used to describe sex was wholesome and non-offensive to me.　　**CD SD NS SA CA**

44. My spouse and I agreed on the difference between sex and intimacy/closeness.　　**CD SD NS SA CA**

45. My spouse and I could talk about our fears or insecurities related to sex.　　**CD SD NS SA CA**

Remember, this evaluation is **not** your new to-do list, replacing the focus on marital restoration. Any couple taking this assessment would find aspects of marital enrichment to work on. Your primary goal in this assessment is to identify if there are concerns about your marriage that are more severe than your spouse's sexual sin.

A secondary benefit of a survey like this is to identify any long-standing marital problems that would undermine the progress achieved during the restoration process. If there are areas of marriage enrichment that need attention *after* the marital restoration is complete, those can be a focus of attention in Step 7, Step 8, and after you complete your G4 journey.

> Marital enrichment solidifies marital restoration; it is not a replacement for marital restoration.

WHAT DO I DO WITH STEP 2 INFORMATION?

As you finish Step 2, in most cases, the healthiest first thing you could do is rest. You have received a significant amount of information that is hurtful and troubling. Some of your fears were proven true. Other fears may seem like they will be unsubstantiated. Disclosure is a hard time; though beneficial and necessary, it is overwhelming as it happens.

Remember, in most cases, the information learned is only "new to you" not "new." Because it is new to you, your mind and emotions are responding as if what you learned just happened. In your world, these things are "breaking news" and carry the emotional weight of an imminent threat. It is important to take some time, even if it's a few hours, to get away from your spouse and let these things settle in as "past events."

The majority of what you will do with this information is covered in the coming steps:

- Step 3—You will grow in your understanding of the impact of these events upon you, your spouse, and your marriage.
- Step 4—You will articulate the destructive scripts often used to make sense of betrayal from a spouse.
- Step 5—You will mourn the reality of what has occurred and the damage done.
- Step 6—You will begin to embrace how the gospel provides a redemptive alternative to the destructive meanings often attributed to our suffering (countering Step 4 content).
- Step 7—You will identify ways to counter the impact of your spouse's sin (Step 3 content).

That is the path in front of you. We want you to take comfort in knowing there is a plan without feeling pressured to enact that plan if you're fatigued from completing Step 2.

G4 GROUP DISCUSSION: STEP 2, PART THREE

As you discuss this material in G4 group, these questions are meant to facilitate a more honest and beneficial dialogue about this material. Anyone is free to respond to whichever questions they choose.

Experienced Members

- When you initially completed this survey, was your pre-betrayal marriage good, adequate, or problematic? How did that impact the way you engaged the rest of your G4 journey?
- How did you feel when you had the opportunity to assess your pre-betrayal marriage? Were you more relieved or confused to be asked to do this? Over your time in G4, how have you seen the importance of making this assessment?

New Members

- Do you currently feel more overwhelmed or encouraged when you look at the path ahead?
- How objective do you feel like you were in assessing your pre-betrayal marriage?
- How can we pray for you?

Everyone

- Are there concerns in your marriage that are more severe than your spouse's sexual sin?
- How are you balancing acknowledgment that marital enrichment work can always be done and the reality that the current focus needs to be on marital restoration work?
- Do we need to discuss any safety-level concerns from the past week?

STEP 3
UNDERSTAND the impact of my suffering.

At the end of this step, I want to be able to say . . .

"I used to fear facing the reality of my marriage, so I would not acknowledge it. I expected myself to live as if the betrayal wasn't real or that bad [describe]. I can now see how the betrayal has affected me [describe]. I interpreted the impact of the relationship as being my fault. The guilt and shame I felt blinded me to God's compassion and grace toward me. Rightly understanding the impact of my marriage helps to quiet my fears and shame. Now I believe there is hope and that finding ways to respond to my spouse is worth it."

STEP 3
PART ONE

TEN FACTORS THAT INCREASE THE IMPACT OF YOUR SPOUSE'S SIN

The video for this part of Step 3 can be found at: bradhambrick.com/truebetrayal3p1.

I t is one thing to experience the impact of your suffering; it is another thing to understand the impact of that suffering. You have been experiencing the impact since the revelation of your spouse's sexual sin, and (likely) even before discovery you were wrestling to make sense of its impact without the central piece to the puzzle. In Step 3, we will begin to understand the connection between what happened and the changes in your life, emotions, marriage, and other relationships.

The rebuttal is that looking at the impact will only make me feel worse. This is partially true, and why it is highly recommended that you complete this study with a G4 group, friend, pastor, or counselor. But it is also largely false. Consider the parallel example of debt. Many people in debt fail to itemize and total their debt for fear it will be overwhelming. But that leaves them powerless to make an effective plan. Naming the impact allows you to create a plan to counter that impact.

In Step 3, we will seek to understand the impact of destructive relationships in three parts.

- **Part One: Ten Factors That Increase the Impact of Your Spouse's Sin**
- **Part Two: The Impact of Your Spouse's Betrayal on You**
- **Part Three: Two Commonly Overlooked Impacts on Your Marriage**

Unfortunately, gaining a better understanding of chaos does not make it orderly. At first, what you read in Step 3 may simultaneously make sense—providing a degree of relief, and make no sense at all—leaving you feeling more overwhelmed. That might tempt you to think that you failed. This simply means that within a storm no amount of education in meteorology (the study of weather) will keep you from getting wet.

At the end of Step 3, you should be able to say some of the following statements: I'm not the only person who has felt this way . . . I'm not crazy . . . There are reasons my spouse and I see things differently . . . That doesn't necessarily mean they are hard-hearted or that I'm overreacting . . . It makes sense why my ability to remember or keep track of time is disrupted, etc.

TEN FACTORS THAT INCREASE THE IMPACT

All sin is equally bad, but not all sin has equal impact. As we prepare to examine the "type" of impact your spouse's sin has had on you and your marriage, it is important to first examine factors that influence the degree of impact. The purpose of this reflection is not to determine the amount of repentance your spouse should give. Amounts have more to do with penance than repentance. Remember, your healing can take place regardless of whether your spouse repents.

The goal is to give a framework for answering these frequent questions: Are my responses—volitional and emotional—proportional to what has happened? What accounts for how hurt I feel? Am I currently trusting in ways that are excessive or restricted based on what has happened? There is no formula for these questions or even a scale for a hurt-quotient or trust-quotient. But understanding the key factors that escalate impact should allow you and your spouse to discuss the influence of their sin in a more open, objective fashion.

While trying to discuss these factors, your spouse may get defensive and say things like the following:

- "I may not be perfect, but at least I'm not [list your faults]."
- "If you won't forgive, then you're the one who is sinning now."
- "Either you're going to trust me or not. I don't see how talking about this is going to help."
- "I said I was sorry. What more do you want from me?"

If this happens, then these discussions should be delayed until they can be done with a counselor or other mediator.

Whether these are discussed with a counselor or alone with your spouse, here are ten factors that increase the impact of sexual sin on a marriage. Most of the information you need to identify these factors should have been revealed during the full disclosure. Because of that fact, you are less likely to learn new information as you have this set of conversations. Instead, you are gaining ways to "weigh" the information you already have.

> Unfortunately, gaining a better understanding of chaos does not make it orderly.

1. **Type of sin.** When we talk about types of sin, it is tempting to try to size or weigh the different types. This causes us to think in terms of greater or lesser sins. However, all sexual sin is a form of betrayal. "Lesser betrayal" is a phrase like "minor surgery." It has the clearest meaning to those who are not experiencing it. This principle should not be used to validate all fears that emerge from the betrayal (e.g., "If my spouse looks at porn, what's to stop them from visiting a prostitute?"). The purpose of the full disclosure is to remove the sense of mystery that makes slippery-slope logic seem plausible.

2. **Duration of sin.** The longer the sexual sin transpired, the less you feel like you know your spouse and the less confident you will be that the sin will stop. Also, the longer your spouse has struggled with this sin, the more impact the sin will have on their character, values, and thinking. When someone is wrestling with changing their core values, they are more likely to have bouts of defensiveness or self-pity during the change process.

3. **Number of lies and extent of lies.** When your spouse lied, they chose to live in an artificial reality. When their sin was discovered, that artificial reality began to collapse, and your spouse was forced to live in the real world, which was new to them. This creates confusion, uncertainty, and anger. Some elaborate deception schemes reach the point of creating a double life. Most offending spouses

are surprised that their lies create as much (if not more) pain than their sexual sin.

4. **Number of times caught.** When sexual sin is not dealt with definitively (Matthew 5:27–30), it almost always repeats itself. That is the reason *True Betrayal* and *False Love* are so extensive. These studies provide a thorough approach to eliminating sexual sin and addressing its impact. Each time a couple feels like "we've been here before," the impact of sexual sin will be larger. Repetition undermines hope that things will be different this time.

5. **Number of incomplete disclosures.** Trust is the primary relational commodity damaged by sexual sin. Incomplete disclosure may deteriorate trust more than anything else. With each incomplete disclosure, the offending spouse is left thinking, *There will always be more no matter how much I know.* The only news that is trusted is bad news. Good news becomes viewed as only an incomplete story.

6. **Social and economic impact.** Who knows now (friends, family, coworkers, etc.)? How many people already knew? How much did it cost (secret credit cards, job loss, job demotion, gifts for adultery partner, etc.)? Both social and economic impacts serve as perpetual reminders and points of shame. Each is a forced sacrifice on the betrayed spouse.

7. **Risk factor of sin.** Risks vary from the worry of "Our kids could find these images on the computer" to sexually transmitted diseases, fireable offenses at work, or a child being conceived. With each risk factor, the less protected and safe the offended spouse feels.

8. **Closeness of people and places involved.** If an affair was with your friend, for instance, the amount of emotional pain increases as the number of life changes required to restore the marriage also increase. In this case, you face a twofold loss: the impact on your marriage and the loss of a friend. If sexual sin, especially adultery, occurred in the home, the emotional pain is increased as the number of memory triggers multiply.

9. **Accusations of spouse to defend their sin.** Before the sin is disclosed or during the "heat" of discovery, the offending spouse often says many hurtful things to defend, explain, or deflect from their actions. Blame-shifting, criticisms, and false accusations are common. The more of these words that are spoken, the more impact your spouse's sin has. You recognize that even when God's grace brought your spouse's sin to light, your spouse chose to attack you rather than cooperate with God's grace.

10. **Interpretation you place on your spouse's sin.** You will add interpretations to what your spouse has done. This is how humans respond to hard times. We try to make sense of it. While you can expect ownership and repentance from your spouse for the first nine items, this last one is different. Your spouse can only give compassion. These are messages that you create and, therefore, your spouse cannot remove these interpretations from your mind or emotions. Because of this, these messages will be the primary subject of Step 4 and will find their replacement through the gospel in Step 6.

    ▶ **Read Genesis 12:10–20 and 20:1–16.** Often, as we read passages like Genesis 12 and 20, we focus on the number of times that Abraham sinned. Or we focus on the impact of Abraham's sin on his relationship with God. Both are valid focal points. But if this is all we focus on, we miss the social fallout of sin. That has been our focus in this part of Step 3. Use the ten criteria above as a filter for these two passages. How many amplifying factors were present in Abraham's betrayal of Sarah? Admittedly, that is not the focal point of these passages. Genesis is about how God's people were formed into a nation and how they got to Egypt. But God gives us these details. We realize even people of great faith sin in severely hurtful ways. From the Bible's example, we see that it is appropriate to talk about these things. Although the Bible is primarily about our relationship with God, it doesn't ignore details that impact our relationships with one another.

CONCLUSION

Imagine being in a severe car accident. There is the initial pain from the injuries you sustained. At first, your focus is on recovering from those injuries. Unfortunately, as you begin to heal, things don't get easier. At that point, as your capacity increases, you begin to face the factors that add to the impact of the wreck. You begin to face things like the cost of property damage, impact on your ability to perform your job, or canceling a vacation you can no longer afford.

> The Bible is primarily about our relationship with God, but it doesn't ignore details that impact our relationships with one another.

That is the equivalent of what we are doing in Step 3. Admittedly, it feels unfair. The hard work of Step 2 gave you more concrete information about what happened. Information that would make you feel crazy if you didn't have it. If your spouse was cooperative, Step 2 was a significant step forward. But now, to fully heal and address the damage done, we must ask Step 3 questions about impact. If that is discouraging, don't feel guilty for being discouraged. It is common to feel bad about feeling bad, but regret and frustration about sin's impact are not wrong.

Again, give yourself the time you need. Review your self-care plan. As much as you want this all to be over quickly, it is not a race, and you do not make the journey easier by rushing yourself.

G4 GROUP DISCUSSION: STEP 3, PART ONE

As you discuss this material in G4 group, these questions are meant to facilitate a more honest and beneficial dialogue about this material. Anyone is free to respond to whichever questions they choose.

Experienced Members

- How did you manage to examine the impact of your spouse's betrayal without being overwhelmed by your hurt or anger?
- What would you do differently if you could do the Step 3 part of your G4 journey again?

New Members

- Which of these ten factors is currently impacting you the most?
- What emotion(s) do you have to manage most as you work through this part of Step 3?
- How can we pray for you?

Everyone

- How did it impact you to study these factors in the life of Abraham?
- In what ways does the recovery from a car accident metaphor describe your current experience?
- Do we need to discuss any safety-level concerns from the past week?

STEP 3
PART TWO

THE IMPACT OF YOUR SPOUSE'S BETRAYAL ON YOU

The video for this part of Step 3 can be found at: bradhambrick.com/truebetrayal3p2.

As you seek to understand the impact of your spouse's sexual sin upon you, it is important to recognize that these impacts come in two varieties: (1) *narrative impacts*—distorted ways of making sense of life, and (2) *volitional impacts*—unhealthy choices or reactions to being hurt and betrayed. These two types of impact are interrelated; narrative impacts make unhealthy volitional impacts seem reasonable or justifiable.

We will consider how to refine narrative impacts in Steps 4 through 6. We will explore how to change volitional impacts in Steps 7 and 8. At this point, we are merely "sorting our laundry." We won't sort it perfectly, but having more distinct piles helps us apply the best-fit remedies to each type of impact. Your goal at this stage in your journey is to merely grow more comfortable with sorting various types of impact.

TEN IMPACTS OF BETRAYAL IN MARRIAGE

The ten impacts of marital betrayal below focus on narrative and volitional forms of impact. You'll notice the various emotions that emanate from these impacts—anger, despair, fear, jealousy, regret, numbness, embarrassment, shame, depression, etc.—are not listed. Each of these forms of impact are the kinds of things that provoke these emotions. Here we want to focus on the things that prompt these (which you can more easily change) rather than the emotions themselves.

1. **Tolerating an unhealthy lifestyle.** Unhealthy marital lifestyle elements might include a lack of awareness of each other's schedules,

no budgeting process to track family expenses, unwise practices in mixed-gendered settings, communication patterns that avoid conflict, lack of accountability in each other's lives, neglect of time together as a couple or family, allowing conflicts to remain unresolved, disinterest in or infrequent intimacy, allowing life to become too busy, or tolerance of controlling or neglectful behaviors. The list could go on. Unhealthy patterns like these easily become a normalized way of life. It feels easier to ignore them than address them, at least until they manifest in a crisis.

▶ **Reflection:** What unhealthy lifestyle patterns did you begin to accept as normal?

▶ **Read Ephesians 5:3–13.** Paul says that the lifestyle associated with sexual sin "must not even be named among you" (v. 3). Paul is not just saying that Christians shouldn't do these things; he is saying that lifestyles that facilitate these things shouldn't be allowed to become normal in Christian homes. Paul is calling us to change atmospheres where sexual sin (and many other sins) are easy. For an alcoholic, changing these things would be the equivalent of not keeping beer in the fridge and finding a route between work and home that doesn't drive past the bar. As Paul talks about the lifestyle changes that would make these sins feel "out of place" (v. 4), he says these changes should be made with thanksgiving. True repentance views freedom from sin as a blessing to embrace, not a punishment to tolerate. That means your spouse embraces these kinds of lifestyle changes with a good attitude and to please God, not merely to appease your preferences.

2. **Changing your role or identity in the marriage.** In a tight social system, like a marriage, when one person acts out, if others don't opt out, they accommodate those changes. Maybe you learned how to function without knowing about the family finances. Perhaps your role becomes adapting to any unforeseen, unexplained change in your spouse's schedule. The longer those accommodations were made, the more they forged into an established role. *That's just how our family operates.* The longer you live in that role, the more that

role begins to become an identity. Rarely does this happen all at once or by demand. Occasionally your spouse may get upset when you don't do what you normally do. Most often, it is an incremental change that becomes increasingly solid.

> ▶ **Reflection:** In what unhealthy ways has your role in your marriage or your sense of personal identity been impacted by your spouse's sin?

> ▶ **Read Ephesians 5:22–33.** For where we are on our G4 journey, we are coming to this passage as a refresher on healthy marriage functioning. While your spouse was hiding sin, your marriage was not functioning according to God's design. It's not that you weren't willing. Hidden sin wouldn't allow your marriage to function properly. In this passage, we see that each spousal role (husband and wife) is secondary to our relationship with God. That is why both the description of a godly husband and wife end with "as to the Lord" and "as Christ." A right relationship with God is necessary for healthy roles to be expressed in marriage. When sin is hidden, it will distort God's design. You are in the process of learning what those sin accommodations were so that you could change them.

3. **Acquiring controlling tendencies.** "I don't want to be hurt again," is the refrain of this impact. In that sense, this tendency has understandable origins. Our rebuttal is often, "I just want my spouse to do the God-honoring and healthy thing. How can that be controlling?" Healthy expectations become controlling if they don't allow the spouse to voluntarily choose what is healthy and good.

   What you will have to face . . . is that you cannot make your husband do the right thing. You cannot talk him into it; you can't shame him into it; you can't police him into it; and you can't threaten him into it. However, what you can do is begin learning the secret of how to entrust him into the hands of the Lord. After all, only God can change his heart. —Kathy Gallagher[1]

After betrayal, controlling responses are enacted more from self-protection than selfishness. But regardless of motive, these tendencies become unhealthy for you and undermine efforts that restore trust during the restoration process. Control promises safety but can't deliver peace. Control reacts to a marriage imbalanced in your spouse's favor (access to information and freedom) by misbalancing the marriage in your favor (influence over decisions). It provides short-term security at the expense of the long-term health of the marriage.

> True repentance views freedom from sin as a blessing to embrace, not a punishment to tolerate.

▶ **Reflection:** In what ways have you tried to control things—in your spouse or others—as you've grappled with the pain created by your spouse's sin?

4. **Becoming inconsistent**. This is an extension of what makes a tendency toward control unhealthy for a marriage. We can't give too much attention to one thing (e.g., our spouse's behavior) without giving too little attention to other things. Overfocusing on one thing means we neglect other things, and the result is that we become less consistent at those other things.

Inconsistency can come into your life in several ways:

- We may find that nothing we do makes a difference in our marriage (at least the kind of difference we want to see), so we give up. Perceived powerlessness leads to inconsistency.
- We make so many declarations about changes that "should be made" that we can't keep up with them all even if they are reasonable. Overcommitment leads to inconsistency.
- We become emotionally overwhelmed and quit trying. Being emotionally saturated detracts from the emotional energy necessary to be consistent.

The purpose of this reflection is not to feel guilty. That would be the equivalent of someone feeling lazy for being fatigued after surgery. If inconsistency has begun since learning of your spouse's sin, you've probably said things like, "I don't feel like myself. I'm dropping the ball on all kinds of things. I don't understand what's wrong with me." In this context, those statements are the equivalent of a marathon runner saying shortly after surgery, "I feel so weak and lazy that I can't complete a 5K."

▶ **Reflection:** In what areas have you been frustrated by your lack of consistency? Do you view that inconsistency through the lens of guilt or compassion?

5. **Growing gullible or cynical.** When we're lied to, we tend to respond in one of two directions: gullible or cynical. You feel torn. "At some point I have to give the benefit of the doubt, right?" But on the other hand, "So much that sounded plausible was a lie—why believe anything but my doubts now?" It begins to feel like the only choice is to believe everything or believe nothing. "Truth," some objective reality that can be known with confidence, begins to feel like a cruel joke. You wanted to know the truth, but each time you thought you did, it changed (e.g., more of the story comes out or another hurtful choice is made). So we drift toward being cynical or gullible.

▶ **Reflection:** When have you become all-or-nothing, gullible-or-cynical about trust?

▶ **Read Hebrews 2:14–18.** This passage raises the question of trust amid suffering. That is the difficult battle you are facing as you seek to resist being either gullible or cynical and learn how to trust wisely amid suffering. We will develop this theme in greater detail in Step 7. Notice that this passage ends with Jesus's compassion for your predicament (v. 18). Jesus too was betrayed by someone he was highly committed to (Matthew 10:1–4), someone he trusted enough to manage his finances (John 13:29), and someone who used affection to betray him (Luke 22:47–48). Perpetual skepticism and uncertainty feel like "lifelong slavery" (Hebrews 2:15). Jesus is with you in this uncertainty (13:20–21) and will ultimately let the truth be known (4:12–13). *True Betrayal* and *False Love* are aids to this truth being known. They strive to allow truth to be known by confession, which is best for your spouse's restoration and the benefit of your family.

6. **Growing passive toward life**. "It doesn't matter what I do." These are immensely painful words. They reveal that we feel like we are losing a sense of agency in our life; that we no longer believe that the choices we make can make a positive difference. They are the words of a parent whose child has a terminal disease, the business owner facing bankruptcy, and the spouse whose partner has been unfaithful. Sometimes these words are healthy. They reveal we are accepting the limits of our choices. Other times, they are unhealthy. They tempt us to grow passive toward choices that— even if they do not produce our most desired outcome—can still enrich and benefit our life. We don't want the healthy acknowledgment of our limits to lead us to the unhealthy neglect of influential choices.

   ▶ **Reflection:** What choices that could make a positive difference in your life, or your marriage, have you begun to neglect as you've felt overwhelmed?

   ▶ **Read Philippians 3:7–16.** Paul knew he did not have what it took to continue (v. 12a) and that what he had been building his life upon was not capable of sustaining him through his current situation (v. 7). He had to remind himself and his readers to "press on" and not allow this sense of being overwhelmed to paralyze them (v. 12b). Paul did not literally forget his past (v. 13). He frequently referenced it (2 Corinthians 11:21–33; 1 Timothy 1:12–17). But Paul wants us to see that our past doesn't have to so define our life that it overshadows God's ability to work in our present and future. This is the mark of maturity for which he was striving and calls on us to strive toward (Philippians 3:15).

7. **Growing insecurity**. When our spouse has hidden sexual sin, we begin to live with a constant barrage of questions about ourselves, our spouse, and our marriage. Perpetually questioning whether these things are "good enough" is the essence of insecurity. Now that what we thought was secure (i.e., good enough to be honored), proved to be inadequate (at least in the sense that our spouse strayed), it is easy to feel like we have no idea what is "good enough" anymore. Our insecurity may express itself through

fear, anger, depression, doubt, or other disruptive emotions. The net effect of living with perpetual questioning is that everything begins to feel personal. It creates a self-referential way of thinking that interprets each action, word, or even silence in your day as a commentary on your worth.

▶ **Reflection:** When do you notice insecurity disrupting your day? Is this a new experience or a heightened struggle with insecurity that predated your spouse's sin?

▶ **Read 2 Corinthians 10:1–18.** Paul was in an intense and personal conflict. As a result, he struggled with how he came across (e.g., weak in person; strong in his letters). Paul wanted to be kind and gracious toward people, even those who disagreed with him, but he also wanted to clearly answer his critics. We can easily imagine how trying to maintain that balance created a highly self-referential style of thinking. We can tell this burdened Paul deeply. This burden wasn't bad. It revealed how important these relationships and the subject matter were. Be encouraged by Paul's vulnerability and learn from his example. You are burdened by something important (e.g., your marriage, avoiding sin, honoring relationships). You are wrestling to maintain a godly focus as you do, or else you would have abandoned this study before now.

8. **Living a one-variable Life.** Chances are, you want one thing more than anything else; that is, for your spouse to demonstrate purity and integrity. It is easy for that one thing to increasingly become the only variable by which you measure a good day, a good week, a good conversation or a good anything. This can happen for several reasons:

- It is natural and right to place a high value on our marriage. When our marriage is threatened, that easily becomes central to almost everything we think and feel.
- There is a clear "one thing" your spouse should do. When the remedy to a major dilemma is clear, it is easy to fixate on whether that thing is or isn't happening.

- As we pray earnestly for the things that ought to happen, our sense of God's closeness and care can become exclusively tied to whether that thing is happening.

However, reducing our life to a single variable has an unexpected effect: It makes our world smaller. The smaller our world gets, the more dominated it becomes by the impact of our spouse's sin. Soon, if our spouse is not responding appropriately, we feel like there is no reason for any hope or encouragement. We become an emotional slave to our spouse's choices. As important as our spouse and marriage ought to be, that is too large a role for them to play.

> We don't want the healthy acknowledgment of our limits to lead us to the unhealthy neglect of influential choices.

▶ **Reflection:** When or how can you see yourself beginning to live a one-variable life?

9. **Relating codependently**. Few terms are harder to define than codependency. It is a pop-psychology term, not a clinical term, so it has no official definition. For our purposes, we will define codependency as a relational style that believes "I can change your bad behaviors with my good behaviors." You can quickly see the appeal. If this were true, you could be good enough to make your spouse stop being bad. When we spell it out this way, it doesn't seem as convincing. But as an unarticulated, subjective feeling of what we wished were true, it is highly compelling.

The appeal is that it gives us a facade of control. The problem is that this control comes at the expense of making you responsible for your spouse's sin; if your spouse is still being bad, it is because you're not being good enough. Taken further, this mindset results in your spouse's preferences becoming your functional god. Your spouse's preferences become the standard or law you must fulfill to be "good enough" and not be punished by the hellish consequence of their sin.

Many partners find themselves making compromises in the relationship that lead to the loss of their sense of self. Examples include acting against your own morals, values or beliefs, as well as giving up on life goals, hobbies, and interests. Other examples include changing your dress or appearance to accommodate the addict, or accepting the addict's sexual norms as your own. . . . You may have struggles with feelings of unworthiness or perfectionism. As a result, you have settled for feeling needed in the relationship and compromised yourself to keep the peace or feel valued. —Stefanie Carnes[2]

▶ **Read Ezekiel 18:1–4.** This passage closely parallels Jeremiah 31:28–30. The problem being addressed occurred frequently enough that God needed to address it through multiple prophets. Ezekiel is confronting a culture-wide problem with how God's people thought about responsibility. Israel believed that children were responsible for the sins of their parents so strongly that it became an accepted proverb of their day (v. 2). In a similar way, you may feel responsible for your spouse's sin. God was very bold in his refutation of this mindset. God wanted his people to know that each person is responsible for their own choices (v. 4). This should give you freedom from whatever fears you may have about there being something you could do—but can't figure out—to make your spouse stop sinning.

▶ **Reflection:** In what ways have you been prone to live as if you could be good enough to compel your spouse to stop being bad?

10. **Experiencing symptoms of post-traumatic stress.** After the discovery of your spouse's sexual sin, it is common to feel as if your fight-or-flight response is chronically left on for weeks or months. If so, you will feel perpetually activated and exhausted at the same time. The betrayal of a spouse can be traumatic in both the descriptive (i.e., overwhelming) and clinical sense (i.e., specific symptoms) of the term.

If you are experiencing the following symptoms three months after the discovery of your spouse's sin, it would be wise to work with a counselor experienced with trauma.[3] The early steps of *True Betrayal* are meant to help you create a safe and transparent home environment that may naturally result in the alleviation of these symptoms. But if these symptoms persist, it is advisable to seek individual counseling.

_____ Intrusive memories of the events surrounding your spouse's sexual sin or your discovery

_____ Recurrent dreams associated with your spouse's sexual sin

_____ Flashbacks where you feel like you are reexperiencing your spouse's sin or the discovery of it

_____ Intense distress when you experience things that remind you of your spouse's sexual sin

_____ Feelings of detachment from your own emotions or other people

_____ Difficulty concentrating at your normal levels

_____ Hypervigilance—chronically anticipating what might go wrong beyond what was normal for you

A resource on trauma, which is built around the same nine steps as *True Betrayal,* can be found at bradhambrick.com/trauma.

▶ **Reflection:** Which of these symptoms are present in your life and persisting even as your home environment stabilizes?

CONCLUSION

It might be hard to know what moral basket to put these ten experiences in. Because these experiences are not good, it can be natural for us to put them in the "bad" basket. However, if we do that, we feel guilty for having a difficult time responding to things that we didn't cause. That would be a sense of false guilt.

That is why it is important for you to put these experiences in the "hard" basket. Some things that aren't good (not God's design) also aren't bad (that is, not immoral); instead, they are hard (an experience of suffering). As you work through Step 3, you'll likely need to remind yourself or your friends in your G4 group many times of this.

G4 GROUP DISCUSSION: STEP 3, PART TWO

As you discuss this material in G4 group, these questions are meant to facilitate a more honest and beneficial dialogue about this material. Anyone is free to respond to whichever questions they choose.

Experienced Members

- Are any of these ten forms of impact still "sticky" for you today?
- Did it feel more like a relief or a burden when you first began to acknowledge these impacts?

New Members

- Do one or more of these impacts currently feel overwhelming for you?
- How are you doing at avoiding a one-variable life early in your G4 journey?
- How can we pray for you?

Everyone

- How well are you differentiating "hard" from "bad" in what you processed in this part of Step 3?
- How are you doing at avoiding a codependent style of relating with your spouse?
- Do we need to discuss any safety-level concerns from the past week?

STEP 3
PART THREE

TWO COMMONLY OVERLOOKED IMPACTS ON YOUR MARRIAGE

The video for this part of Step 3 can be found at: bradhambrick.com/truebetrayal3p3.

Your spouse's sexual sin doesn't just impact you as an individual. It also impacts the marriage in ways that are distinct from its impact upon you. Consider the experience of having a child. That experience had an impact on each spouse individually and an impact on the marriage. Both are valid and need to be understood. In this part of Step 3, we will be exploring the latter.

You have likely already been experiencing these impacts but were unable to articulate them. Even once you begin to understand "What is going on with me?" you may still be wrestling with "What is going on with *us*?" We'll try to address this by considering two often overlooked challenges that face a marriage recovering from betrayal.

BEING ON TWO DIFFERENT TIMETABLES

Many couples find the concept of being on two different timetables to be one of the most beneficial and enlightening dynamics to understand. To use the metaphor of a movie, the two of you are watching the same film, but your spouse began long before you did. To use the parallel of a tragic car accident, the two of you are living in the aftermath of the same wreck, but you were, metaphorically, in a coma (i.e., unaware of what was happening) until you discovered your spouse's sin.

To state it plainly, the two of you are experiencing the same crisis, but your spouse has been aware of the crisis for weeks, months, or perhaps even years longer than you have. This accounts for some (not all) of the differences the two of you have in how you're responding to this crisis.

We will use the stages of grief to help visualize these two timetables. Your spouse likely began their journey when the initial temptation to sin emerged. Their emotions may have sounded something like this:

- **Shock**—Disbelief that someone is interested in them or that it could be this easy to find stuff on the internet.
- **Denial**—Thinking, *We don't mean anything by what we're doing. We're just being friends.* Or *It's just porn and no one will find out.*
- **Anger**—A sense of self-condemnation for doing something they knew was wrong.
- **Bargaining**—Convincing themselves it's not that bad. Drawing a line, a little farther into sin, and saying, "I won't cross *that* line."
- **Depression**—A sense of guilt and hopelessness when they wanted to get out of their sin but felt trapped.
- **Acceptance**—Once sin became normal, it seemed as if they could get away with it.
- **Forgiveness**—The longer they sinned, the quieter their conscience became. The felt sense that forgiveness was needed slowly becomes muted. This is what the Bible refers to as a seared conscience (I Timothy 4:2).

Most often, the betrayed spouse does not learn about the affair until the latter two stages. Early on, the offending spouse is diligent about keeping their sin hidden. It is often not until the offending spouse becomes comfortable with the presence of their sin and gets sloppy that they get caught. However, during the mental distraction of bargaining or the down emotions of depression, you may have begun to feel like something was "off." That would have been the beginning of your comparable emotional journey.

- **Shock**—"Could my spouse really be cheating? Is my spouse hiding something from me?" Even asking the question may have evoked a sense of guilt.
- **Denial**—"No, there has to be another explanation." You try to find a different explanation for the clues that are emerging.

- **Anger**—As certainty builds or discovery hits, the wrongness of your spouse's actions is met with the appropriate emotional response—anger.
- **Bargaining**—This is another stage of question-asking. It feels like if you could only get your mind around the "why" question, you would be able to figure out what to do.
- **Depression**—You realize that no matter how many questions you ask, you are not going to be able to unwrite these chapters from your story. It hurts. You feel like giving up.
- **Acceptance**—You're not accepting your spouse's sin, as if you're declaring it okay. But you accept that this betrayal is part of your story and begin planning a future in light of that reality.
- **Forgiveness**—Whether forgiveness results in restoration, forgiveness is part of finding emotional freedom from this painful season of life. It is something God wants for you, for your good. The question of trust, marital restoration, and divorce is one we engage more directly in Step 7.

> The two of you are experiencing the same crisis, but your spouse has been aware of the crisis for weeks, months, or perhaps even years longer than you have.

Hopefully, you can begin to see why it has been so hard for the two of you to communicate. Your spouse may have seemed cold, indifferent, or relieved because they were hiding this information for weeks, months, or years. You were likely hot, panicked, and taken off guard. For you, this was breaking news about something brand new.

Even when you and your spouse agree on the facts, it is hard to have a productive conversation in that environment. You feel like your spouse doesn't "get it" because (at least in part) they are not where you are. They keep telling you that "you don't understand" because (at least in part) you are not where they are.

This also explains why there are so many cross-references between *True Betrayal* and *False Love*. What is changing is not just choices but timetables. We're not just trying to get you accurate and complete information but also to bring you and your spouse closer to the same timetable with that information.

Some couples get discouraged by this concept, asking, "How will we ever get on the same page?" If you feel discouraged, remember what we said early on: Honesty and cooperation with the process are the best predictors of progress. If your spouse is still being honest and cooperating, don't allow the articulation of new challenges to discourage you.

FALLING INTO THE PRINCIPLE OF LEAST INTEREST TRAP

Here is the principle of least interest: *The person who is least interested in a relationship holds the most power.* This is true in business, real estate, and marriage. However, when this principle becomes active within a marriage, it is never healthy. A marriage that begins to operate based on power and leverage rather than love and sacrifice is a marriage in decline. When this happens, marriage quits being a microcosm of the gospel and becomes a microcosm of the world.

Betrayal is a common trigger that prompts a marriage to start operating on the principle of least interest. In many marriages, the progression looks something like this:

- Your spouse has a growing dissatisfaction in the marriage as their sin increases. You feel the drift, so you concede or sacrifice more to care for your spouse and your marriage. This continues.
- You start to feel used, or at least that the marriage is too one-sided. You voice your concerns. Out of guilt and not wanting to get caught, your spouse invests more in the marriage for a season.
- Because their sin is still present and authenticity cannot be present, your spouse drifts away again. The cycle repeats.
- Eventually, you find out about your spouse's sin. You are deeply hurt. You pull back in anger and fear. Out of guilt and penance, your spouse invests more in the marriage.
- When you become more open to the possibility of restoration, your spouse gets fatigued by their elevated level of investment and pulls back since it now feels safer to do so.
- You are hurt by their lack of continued effort. You get upset. This creates fear in your spouse and increases their investment in the marriage again.
- And so on . . . and so on. The person who shows more interest loses voice and influence. The person who shows less interest gains voice and influence.

Frequently, this power play dynamic existed to a lesser degree in the marriage before the crisis emerged. When this is the case, both spouses are familiar with the "rules of the game." After the marital crisis, the couple can play their old game with more powerful weapons. In these cases, mutual repenting for playing games with the marriage long before the sexual sin is a prerequisite to continued progress.

The question becomes, How do we get out of this power play dynamic? Here are several points to help you exit the principle of least interest trap:

- A new motive for change must emerge. Personal preference and emotional self-protection cannot remain the reason you pursue a more functional marriage. These motives feed the principle of least interest. Change must be pursued because you want to pursue a God-honoring marriage. When this happens, you pivot toward a marriage marked by mutuality expressed through sacrifice and honor. It's a new economy for your marriage.
- The offending spouse should lead in sacrifice by doing all that is possible to alleviate uncertainty. When this sacrifice is not voluntary, it undermines a mutual marriage. Patterns of past deceit are power because, as the saying goes, information is power. Surrendering the ability to deceive brings balance. This voluntary sacrifice should be seen as part of genuine repentance, not appeasing or making concessions to one's spouse.
- Abstain from requesting change with statements such as "If . . . , then . . ." or "Because . . . , you should . . . ." These feed a morally-generated power differential in marriage. Even when the request is honored, the nature of these requests do little to restore mutuality. Requests based on a moral high ground do little to regrow trust. It is better for you and your marriage to let your request stand alone. For instance, "It would help me recover [relax, trust, etc.] if you would [desired action]." Softer requests allow trust to grow.
- Recognize this is a unique season. Do not begin to think, *This is how things are going to be from now on.* That mindset feeds despair. Despair tempts us toward more power-based, immediate-result approaches. This season in your marriage, if handled well, can be just that—a season.

In each of these points, we are separating "change" from "power." Actually, separating change from power is just another way of defining healthy trust. *Trust is the belief that reasonable requests will be honored without the need for relational leverage.* This definition should allow you to begin to build trust without thinking trust has to mean putting yourself in a position to be hurt by the other again." When leverage is required, trust is not warranted yet. Cultivating trust wisely will be discussed more in Step 7.

> ▶ **Read 1 Corinthians 9:8–14.** Paul was in a conflict that had the strong potential to devolve into power play dynamics—some in the church at Corinth were accusing him of being in the ministry for money. Notice that Paul begins by stating what is healthy and holy (v. 8)—those who labor deserve compensation; this is what God established. After stating this, Paul was careful to allow the focus to remain on the point where his audience most needed to understand the gospel (v. 12). Similarly, as you walk through understanding the impact of your suffering with your spouse, your goals should be (a) clearly stating what is healthy and holy for marriage, and (b) keeping the focus on where your spouse needs to embrace the gospel to experience lasting change.

CONCLUSION

We are coming to an end of the first cluster of steps. We have spent the first three steps focusing on creating stability. Stability by preparing for the difficult journey ahead. Stability by getting as much accurate information as possible as a foundation for future decisions. Stability by understanding the impact of what has happened so that we feel less crazy and know what to account for in the steps ahead.

As you transition to Step 4, there will be a new focus. We will pivot toward working on the ways we make sense of these experiences. Even if your spouse is repentant and faithful moving forward, there are many ways to make sense of hurt that would undermine personal health and marital restoration efforts. If your spouse is uncooperative, how you make sense of this experience will be foundational to your long-term emotional and relational health. Either way, that is why we'll focus our attention there in Steps 4 through 6.

G4 GROUP DISCUSSION: STEP 3, PART THREE

As you discuss this material in G4 group, these questions are meant to facilitate a more honest and beneficial dialogue about this material. Anyone is free to respond to whichever questions they choose.

Experienced Members

- If your spouse was cooperative, how long did it take for the two of you to harmonize your timetables again?
- What was the hardest part for you in surrendering the power of morally rooted requests for change?

> Trust is the belief that reasonable requests will be honored without the need for relational leverage.

New Members

- In what ways do you most feel the effects of being on two timetables?
- Where are you now in the grieving process over your spouse's sin?
- How can we pray for you?

Everyone

- Do you currently feel more encouraged/equipped or discouraged/overwhelmed as you study the impacts of your spouse's sin on the marriage?
- Which strategy for avoiding the principle of least interest trap do you currently need to apply most?
- Do we need to discuss any safety-level concerns from the past week?

Is What I'm Thinking True, Right, Real, and Helpful?

STEP 4
LEARN MY SUFFERING STORY, which I use to make sense of my experience.

At the end of this step, I want to be able to say . . .

"My spouse's betrayal shaped my beliefs about myself, life, relationships, and God based on my suffering [describe each]. I lived out of those beliefs because they were all I knew, and they seem to fit [describe how]. Those beliefs became guiding themes for my life story. Putting those beliefs into words unsettles me [describe why]. I reject these destructive scripts and am committed to learning how my life fits into God's great story of redemption."

STEP 4
PART ONE

HOW WE NARRATE OUR LIVES

The video for this part of Step 4 can be found at: bradhambrick.com/truebetrayal4p1.

I t has been said that animals divide between herbivores (those eating plants) and carnivores (those eating meat), but that humans are verbivores—we live off words, or, more accurately, off the meaning we give to life through words. This is why we will emphasize the themes of story, journey, and identity in Steps 4 through 6. They are how we digest life.

But you don't have to enjoy literature to benefit from Step 4. You just need the courage to put into words what and how you think. In the last couple of steps, you've put into words what you have experienced and how it has impacted you. In those steps, we looked at experiences, emotions, and relational dynamics. Now we're going to consider how you talk to yourself and how you make sense of the things that have happened.

In Step 4, we will look at the unhealthy ways people commonly make sense of betrayal. That means you may disagree with everything you write down in Step 4. A common refrain for you may be, "I know this isn't true, but . . ." or "If I heard one of my friends talk about their situation like this, I would try to help them see it differently." That's okay. More than that, it's actually good. Part of changing the way we think is putting our beliefs into words so we can examine them.

We'll put most of our Step 4 work in the category of *real but not true*. Think of the child who grows up in a verbally abusive home. From their earliest memories, the child is told, "You're no good. It's your fault our life is hard. I wish you were never born. Why do you make me yell at you?" Here is the abbreviated version of that child's Step 4 work.

- "I am a mistake."
- "I make other people's lives harder."
- "At best, God doesn't care about me; at worst, God hates me."

Are any of these statements true? No. Are these real experiences that accurately capture how this child is making sense of life? Yes. What good is putting real-but-not-true beliefs into words? It helps us begin to doubt them. That's really our complete goal in Step 4. If we begin to doubt the destructive messages of our suffering, we will have created a crack in a veil of darkness to let light in.

▶ **Read Psalms 10:1; 13:1; 22:1–2; 44:23–24; 74:1; and 102:10.** Notice how many false statements about God are in these psalms. By inspiring these psalms, God is not affirming these statements. God is demonstrating his willingness to put compassion before instruction. God's compassion toward our felt experience—even when false—strengthens us enough to be able to embrace the truth. Realize you are not coming to God against his permission when you wrestle with thoughts like these. *God wants to transform our suffering story, but he is willing to enter it where we are and transform it from within the story.*

One bold message in the book of Job is that you can say anything to God. Throw him your grief, your anger, your doubt, your bitterness, your betrayal, your disappointment—he can absorb them all. . . . God can deal with every human response save one. He cannot abide the response I fall back on instinctively: an attempt to ignore him or treat him as though he does not exist. That response never once occurred to Job. —Philip Yancey[1]

In the next parts of Step 4, we will walk through the same process several times.

1. We'll introduce two big questions: Who is God? and Who are you?
2. We'll break the big question down into smaller questions.
3. You'll be asked to be honest (accuracy can wait until later).

4. We'll introduce enough of the Bible to create healthy doubt toward the things that are untrue, but we won't rush you to feel differently simply because you understand more.

After we've walked through four big questions, we'll help you congeal these narrative elements (i.e., the answers to the various questions) into a story in the final part of Step 4. We'll begin to see the story by which you've made sense of your marital disruption. That work will set up what you do in Step 5 and Step 6.

> God wants to transform our suffering story, but he is willing to enter it where we are and transform it from within the story.

In Step 5, we'll explore how to grieve the pain and losses associated with your spouse's action without embracing the narrative elements that are untrue. For too long, any grieving you have done has likely (though unintentionally) reinforced these destructive messages. Then in Step 6, we'll seek to replace these untrue scripts with accurate and redemptive themes from the gospel.

PAIN VS. SUFFERING?

Medical professionals who work with chronic pain often differentiate between pain and suffering. Pain is the physical experience (e.g., a pinched nerve) that travels from nerve to nerve and registers in the brain. Pain is treated medically. Suffering, however, is the sense of hopelessness or despair that attaches to pain. It does not travel via nerve endings; instead, it is part of our immaterial mind (not our physical brain). Hence there is no medical treatment for suffering. That work is done in the soul, not the body.

As we examine the suffering story we use to make sense of our experience, we are examining suffering (i.e., the meaning you have given to your experience) rather than pain (i.e., the act of betrayal or how you learned of it). As in chronic pain, both *pain* and *suffering* are real and should be treated. In Steps 4–6, we will treat the suffering. During this time, your spouse should continue working through *False Love*. Then, in Steps 7–8, we will return to the pain of your experience.

You might ask, Why are we dealing with the suffering before the pain? Can't we do both at the same time? We are. If your spouse is working through *False Love*, that is the most important component of working on the pain that can be addressed at this stage.

At this time in your spouse's work, they will be learning to genuinely repent to God; how to confess their sin to you (humbly seeking forgiveness, not just giving you an accurate history), and to fulfill reasonable expectations during the restoration process. This is an important time for your spouse, but these steps may not be as conversationally interactive as the previous steps.

> Pain is the physical experience that travels from nerve to nerve and registers in the brain. Suffering is the sense of hopelessness or despair that attaches to pain.

Unless we take some time to work on the suffering side of your experience, it would be tempting for you to grow increasingly passive, impatient, or bitter as your spouse transitions from steps where there is a high information transfer to steps that produce less information to share.

These do not have to be "the silent steps" for you. They can be a time when you process the information you have gained in the first three steps of your journey. You have taken in an unsettling amount of information. It would be unwise to quickly move forward without taking time to assimilate what you've learned, distill the destructive messages (Step 4), grieve the betrayal (Step 5), and reframe these painful events in light of the gospel (Step 6).

CONCLUSION

You now know where we're going. Don't feel any pressure to feel better. Studying a map and knowing the next steps is one thing. Walking the journey is another. In this first part of Step 4, all we've done is drawn a map to clear a path. We've named and sought to remove emotional obstacles. If you have a sense for how the next several steps fit together, you've gleaned everything you need from this part of your journey.

G4 GROUP DISCUSSION: STEP 4, PART ONE

As you discuss this material in G4 group, these questions are meant to facilitate a more honest and beneficial dialogue about this material. Anyone is free to respond to whichever questions they choose.

Experienced Members

- The concept of story or scripts can be confusing. Having worked Steps 4, 5, and 6, how would you explain them?
- How has the category of "real but not true" helped you navigate difficult emotions and beliefs?

New Members

- Was the humble goal of doubting your destructive beliefs encouraging or discouraging?
- How did the medical parallel of pain and suffering help you grasp the type of work that is done in Steps 4, 5, and 6?
- How can we pray for you?

Everyone

- What things do you say to yourself frequently that you already know are part of the destructive scripts making up your suffering story?
- How did the devotional on false statements in the psalms encourage you?
- Do we need to discuss any safety-level concerns from the past week?

STEP 4

PART TWO

WHO IS GOD? WHO ARE YOU?

The video for this part of Step 4 can be found at: bradhambrick.com/truebetrayal4p2.

Suffering distorts our view of everything. Pain blurs how we think about life. Because we're processing pain prompted by someone as close as our spouse, this is even more true on your *True Betrayal* journey. That is why we set aside an entire step to articulate and begin to doubt the distorted messages about life that we've begun to believe.

In this part of Step 4, we will explore two foundational questions for how we make sense of life: Who is God? and Who are you? With each question we'll seek to put into words the kinds of distortions that commonly emerge when we've faced the hardship of betrayal in a marriage.

As you read each false message, it is important to realize that each likely began as a feeling that became cemented as a belief. In other words, *each false message began as an emotional response that became a guiding principle you used to make sense of life.* For instance, we feel alone and then come to believe that God abandoned us. You didn't set out to embrace these beliefs. They just seemed to solidify as the best explanation as life remained difficult.

Realizing this helps us be less defensive. This step is not about confronting heresy. It is about holding these beliefs with an open hand so we can say, "Yeah, I've begun to think this. I'm not sure if I believe these things are true, but they feel real. I'm willing to ask questions about these beliefs." If we get that far in this step, we will have set ourselves up to make significant progress in the steps ahead.

A Bible passage and devotional reflection is provided after each theme. These are not meant to be holistic rebuttals to each destructive script. That would move you too fast—like an orthodontist proposing to fix a teenager's gaping teeth in only two months. Instead, these devotions are meant to do two things. First, allow you to see that God chose to speak to the kind of hard questions you're grappling with. God hasn't ignored your pain. Second, to introduce a new perspective. After prolonged pain, our distorted beliefs have the home field advantage in our mind. During Step 4, be content to "try on" these alternative beliefs and experiment with the possibility that these things are true.

HIDDEN SIN'S UNIQUE IMPACT

Suffering rooted in deceit has a unique capacity to disrupt our life; it affects our sense of who we are and what feels safe. Suffering not rooted in deceit only affects the present and future. It may be intense, but it is "now." We have some capacity to decide what to do with it. For example, if you have cancer, you consult with doctors and make decisions about treatments. That is different from hidden sins of betrayal.

Hidden sin is "then" before you knew about it "now." It feels impossible to fight the past. Yet this unknown past is part of your story. Strangely, you are asking questions about your life in the same way that you read a novel—wanting to know what happened next. You are like an adopted child hearing a story from his adopted parents about a time before he became a part of the family and asking, "Do I remember that?" The mere fact that you don't know your own story is simultaneously unsettling, infuriating, and frightful.

> One wife said to me as she became aware of her husband's affairs, "Give me my life back! Take me back to twenty minutes before we started talking; I want my husband back just as he was!" —Harry Schaumburg[1]

The fact that you do not know your own story makes it so much easier for false (even if partially true) storylines to begin to dominate how you make sense of your life. Things that might only be true of this situation can easily be generalized to apply to all of life. When this happens, fear, anger, insecurity, or other emotions that you feel become a permanent part of your life.

It does no good to say, "The rest of your life will not be like this season." You didn't see this season coming. When you have an enemy you can't see, it only makes sense to always be on guard, right? Deception makes sexual betrayal feel like a ghost. It was haunting your life before you knew it existed.

THREE DISTORTED THEMES ABOUT GOD

Give yourself the freedom to admit you hold these distorted beliefs if you do. Acknowledging what we believe is not irreverent. In this context, it's simply a form of saying to God, "I've been through some hard things. I've tried to figure out where you fit in those hardships. I'm not sure I agree with my conclusions, but here they are. Can we talk about them?" That is the kind of prayer posture we'll maintain throughout Step 4. Actually, the fear that you cannot be honest with God about what you believe about him (even when false) would only ratify the idea that God is who you fear he might be.

1. **God is not good.** We can be prone to think, *If God is in charge and God is good, how could my marriage be like this? How could God be good when this much pain is possible? I know saying bad-God may feel like saying dry-water or cold-fire, but it represents my experience even if it doesn't make sense.*

    Unhealthy ideas often follow good logic. That is the case above. The paragraph above is not irrational. However, when we embrace the idea that God is not good, we lose any foundation for peace, hope, or stability. The world becomes governed by a survival of the fittest principle in which everyone is either predator or prey; everyone is either unfaithful or betrayed. If you are unwilling to betray others, then you must live in fear. That's not satisfying, and we have an innate sense that it's not true.

    In the same way that our desire for food (hunger) indicates that food exists, our desire for goodness (a moral order) indicates that God is good. We do not have fundamental appetites for things that don't exist. Humanity's near-universal assessment that betrayal in marriage is wrong reveals that the God in whose image we are made does not approve of what your spouse did. The Genesis 3 fall may have wreaked havoc on how people live, but the character of the God who made us is good.

▶ **Reflection:** When are you most prone to think God is not good? What kind of temporary comfort does letting go of a belief in God's goodness provide? What sense of futility emerges when you doubt God's goodness? When you question God's goodness, what do you tend to say to yourself?

▶ **Read Psalm 34.** You might read "taste and see that the LORD is good" in verse 8 and think: *Great, the Bible disagrees with me, so now I feel worse.* But realize that God includes phrases like "the LORD is good" in Scripture because he knew we would need this reminder. The Bible says "fear not" so many times because God knows this fallen world is a scary place and we would need that reassurance. *The fact that the Bible speaks to our doubts is a sign of compassion, not condemnation.* With that in mind, notice the phrases that reveal the context of this reminder about God's goodness. As David wrote this psalm, he needed God to be his refuge (v. 8) because he was afraid (v. 4) and in need (v. 6). David knew these experiences were common enough that he put them in the hymnal of God's people. In this psalm, God reassures us that he hears our prayers (v. 17) and that our affliction is not a sign he has rejected us (v. 19).

2. **God does not care.** "Maybe God is good, but he's just not concerned enough. After all, there are plenty of people with a strong moral fiber who are unmoved about important issues going on around them. Perhaps that explains what is going on with God. I can understand. With all God's got on his plate, maybe he just overlooked my life."

   When we've experienced major relational brokenness, it can be easy to view God as the "CEO of All Creation, Inc. LLC" rather than our loving heavenly Father. It eases the internal disruption by depersonalizing God. If God were a system of beliefs, a machine, or even an accountant, then our questions about his seeming lack of involvement or concern would be less painful.

   But if God does not care, it makes no sense to pray or read our Bible. Prayer would just remind us that God is not listening. Reading our Bible would just be reviewing instructions for life that don't seem to be working for us. This distorted theme transforms two of our primary sources of comfort and strength into reminders of our worst fears.

▶ **Reflection:** When are you most prone to think, *God does not care*? What kind of temporary comfort does letting go of a belief in God's care for you provide? What life-giving activities do you begin to neglect when you doubt God's care? When you question God's care, what do you tend to say to yourself?

> The fact that the Bible speaks to our doubts is a sign of compassion, not condemnation.

▶ **Read John 11:1–44.** Don't just read that "Jesus wept" (v. 35); notice why and when he wept. Jesus knew he was about to raise Lazarus from the dead (vv. 43–44), yet Jesus did not withhold his compassion from his friends in their moment of grief. Jesus doesn't rush us in our pain. Notice that Jesus being moved this way was not a one-time occurrence; it happened multiple times (v. 38). Jesus's response was not a one-time exception because he was so close to Mary, Martha, and Lazarus. It was and is his character. That means it is something we can still rely on. This passage is powerful not merely because it reveals that Jesus, as our Great High Priest (Hebrews 2:14–18 and 4:14–16), has the capacity for tender emotions, but it shows that God is moved by our hardships.

3. **God is not able.** "Well, if God is good and he cares, maybe he's just not able. I guess I must accept that people are free enough to hurt one another and there's not anything that anyone—including God—can do about it."

    In the next part of Step 4, we will consider how to think about the choices of others who hurt us. People do have enough freedom to make choices that hurt their life and ours. But we need not embrace this reality with resignation that renders God as powerless.

    We often miss that if other people are free to make choices that matter, we are too. Not only your spouse, but you also can make choices of consequence. God is active in both—calling your spouse to repentance and inviting you to assess the situation and respond wisely. *True Betrayal* is about identifying and enacting choices that fit your spouse's response to their sin. We often think God is powerless because we believe he is asking us to live passively. That is not true.

▶ **Reflection:** When are you most prone to think, *God is not able?* What temporary comfort does letting go of a belief in God's power provide for you? What choices of consequence do you think God is inviting you to consider? When you question God's care, what do you tend to say to yourself?

▶ **Read Numbers 11:16–23.** Before you read this passage, keep one finger in Numbers 11 and pinch it together with the pages that start with Exodus 1. The pages between your fingers are the biography of Moses's life, to whom God said, "Is the LORD's hand shortened? Now you shall see whether my word will come true for you or not" (v. 23). Moses had a long history of pain and provision in his walk with God. We can understand Moses's doubt. Too often we read our Bible as if people like Moses lived a series of epic moments instead of a long lifetime with hardships like we do. Yes, Moses had a burning-bush moment and saw God part the Red Sea, but he also had far more ordinary days when he needed to be reminded of God's power. Most of our life is lived in ordinary days when it is easy to doubt whether God will keep his promises. When we need to be reminded of who God is, we are far more like the heroes of the faith than we realize. Your doubt is no more a sign of God's absence in your life than Moses's doubt was an indicator that God had abandoned him.

FOUR DISTORTED THEMES ABOUT YOURSELF

The two main characters in your life story are God and you. When your marriage is in upheaval, your spouse's choices can tend to usurp both God and you in your story. You begin to live in reaction to what your spouse is or is not doing. Their influence in your life becomes larger than God's or your own.

This helps us understand the priority of our first two questions (Who is God? Who are you?). We don't merely want to recognize that pain may have distorted our answers, we want to see how the order of our questions has become disrupted. By the time we finish our G4 journey, we not only want more accurate answers to these important questions, but we also want to have a better prioritization of our questions.

As we move into questions of personal identity, it's important to realize that distorted beliefs about ourselves amid a marital betrayal are usually rooted in a desire for more control than we have. If we want more power over the situation than we have, we view ourselves as weak. If we want more answers than we can have, we call ourselves stupid. In this, we see that a more accurate set of beliefs about ourselves serves as a buffer against many of the following self-condemning statements we're prone to believe:

1. **Something is wrong with me.** After betrayal through sexual sin, it is easy to begin comparing yourself to your spouse's adultery partner or favored pornographic images. Whatever is different between you and them becomes what you believe is "wrong" with you. It is not long before you begin comparing yourself to the most favorable qualities of every person you meet. Every good quality in someone else becomes a standard, a point of insecurity, and ultimately a threat. Life becomes a cruel emotional game where your weaknesses must compete with everyone else's strengths.

   The world begins to feel increasingly less safe. We can drift toward assuming that our deficiencies are more obvious to the rest of the world than they are to us. Compliments and words of encouragement can be perceived as words of pity offered to someone who "obviously needs them." If this persists, only relationships where you have a clear function with measurable outcomes (e.g., work) or where you serve a clear caretaking role (e.g., children or parents) may feel safe.

   This distorted theme assumes that my excellence is the only barrier between my spouse and sin, or between me and pain. Before long, our inability to do things "right" is *the* reason any and everything goes "wrong." We begin to reverse engineer this theme; we trace any problem or hardship in our life back to the deficiency in us that caused it.

▶ **Reflection:** When are you most prone to think, *Something is wrong with me*? How does this sense of inevitable deficiency become the default explanation for hardships in your life? When are you prone to apologize for things that aren't your fault because you assume you contributed to the problem? What aspects of your appearance, personality, or aptitudes are you most prone to blame for life being hard?

▶ **Read James 2:1–13.** This theme assumes the sin of partiality. It assumes that those who are "better" by a cultural preference standard (e.g., wealth and fashion) are more deserving of being treated with honor. We often only read this passage as instructions about how we should treat others. But it is equally applicable to how we speak to ourselves. Read the paraphrase of James 2:12 as written to you, "Think, speak, and act as someone who is not judged by physical appearance or performance, but by the requirements of God, who rejoices when humble hearts live free of condemnation." That is how God wants you to see, speak to, and treat yourself.

2. **It's my fault or I deserve this.** This theme is a step beyond the previous theme that something is wrong with me. In the previous theme, you were merely acknowledging what you perceived to be an unpleasant fact. In this theme, those untrue destructive scripts become explanations. They answer the pernicious "why" question about your spouse's betrayal.

    The tempting part of this theme is that it provides a facade of control. If it really was your fault, then you could make sure it (whatever it is) never happened again. That would be blissful. We would accept any degree of guilt if it meant our spouse did not betray us again.

    This theme is false because we're not responsible for another's choices. Changes in our life cannot force change in anyone else's life. Even if I'm wrong about something, that doesn't excuse you being bad. Even if I'm deficient in how I do something, that doesn't produce depravity in you.

    You can't be good enough to make your spouse be faithful. That's not the equivalent of saying you cannot make enough money to pay off their debts. Instead, it's the equivalent of saying you cannot be smart enough to increase their IQ.

When we try to outperform our loved one's depravity, we turn everything we do to bless our relationships into acts of self-protection. When our self-protection fails, we get bitter. This distorted script results in us feeling used. We sacrifice more and more, but that doesn't guarantee anything gets better. Then, not only is everything our fault (this theme), but we feel like a failure on top of that.

▶ **Reflection:** When are you most prone to think, *It's my fault*? How does this sense of false guilt build up to become a sense of perpetual failure? When do you blow up and then experience a combination of false guilt and true guilt that confuses your situation further? When you're blaming yourself for your spouse's unfaithfulness, what words do you use?

▶ **Read John 9:1–7.** The pattern of explaining suffering (in your case, your spouse's unfaithfulness) as if it must be the consequence of personal sin has a long history. This isn't just a mindset that Job's friends struggled with but something common to all people. If you are prone to thinking this, you are not alone. In John 9, Jesus was still refuting this mentality. Take comfort that Jesus did not assume because this blind man's life was hard that he had been bad. For anything you've done wrong, rest in the gift of forgiveness. For those things that make your life hard but are not your responsibility, feel the freedom to release the sense of responsibility (i.e., guilt) you feel.

3. **I am crazy.** If we don't embrace false guilt, the next most common distortion may be assuming we're crazy. "Maybe I have no idea what I'm doing. Maybe I'm blowing everything out of proportion. Maybe what I think is reasonable, good, or healthy is all out of whack."

    This theme emerges more often when your spouse blames you for their sexual sin or denies that their sin is occurring. When this happens, not only are you dealing with the emotional pain of their sin, but you begin fighting to prove simple, obvious realities. This makes you feel crazy. It makes you wonder if the things that seem evident and reasonable to you are true.

A common (although ineffective) way to try to gauge whether we're being reasonable is to compare our thoughts and reactions to people in other marriages. Whether overtly in conversation or by observation we ask theses kinds of questions:

> - "How do you respond when your spouse is out late or doesn't let you know where they are?"
> - "How do you respond when your spouse is defensive about how they spend their time at home alone?"
> - "How do you respond when your spouse skips small group (i.e., place of same-gendered accountability)?"
> - "How do you respond when your spouse is unresponsive or disinterested in conversation?"

> You can't be good enough to make your spouse be faithful.

If their answers are less alarmed than yours—because their marriage is in a healthier place—you begin to doubt the soundness of your judgment. What is "reasonable" in a healthy environment can easily make you feel crazy for what is "necessary" in marriage where sexual sin has been prevalent. This is why an environment like G4 is valuable. It provides you with a setting where people understand because their situation is more comparable to your own.

▶ **Reflection:** When are you most prone to think, *Am I crazy?* When does your loved one's reactions make you wonder whether your expectations are unrealistic? What healthier situations do you compare your marriage to that make you feel exaggerated? When you use an insulting term like *crazy* in your self-talk to describe yourself, what other negative words do you use?

▶ **Read Luke 20:19–26.** Notice that the scribes and priests were not coming to Jesus in good faith. Their intent was to discredit Jesus by catching him in his words about a highly political issue (vv. 19–20). If their question was sincere, Jesus would likely have engaged them in a conversation. Instead, in this case, Jesus was cagier. The response Jesus gave would have been rude or dismissive in a more authentic relationship. As religious leaders, one would assume Jesus should have been closer with the scribes and priests. In the same way, some people may assume you should be more trusting of your spouse. But Jesus didn't assume this suspicion meant he was crazy. Instead, he responded as the situation warranted.

4. **I am the unwanted one.** It is easy to fall into a comparable version of a romanticized fiction, as your spouse did. This can be done overtly by wanting someone to desire you and risking everything for you like they did for your spouse. Or it can be more subtle, through jealousy of being that wanted.

> And I was angry! Gary and his partner had "repented and been forgiven." They could move on with their lives. Well, I couldn't! I resented the fact that I had not committed this sin, yet I still had to carry the pain. Why didn't they just run away together? By now I could have been moving on with my life instead of being stuck. And at least I wouldn't have had to suffer in silence; everyone would know if they'd run off. Even as I thought these things, I knew the absurdity of them. We all suffered. We all were suffering. But it was so unfair. No one had ever wanted to have an affair with me! There had been no desire so strong that I had risked everything to satisfy it. Gary had risked everything and everyone for her. What had he ever risked to have me? Maybe I wasn't worth having. Maybe I should just disappear. —Gary and Mona Shriver[2]

Even if you do not try to become "the wanted one" through some extramarital means, "the unwanted one" theme can still be very strong. It may manifest itself in listing and rehearsing all the things the other person got from your spouse that you didn't.

Another common manifestation of this theme is retreating to relationships where others are dependent upon you and your role is very clear (e.g., children or workplace). These relationships can be used to hold at bay the feeling of being unwanted. However, when we use these relationships to counterbalance this destructive theme, we allow these relationships to be over-defined by the struggles in our marriage.

▶ **Reflection:** When are you most prone to think, *I am the unwanted one*? When you feel unwanted, to what do you turn to numb this feeling? What roles or relationships have become over-defined by proving you are wanted and needed? When you talk to yourself about feeling like the unwanted one, what words do you use?

▶ **Read I Peter 2:9–10.** This passage can be summarized in a single statement, "You are wanted!" Peter draws on image after image to reinforce his point. Though it is sometimes hard to accept, this passage teaches that our being chosen by God as a "people" is not based on anything about us (Deuteronomy 7:6–7). This means we cannot lose this identity or have it stolen from us. We do not have to compete to keep it because we did not compete to receive it. Allow this to provide the foundation and courage from which you face the pain of your spouse's sin. It has often been said, "Your identity is what the most important person in your life thinks of you." When the intensity of the pain caused by your spouse's sin tempts you to define yourself by the "unwanted" message, remind yourself of how God—your ultimate relationship—sees you.

CONCLUSION

Even if you disagree with everything you wrote in this part of Step 4, that's okay. That's what this step is all about. You're putting into words the lies and distortions you've embraced as you've tried to make sense of your spouse's sin and its impact on your marriage. The first step toward replacing these destructive scripts is doubting them. We'll continue this work in the next part of Step 4 as we explore two more big questions that impact how we story our lives.

G4 GROUP DISCUSSION: STEP 4, PART TWO

As you discuss this material in G4 group, these questions are meant to facilitate a more honest and beneficial dialogue about this material. Anyone is free to respond to whichever questions they choose.

Experienced Members

- In your view of God, what distortion was the most difficult to admit?
- In your G4 journey, how have you seen the truth of the statement, "The fact that the Bible speaks to our doubts is a sign of compassion, not condemnation"?

New Members

- Where do you feel a false sense of guilt (e.g., "It's my fault") because of your spouse's betrayal?
- From the I Peter 2 devotional, can you begin to view yourself as wanted by God?
- How can we pray for you?

Everyone

- What is the most pervasive sense of "I must be crazy" that you experience?
- Which of the Scripture devotionals in this part of Step Four best helped you doubt parts of your suffering story?
- Do we need to discuss any safety-level concerns from the past week??

STEP 4

PART THREE

WHO IS MY SPOUSE? WHAT IS LIFE?

The video for this part of Step 4 can be found at: bradhambrick.com/truebetrayal4p3.

In Part Two of Step 4, we defined the two main characters in your story: God and you. In Part Three, we will explore how you think about your spouse and life in general. Regardless of whether your marriage is restored, how you think about your spouse will have a profound impact on your life moving forward. Also, overgeneralizing the pain you feel can create a jaded and cynical perspective on life.

Allowing these narrative distortions to go unquestioned can have as large of an impact as the initial betrayal in your marriage. That's a big statement, but not hyperbole. When our default disposition toward others is fearful skepticism and our innate perspective is that life is a game we'll never win, the negative impact on our life is profound.

But like our previous two big questions, it does us no good to merely say we shouldn't think that way and feel guilty about it. We need to articulate how we're thinking, understand the implications, and begin to doubt the distortions that make up our suffering story. That sets us up to compassionately disagree with these common distortions.

THREE DISTORTED THEMES ABOUT YOUR SPOUSE

After a significant marital betrayal, it can be very difficult to discern the difference between "safe pain" and "unsafe pain." The unfortunate reality is that even in a healthy marriage, we will be disappointed, offended, and hurt. Because every relationship is between two sinners, safe pain is inevitable.

But when a relationship as central as marriage is a source of betrayal, it is easy to generalize that everyone is unsafe. If we allow this tendency to go unchecked, we will often go through cycles of isolation and blind trust. We will be prone to do this with our spouse and other relationships. Fear will cause us to pull away from people until we are relationally famished. Then in reaction to our exaggerated mistrust, we'll convince ourselves "we just have to trust" and blindly trust at the next opportunity.

Taking the time to articulate and doubt these distorted themes about other people is a key part of breaking this cycle.

1. **Trust is dangerous or naive.** Love was intended to make us feel safe (1 John 4:18). Love assumes, or is built upon, trust. This is why the betrayal of sexual sin hurts so badly. Fear of experiencing that pain again is what makes it hard to view trust as something that could be good. Hence, it is easy to begin viewing trust through a negative lens and write trust off as the practice of young fools or people who don't live in "the real world."

   Premature trust is dangerous and naive. This is why in Step 7 we will discuss what wise trust looks like. You prepare yourself for that step by resisting the tendency to treat trust like it is the exclusive property of horror movies. Trust did not hurt you. Sin hurt you. If someone woke up from sleep because of an earthquake, they should realize that sleep did not destroy their house; the earthquake did.

   Trust is the soul's rest. When you allow the theme of trust to become disparaged, you begin to write a very weary life story. While you may need to learn what warning signs to give more credence to, that does not mean that trust is dangerous or naive. It just means that we need to become wiser in how we bestow trust.

   ▶ **Reflection:** When do you notice yourself viewing trust as dangerous? When has your trust been premature, and you need to learn to be wiser? When was your trust appropriate and the other person acted out of character? When you are suspicious toward trust, what words do you use as you talk to yourself?

   ▶ **Read Isaiah 50:10–11.** Isaiah helps us see that the only place where fear and trust can coexist without risk is in our relationship with God—the fear of the Lord and trust in the name of the

Lord (v. 10). However, this does not mean earthly trust is foolish, nor that it's futile to take wise steps to increase security. Isaiah then uses the metaphor of torches (i.e., instruments that give light) and darkness (i.e., places of uncertainty). Instruments like torches are gifts from God's hand (v. 11b) and, therefore, appropriate to use. However, when our trust is in the torch (our ability to find information) more than the giver of the torch (God's faithfulness to make known what is vital to know), then we will have no rest (v. 11c).

> Trust did not hurt you. Sin hurt you.

2. **If you loved me, then . . . .** This theme tries to make life simpler than it is. This theme is most often applied retrospectively, "If you loved me, then you would not have . . . " while summarizing your spouse's sin. Other times, this theme is absolutized into the future, "Because you did this, then it means you could never love me." Either way, this theme is built on the premise that you can't love someone and hurt them. We wish that was true. Life is not that neat. Simple if-then statements don't capture the complexity of real life.

> Quite often I hear in counseling, "If he loved me, he wouldn't have had the affair." I sadly respond, "He loves you and he had an affair." —Doug Rosenau[1]

It is accurate to say, "If you loved me *well*, then you would not have been unfaithful." Your spouse's sexual sin was a contradiction to the covenant they made with you. Purity, integrity, and honor are perfectly reasonable expectations to place on your spouse. As we explore the destructiveness of this theme, we do not want to minimize that.

The danger of this theme is that it oversimplifies life. You are facing major decisions. You don't want to make those decisions with faulty scales. Imagine you were deciding your future career. Now imagine someone gave you a simple if-then statement to determine that decision: If you like dogs, you should be a veterinarian. While not wrong or illogical, this is an inadequate formula

for such a weighty decision. We want to avoid things that introduce reductionistic logic into major decisions.

Understanding the destructive influence of this theme allows
us to be both hurt and hopeful. It allows us to resist the tendency
to make betrayal the defining event of our marriage. At the same
time, it gives us the freedom to make decisions based on more
accurate and holistic scales. We will explore those variables more
in Steps 7 and 8. For now, it is enough to resist the urge to oversimplify the basis for how you make decisions.

▶ **Reflection:** What oversimplified if-then statements are you
most prone to believe? When are these statements stickiest in
your mind? Is it when you're tired, after an argument, when you
see something that reminds you of your spouse's sin, etc.? When
you oversimplify things, what words do you use as you talk to
yourself?

▶ **Read Revelation 2:1–7.** Ephesus was a great church. The letter
that bears its name, Ephesians, has some of the richest theological reflection in the New Testament. Paul had a powerful bond
with the church at Ephesus and they felt the same toward him
(Acts 20:36–38). But now, some years later, Jesus rebuked the
church at Ephesus, "You have abandoned the love you had at
first" (Revelation 2:4). But Jesus did not give up hope. Rather he
called for decisive change (v. 5), acknowledged their good qualities (v. 6), and placed responsibility to change on them while
maintaining hope for a positive outcome (v. 7). That kind of
demeanor is the alternative to this destructive script: Call for
change, acknowledge what has been good, and place responsibility to change on your spouse.

3.   **Intensified male/female stereotypes.** A big part of our work in this
question has been about avoiding overgeneralizations. Perhaps the
easiest overgeneralization to make is related to gender. If you were
betrayed by your husband, it is easy to think, *This is just how men
are.* If you were betrayed by your wife, it is just as easy to think, *All
women are this way.*

Whatever real differences exist between men and women, allowing our pain to define an entire gender is unwise. But why? When we do, an unhealthy set of rules emerge for relating to the opposite sex (e.g., always give them what they want or they'll betray you, never trust them, put them in their place, etc.). If you begin to live by these rules, many relationships in addition to your marriage will deteriorate. And when they deteriorate, it will seem as if these rules were proven right. In reality, however, these intensified stereotypes become their own self-fulfilling prophecies rather than true statements about all men or all women.

▶ **Reflection:** How can you see intensified male/female stereotypes beginning to emerge? What things are true about your spouse but not true about everyone who shares their gender? When have you been prone to mistrust those who do not share your bias? How has this increased the influence of this betrayal in your life?

▶ **Read Genesis 1:26–31 and Genesis 3.** God created both genders, male and female. God called both genders good. The fall impacted both genders. Characteristic weaknesses and faults emerged that were more prevalent in one gender than the other. But throughout the Bible, God continued to use both men and women to accomplish his purposes. *When the Bible tells the story of a man or woman who should not be trusted (which it does frequently), that mistrust is attributed to that person's choices, not a characteristic fault of their gender.* Therefore, whatever reason we have to trust or mistrust a person should be based upon their character, not whether they have an XX or XY chromosome.

THREE DISTORTED THEMES ABOUT LIFE

Life is hard in a broken world. Life in a broken world after a marital betrayal is harder. How we make sense of that hardness has a significant impact on the quality of life we will experience in this broken world. That is why we will explore common distortions about how we make sense of life in this final question. We won't try to explain away the hardship. That would be ineffective and offensive. We will grapple with the distortions that emerge amid hardship and make life harder.

1.   **Sex is ultimate.** Another twisted theme that emerges after a spouse's sexual sin is the idea that "sex is ultimate." This destructive script can take several forms: A good marriage is defined by a good sex life, a good spouse is defined by their ability to perform sexually, or the value of a person is defined by their attractiveness. Hopefully, this theme rings false when stated in short, concise statements.

     This theme can be reinforced when you are told by your spouse (and too often also by friends or a counselor) that the reason for sexual sin was that you were not "filling your spouse's love tank." The message becomes that sex is ultimate because I am only safe from future betrayal if I consistently meet the ambiguously defined, romantic standard of someone who just hurt me. If I don't, then our marriage is unworthy of being honored.

     "Sex is ultimate" gets further reinforced when sexual sin changes your spouse's expectations about sex. Pornography creates an expectation fueled by a fantasy world of professional sex athletes enacting stories created by professional writers. Adultery creates an expectation fueled by the elevated level of planning and risk accompanying each sexual encounter. Both dynamics create an artificial high for sex. Until sex is less than ultimate, we will not find contentment and enjoyment in sex as God intended.

     ▶ **Reflection:** How have you been tempted to interpret "sex as ultimate"? What messages from your spouse, friends, or a counselor have reinforced this theme? When you are prone to think of sex as ultimate, what words do you use as you talk to yourself?

     ▶ **Read 1 Corinthians 6:19–7:5.** Too often, the end of I Corinthians 6 is separated from the beginning of I Corinthians 7. This passage, as a whole unit, speaks of the two people who have authority over our body: Christ, as our Savior, and our spouse (if married). We see that sex within marriage does have a role in averting temptations (7:2), but Paul does not take the next step to say that the absence of sex in marriage excuses sin. Rather,

Paul goes on to say that there is never an excuse to sin (10:13). In this passage, he says the reason for sin is an individual's "lack of self-control" (7:5). The point to be taken from this passage is that sex is good and should be enjoyed frequently in marriage, but it is not ultimate.

2. **Life would be easier if . . .** This theme searches for quick relief. It can sound like, "Life would be easier if we just went ahead and divorced . . . My spouse had left with their adultery partner . . . We had never gotten married in the first place . . . I was still living in ignorance about their sin." Each of these if-statements has the advantage of not being real. We can easily assume these imagined situations would be better because our current circumstances are hard.

    When you escape into these if-statement stories, it is a form of fantasy. As you wrestle with this theme, you will gain an appreciation for how enticing fantasy can be. This can be a window into your spouse's motives. Fantasy and escape are common motives for sexual sin. This does not mean their actions and your daydreaming are moral equivalents. They are not. But it may help you better understand their temptation.

    It is helpful to remember how unfair the playing field is for these if-statement stories. Imagine you had to choose between two jobs. If you took job A, then whenever job A was difficult (e.g., demanding boss, long hours, bad commute), it would be tempting to think, *I bet job B would not have been like this.* Because Job B is hypothetical, it would never have problems. Similarly, none of your if-statement stories ever have problems.

    ▶ **Reflection:** What-if statements that you are prone to escape into? How does escaping into these stories that never have to bear the weight of life make your current life more challenging? When you start to entertain one of these if-stories, in what ways do you talk to yourself early in the narrative development?

    ▶ **Read Matthew 6:25–34.** If-statement thinking is very similar to anxiety—which is also builds on "what if" thinking. Both are rooted in hypotheticals that never have to be lived out; they get the advantage of existing only in our imaginations. In that way, we are in control of our pain—the control we long for when we are in the middle of a trial. Jesus is honest about life having troubles (v. 34). He also knows that God is faithful and that our hands are full with today's reality without adding our hypotheticals.

3. **Everything is second class now.** This theme has the strange ability to assume the best and the worst at the same time. It assumes your spouse can put their sin behind them, that the marriage can be reconciled, and there could be a long future for your marriage. That's assuming the best. But it also assumes that this best-case scenario will always be a notch below what it could have been. No mark of progress comes without a sigh. That's assuming the worst about the best.

> Honesty is what brings light into darkness, even when we're being honest about dark things.

The affect is that every good aspect of marriage is met with "it would have been better." Our imagination always allows for this. We can imagine a building one story taller, a strawberry just a bit sweeter, a sunset just a bit more vivid, or even the Grand Canyon just a bit deeper.

> You may think if your marriage survives, it will always be a damaged, second-class relationship. This is not true. All marriages are damaged in one way or another. A marriage becomes beautiful when the husband and wife face their brokenness and invite Jesus to work in them. . . . The resurrection marriage isn't less beautiful because it has passed through death; it's more beautiful.
> —Winston Smith[2]

This brings us face-to-face with one of life's great mysteries. God chose to create a world where people were free but in need of redemption instead of a world where people were unfree but redemption was unneeded. We can debate which we think would have been better until we get migraines, but it wouldn't do any good. We can admit we are confused by it and be in the emotional company of the angels in heaven (1 Peter 1:12).

▶ **Reflection:** When are you prone to think the worst about the best outcome? When do you catch yourself sighing when there is reason to be hopeful? When you think about everything being second class now, what words do you use as you talk to yourself?

▶ **Read Hebrews 7:15–25.** Our God is not a God of limited restoration. The worst part of this theme is not how glum it makes us feel but how small it makes God appear in our eyes. The author of Hebrews repeatedly points out the superiority of Christ. In this passage he pointed out how Christ offers "a better hope" (v. 19). The quality of this hope is so great that "he is able to save to the uttermost" (v. 25). When the second-best theme begins to cloud your appreciation for what is or can be done for your marriage, remind yourself of who is active in your marriage—Christ, your High Priest, interceding on behalf of your marriage.

CONCLUSION

Remember, Step 4 is more about being honest about inaccurate thoughts than it is about learning right answers. Step 4 isn't preparation for a quiz you're trying to pass. Instead, it is like a journal entry you can show someone and say, "This is me." Even if you know many of the things you've written in your reflections are inaccurate, it is good to honestly write them down.

So much of navigating betrayal in a marriage involves thinking about things you wouldn't share with a casual acquaintance. Your spouse's sin was hidden. Now you're reflecting on things you wouldn't casually share. That can feel like you are participating in the hiding. You're not. The honesty of Step 4 is you saying, "No more!" to a life of hiding. As honesty increases, so does hope. Honesty is what brings light into darkness, even when we're being honest about dark things.

G4 GROUP DISCUSSION: STEP 4, PART THREE

As you discuss this material in G4 group, these questions are meant to facilitate a more honest and beneficial dialogue about this material. Anyone is free to respond to whichever questions they choose.

Experienced Members

- Are you at the point in your journey where you can see that everything doesn't have to be second class now? If so, what was the journey like to embrace that reality?
- How did you work to resist intensified male or female stereotypes?

New Members

- When are you prone to give in to the "life would be better if . . ." script?
- What parts of the Matthew 6 devotional are more relevant to where you are on your journey?
- How can we pray for you?

Everyone

- What are some recent examples of "safe pain" and "unsafe pain" in each of our lives?
- How has your time at G4 helped you realize that trust doesn't have to be dangerous?
- Do we need to discuss any safety-level concerns from the past week?

STEP 4
PART FOUR

ARTICULATING YOUR SUFFERING STORY

The video for this part of Step 4 can be found at: bradhambrick.com/truebetrayal4p4.

This part of Step 4 isn't about doing fresh work. It's about contextualizing your Step 4 work with what you did in Step 2 and Step 3. It would be easy to feel like Steps 2 through 4 are helpful but disconnected. We want you to understand the flow of the work you've been doing.

Most of Step 4 has involved you responding to reflection prompts. This final part of Step 4 will have less structure and more freedom. Use the four broad prompts below to summarize your Step 4 work. Once you've done that, we'll connect the narrative work with your history (Step 2) and impact (Step 3) work.

▶ **Reflection (Self):** In your own words, how has your marital disruption impacted the way you view you? You can use your notes from Part Two of Step 4 if it is helpful. Summarize how you view yourself differently because of what you've been through? What parts of this are inaccurate, distorted, or destructive?

  • What parts of your view of self are accurate, helpful, or redemptive? Hold on to these thoughts. We'll review them again in Step 6.

▶ **Reflection (God):** In your own words, how has your marital disruption impacted the way you view God? You can use your notes from Part Two of Step 4 if it is helpful. Summarize how you view God differently because of what you've been through? What parts of this are inaccurate, distorted, or destructive?

- What parts of your view of God are accurate, helpful, or redemptive? Hold on to these thoughts. We'll review them again in Step 6.

▶ **Reflection (Spouse):** In your own words, how has your marital disruption impacted the way you view your spouse? You can use your notes from Part Three of Step 4 if it is helpful. Summarize how you view your spouse differently because of what you've been through? What parts of this are inaccurate, distorted, or destructive?

- What parts of your view of your spouse are accurate, helpful, or redemptive? Hold on to these thoughts. We'll review them again in Step 6.

▶ **Reflection (Life):** In your own words, how has your marital disruption impacted the way you view life? You can use your notes from Part Three of Step 4 if it is helpful. Summarize how you view life differently because of what you've been through? What parts of this are inaccurate, distorted, or destructive?

- What parts of your view of life are accurate, helpful, or redemptive? Hold on to these thoughts. We'll review them again in Step 6.

What you've just done is articulate your suffering story—those inaccurate, distorted, and destructive beliefs that emanate from your experience of suffering that we use to make sense of our life. Even if we cannot change our spouse, we can let go of these beliefs and begin to make sense of life in healthier, more redemptive ways. That is what we're in the process of doing.

It would be shortsighted to just interact with our suffering story intellectually. These beliefs are more than thoughts. They are more than ideas. These beliefs cause and amplify pain. These beliefs can prompt you to pull away from sources of hope and healthy relationships. These beliefs pollute your soul with shame, despair, and angst.

▶ **Reflection:** How has your suffering story—the beliefs that emerged amid your marital disruption—caused pain in your life? What good choices did your suffering story distract you from or make you feel were impossible? What unwise choices did your suffering story make seem inevitable or logical?

- Stated another way, if you relinquished the false or destructive elements of your suffering story, how would your life get better?

Remember, our goal for Step 4 is modest. We merely want to articulate and doubt our suffering story. This story has deep roots in your life. We don't have to yank them out fast. But the more clearly we see the damage this suffering story has done, the less we'll trust it. If the destructive things that once seemed true now seem suspect, we're making great progress.

▶ **Read Mark 9:24.** Make this your prayer for this stage in your journey: "I believe; help my unbelief." When elements of your suffering story feel convincing, pray this prayer. Like the father in Mark 9, you may know the truth and still doubt it at the same time. Realize this story is in the Bible because it represents how many of us live. This father knew Jesus could heal his son, but doubted if he would. This father knew Jesus loved the poor and vulnerable, but doubted if Jesus would love him. Notice how honest this father is. Be just as honest as you wrestle to relinquish your suffering story. God affirms and admires this kind of faith.

THE JOURNEY FROM THEMES TO STORY

How do we develop an experience or set of experiences into a story? The answer is unique to each person. While we may all interpret painful life experiences with similar themes, the way we move from events to story is not uniform.

We want to provide you with a chart to help you see how the work you've done in Step 4 connects with the work you've done in Step 2 and Step 3, as well as set up work you will do in Step 7. While each step can immersive, we don't want you to lose the whole of your journey as you focus on one part of the experience.

As you work on this chart, we need to make two cautions. First, realize there are no relational–emotional formulas. You are simply describing your experience. Other members in your G4 group may have had similar experiences (Step 2), but have been impacted differently

(Step 3), derived different destructive scripts (Step 4), or developed different maladaptive behaviors that need to change (Step 7). Every person's response to a painful situation is different. *There are no right answers to this chart—that is, answers that fit everyone—only accurate answers—that is, answers that represent the connections that exist in your life.* When we forget this, we can impose our experience on others or feel like we did the assignment wrong when someone else has different answers.

> The more clearly we see the damage this suffering story has done, the less we'll trust it.

Second, understanding does not mean justifying. Too often, these two terms are used as synonyms. For instance, a spouse might say, "If you understood why I was upset, you wouldn't think I'm overreacting," or an alcoholic might say, "If you understood why I drank, you would accept that it's necessary." We can be sympathetic toward the first clause of each statement without accepting the conclusion of the second clause. We want to understand; we don't want to make excuses. We want to be able to do that with others and we want to be able to do that with ourselves. That is how we want to relate to our suffering story. We want to sympathetically disagree with our suffering story so that we can begin to make choices that aren't as influenced by those distorted scripts.

The chart below is modified and adapted from a comparable chart in Leslie Vernick's *How to Act Right When Your Spouse Acts Wrong.*[1] Steps from the G4 model have been added to the column headers. We've provided two examples to help you begin using this chart to sort your own life.

SINFUL SITUATION (STEP 2)	IMPACT ON YOU (STEP 3)	DESTRUCTIVE SCRIPT (STEP 4)	BEHAVIORS (STEP 7)
Spouse claims to be abstaining from pornography. Has a new, more elaborate means of hiding their sin. Weeks later you discover their sin.	You begin to feel like good news is merely an incomplete story. You equate trust with naivety.	Trust is dangerous. Trust is what weak people do so they don't have to be alone. I must either be strong or lonely.	Remain emotionally distant. Go along to get along. Berate yourself when you trust. Living expecting the worst.

SINFUL SITUATION (STEP 2)	IMPACT ON YOU (STEP 3)	DESTRUCTIVE SCRIPT (STEP 4)	BEHAVIORS (STEP 7)
Spouse commits adultery with an out-of-town colleague while on a business trip. You see pictures of this person and believe they are more attractive than you.	You feel a growing sense of insecurity about your appearance and whether your spouse finds you attractive.	I will never be attractive enough to win my spouse's attention. My spouse will feel like they have a second-class life as long as they're married to me.	Workout excessively. Begin to feel shame each time you look in the mirror. Compare yourself to others in social settings. Deflect compliments from your spouse.

How many people knew about the affair? I didn't know and would never know. . . . I felt as if I were wearing a sign that read "NOT GOOD ENOUGH!" . . . *God, I need a miracle here. You're the great Healer. Heal us! Let me wake up from this nightmare. We're sitting here breathing, and yet as surely as there is air moving in and out of my lungs, I know we're dying. But I want to know why I have to die when the sin is not mine! I didn't do this. . . .* In my weary brain there were only three alternatives: lying to myself, being lied to, or pain. If there was no pain, then someone must be lying. —Gary and Mona Shriver[2]

> We want to sympathetically disagree with our suffering story

On this chart, we are currently examining column three. We want to understand how our marital disruption has resulted in an inaccurate way of interpreting life. Column four is foreshadowing. In column four, we note the unhealthy ways we've tried to manage the destructive scripts of column three. The clearer we see this connection, the more we will be ready to make choices that represent who we want to be and the values we want to pursue.

Right now, we've gained clarity about where our existing choices come from, why they make sense to us (at least in the moment), and what we would need to see differently if we are going to make different choices. Even if it's uncomfortable, we must realize the choices we've made reveal how we've made sense of life. If we want to do more than make reactive choices in moments of exasperation, we will have to make sense of our situation differently. That is what we're taking the time to do.

CONCLUSION

It is helpful to remember again that you may disagree with almost everything you wrote in Step 4. But Step 4 can still help. The point of Step 4 was to put into words what we actually think so that we can examine it and its implications; not to write what we ought to think. If you were honest, you harvested information that will be helpful to you in the steps ahead.

The more we need to purge Step 4 thinking from our life, the more exhausting Step 4 can be. The more we need Step 4, the more discouraged we may be about the things we wrote down. If that's the case, give yourself the freedom to rest physically and emotionally. Don't rush to Step 5 simply because it's next.

When you're ready, here's what we're going to do next. You're going to bring everything you learned in Step 2 and Step 3 to God as if all the destructive scripts you articulated in Step 4 are false. That process is called mourning or grief. It is a process of accepting bad things as real without taking responsibility for what's not your fault. It is an opportunity to receive God's comfort and compassion for the hard things you've faced in ways that have been disrupted by a sense of guilt and self-doubt. That's where we'll turn next, and when you're ready, it is something you can look forward to.

G4 GROUP DISCUSSION: STEP 4, PART FOUR

As you discuss this material in G4 group, these questions are meant to facilitate a more honest and beneficial dialogue about this material. Anyone is free to respond to whichever questions they choose.

Experienced Members

- How did you feel when you initially summarized your suffering story?
- How did articulating your suffering story help the grief (Step 5), redemptive story (Step 6), and life changes (Step 7) work ahead? In other words, how did you come to see that Step 4 was worth it?

New Members

- What behaviors did you put on your chart that you anticipate wanting to change as you move toward Step 7?
- How did this part of Step 4 help you begin to doubt some of the false or distorted beliefs you've held?
- How can we pray for you?

Everyone

- How did the Mark 9 devotional help you relate to the inaccurate or contradictory beliefs that exist within your suffering story?
- What pain in your life has been exacerbated by your suffering story?
- Do we need to discuss any safety-level concerns from the past week?

STEP 5
MOURN the wrongness of what happened and receive God's comfort.

At the end of this step, I want to be able to say . . .

"I now realize God sees my experience of my spouse's sin as suffering. I can see that God does not just want me to 'get over this' as if it is my fault. Instead, God has compassion for my hardship and mourns with me. I see that 'blessed are those who mourn, for they shall be comforted' (Matthew 5:4) is occurring through this G4 group as one way God keeps this promise. Mourning my suffering with God and this group has changed me in many ways [describe]."

STEP 5

PART ONE

IDENTIFYING WHAT WE ARE MOURNING

The video for this part of Step 5 can be found at: bradhambrick.com/truebetrayal5p1.

Many of the previous steps took *strong courage.* That is, the kind of courage where you muster strength to acknowledge things that were hard to acknowledge. Step 5 is different. It requires *weak courage.* That is, the kind of courage to invite God and others into sensitive areas that require vulnerability more than strength.

Weak courage is a *key component to mourning—inviting God and others into sensitive areas of life marked by loss, pain, or disappointment.* In this step, you'll be asked to be vulnerable in a new way—a good way—which opens the door to another level of care and healing for the brokenness you've experienced.

> ▶ **Read Matthew 5:4.** Notice what this passage doesn't say. It doesn't say "you are blessed *because* you mourn," as if suffering earned you a merit badge in heaven. Instead, it says, "Blessed are those who [do] mourn." Why? "Because they will be comforted." The blessing is in the opportunity mourning creates—namely, to be comforted—not the experience of being sad or hurt about something hard. As you do the work of Step 5, that is the benefit you can begin to receive from your vulnerability. You won't be alone in your suffering. You will be able to receive the compassion and comfort God has wanted to provide, but was hindered by your suffering story.

For many of us, it is surprising to realize that God does not think we are whining when we acknowledge that the relational pain has been a heavy burden. God has been inviting that kind of honesty for a long time. Imagine you have a child who has been fearfully carrying a secret about intense suffering. When your child finally shares that secret with you, how would you feel? Not judgmental or angry, but thankful for the trust this disclosure reveals and grateful for the opportunity to show your compassion. That is how God responds as you traverse Step 5.

We will explore the subject of mourning in three ways:

1. Identifying What We Are Mourning
2. What Is the Difference Between Mourning and Bitterness?
3. How Do We Mourn?

IDENTIFYING WHAT WE ARE MOURNING

Many of the losses that emanate from a marital betrayal are not as tangible as we might imagine. The losses are rarely as concrete as a death that results in a funeral. That can make us wonder, *Should I just get over it?* The ambiguity of our losses causes us to question our emotional responses and wonder if we're overreacting.

> We found that not recognizing the loss, not mourning, only made it worse. . . . It took us a while to identify the things we had lost, and even when we did, accepting that they were really gone was more difficult than we expected it would be. However, once we were able to name them, it seemed we had taken another step on the path of healing. We didn't feel so stuck. —Gary and Mona Shriver[1]

In this part of Step 5, we will explore ten losses commonly associated with marital betrayal. Our goal is to find tangible, accurate answers to the question, What have I lost and why is it important for me to grieve? These losses are real, and they matter. As you make decisions about how to navigate the future of your marriage, it is helpful to articulate what these losses are.

As a word of caution, don't use these losses as a weighing system to compare your hardship to the hardship of others. This list is meant to make vague things clearer, not to serve as a basis for comparing situations to determine which is worse.

1.   **Loss of your marriage as it once was.** There is no unwriting history. Those words carry the sting of grief. While the future can be

good, even brighter than the past, your marriage will lack some of the innocence it had before. Your marriage will be something new and different. "New" may be better, worse, or just different. That has yet to be determined. But grieving the loss of what was is an important part of moving toward that new relationship.

2. **Loss of your dream marriage.** No one dreams of their marriage being disrupted by sexual sin. Processing these events is definitely off script. The impact of this is more than just saying, "This is not what I wanted to happen." The dreams that you have for your marriage become part of your identity and how you evaluate life. So when this dream gets changed, it influences many areas of life. This is why mourning the impact of your spouse's sin can have a significant disorienting effect.

3. **Loss of the purity of the marriage bed.** This is a form of mourning that often spikes with emotional intensity. This response is logical because sex is emotionally intense (for better or worse). So, if you have grief related to sex, that mourning will be more extreme. Each of you may wonder, *What is my spouse thinking about?* while having sex. Underlying that question is grief. It is a time when the destructive messages of your suffering story come crashing back. Your goal is to experience them as mourning rather than retreating into anger or the self-protection of being aloof. The return of vulnerability in the marriage, even through grief, is part of restoring intimacy.

4. **Loss of faithfulness.** God made sex to be a sign of fidelity—an exclusive bond that exists between husband and wife. When what God intended to be a reminder of faithfulness is warped with unfaithfulness, the pain echoes. For a while, every hug reminds you of rejection, and every compliment echoes your insecurities. Relational glue has become a repellant. If you try to just fight through this dynamic without mourning, you will either (a) feel like you are pretending nothing happened, or (b) angrily cry out, "I just can't do it!" and walk away. This is a loss that must be mourned before it can be restored.

5. **Loss of trust (emotional safety).** One way to define trust is a sense of being emotionally safe with another person. When betrayal happens in marriage, it disrupts a primary relationship of trust and a primary location of trust (home). The person you most want comfort from is the same person who caused your pain. The place you would normally retreat to is the place with the most reminders of what you're retreating from. Even though this need not be permanent, it is sad and should be mourned as a loss—or else you may think you are being silly and overreacting.

> The return of vulnerability in the marriage, even through grief, is part of restoring intimacy.

6. **Loss of sexual safety.** A sense of safety dissipates when there is a gap between reasonable expectations and life events. That gap prompts a multitude of unpleasant emotions. This gap causes us to feel unsafe, even if there is no immediate danger. God created sex to communicate, "I am my beloved's and my beloved is mine" (Song of Solomon 6:3). Uncertainty emerges when that affirmation is called into question. If you do not grieve this loss, then you will try to just be stronger or braver, but this type of self-willed strength undermines the tenderness and vulnerability that are intended to mark sex.

7. **Loss of financial stability.** Mourning can be as practically triggered as it is emotionally triggered. Sexual sin can affect finances in many ways: the loss of a job, incurring debt while sinning, blocking a promotion, or needing to turn down opportunities to protect the damaged trust of the marriage. These are involuntary sacrifices forced upon you. You got no vote on the choices that prompted these sacrifices. Unless these changes are grieved, they will become roots of bitterness. Mourning allows you to healthily avoid being silenced about these losses.

8. **Loss of identity (personally and as a couple).** It can be easy to miss how grief always involves shifts in our sense of identity. A primary question of grief is, Who am I *now*? Personally and maritally, this is another time when the destructive scripts from Step 4 emerge. Like you did in Step 4, be honest about the pain and

hold these interpretations loosely. As you grieve, you will become increasingly able to define the marriage by its current health rather than these past events and increasingly able to embrace the identity God has for you rather than embracing your pain as your identity.

9. **Loss of connection with your church.** Church will feel different, at least for a while. If you and your spouse keep the sin completely secret, then your church involvement will likely feel increasingly superficial as you think, *No one here really knows what we're going through* and wonder, *How would they respond if they did?* This is why *False Love* and *True Betrayal* guide you and your spouse to confide in strategic people within your church. Without these conversations, you will likely add the erosion of many Christian relationships to the list of things you are grieving. Even with wise disclosure and a supportive church, church life and personal faith may feel different. You may also look back and see this as one of God's greatest blessings during this time. Even if this is the case, it is appropriate to grieve the changes, so that God's blessing does not become a reason for living in denial.

10. **Loss of the sense of god's presence.** When pain is near, God feels far. When pain is up in our face, God often feels out of sight. Pain is such an intense, internal experience that the idea of God being with us, near us, or in us no longer matches up with our experience of life.

▶ **Reflection:** Which of these losses have you experienced because of your marital disruption? Which losses were most difficult to put into words until now? Which losses are most painful to you? Which losses are least understood by those around you?

▶ **Read Joel 2:25–27.** It is easy to read this promise and miss the grief. The promise to restore what was lost does not remove the experience of being deprived. Notice that this verse references the *years* that were lost (v. 25). Notice the multifaceted cause of loss: various insects and pestilence (v. 25). Notice there is no guarantee that the fulfillment of this promise will be immediate. If you read the larger book of Joel, you see that God's people will need to make significant choices in cooperation with the fulfillment of this promise. But even with that, notice that God does not ignore the painful emotional experience—in this case, shame (v. 27)—associated with these losses. God has the same compassion toward your losses.

CONCLUSION

It is common as you conclude this part of Step 5 to feel an odd combination of relief and sadness. Relief at finally being able to put losses into words. Sadness because these losses merit being grieved and, now that you can put them into words, you are able to honor these losses with grief.

> When pain is near, God feels far.

This mixture of relief and sadness may not be understood by everyone in your life. It is easy to think that where relief is present, sadness should fade. That is the value of working through *True Betrayal* with a G4 group. The group provides a place to be understood as you articulate, feel, and mourn these losses with people who understand the importance of this step.

G4 GROUP DISCUSSION: STEP 5, PART ONE

As you discuss this material in G4 group, these questions are meant to facilitate a more honest and beneficial dialogue about this material. Anyone is free to respond to whichever questions they choose.

Experienced Members

- How has grieving more intelligently and intentionally aided your G4 journey?
- Which loss was most difficult for you to acknowledge when you reached Step 5 in your journey?

New Members

- How hard is it for you to acknowledge the losses you've incurred?
- How did the Matthew 5 devotional help you see the value of being vulnerable in your grief?
- How can we pray for you?

Everyone

- Which losses currently have the most significant impact on your life?
- How do you respond constructively when these losses are misunderstood by friends or family?
- Do we need to discuss any safety-level concerns from the past week?

STEP 5
PART TWO

WHAT IS THE DIFFERENCE BETWEEN MOURNING AND BITTERNESS?

The video for this part of Step 5 can be found at: bradhambrick.com/truebetrayal5p2.

As you grieve the losses created by your spouse's sin, one of the rebuttals you are likely to face is "you're bitter." By the time you arrive at Step 5, you found out about their sin weeks or months ago. Why are you still upset? If you had truly forgiven, wouldn't you be "over it" by now? These are just a couple of the logical fallacies that may come your way as you grieve.

These kinds of logical fallacies are not always malicious; often they are just naive. They assume the temporal impact of the gospel to be as immediate and pervasive as the eternal impact of the gospel. But let's use the parallel of pride. When we embrace the gospel, our pride is forgiven immediately, and it no longer has any ability to hinder our entrance into heaven. However, in our day-to-day life, we still struggle with pride and its presence still influences our relationships. The same applies to grief. Expectations of grief related to a painful betrayal should be approached with even more patience. But, in that patience, we don't want to drift into bitterness—it's not good for our soul or our marriage. That's what we're going to wrestle with in this part of Step 5.

HOW ARE MOURNING AND BITTERNESS SIMILAR?

You may find it odd that we're paralleling mourning and bitterness. We don't often think of these two experiences as siblings or cousins. Maybe we think of them as classmates or work peers. But mourning and bitterness share a lot in common, enough in common to be opposites.

Consider this thought experiment. What do east and west have in common? They are both directions. What do hot and cold have in common? They are both temperatures. What do high and low have in common? They are both elevations. With this mindset, consider what mourning and bitterness have in common.

- Both are triggered by events that are intensely personal and undesired.
- Both exist on the unpleasant end of the emotional spectrum.
- Both feel very justified and make sense in light of the event that prompts them.
- Both feel very natural—like we are not in control of them, but they are happening to us.
- Both involve a high degree of mental repetition.
- Both are seeking to make sense of life in light of a negative event.
- Both shape the way you anticipate and prepare for the future.
- Both change the way that you think of past events.

What do you gain from this bulleted list? A realization that none of these criteria, on their own, can differentiate mourning from bitterness. Each criterion is true for both. It is as if you were asked to distinguish a square from a rectangle. You could say, "The shape has four sides, and each corner forms a ninety-degree angle." These statements are true for both a square and a rectangle, so it does not help you differentiate the two shapes. Some people may say you are bitter because you fit the descriptions above, but these data points are insufficient to make that determination.

When someone has the experiences listed above, all we know is that they're hurting. It is not clear whether this pain is being processed in a healthy (mourning) or unhealthy (bitterness) way. We want to process our pain in a healthy way. The reality is our emotions and motives will never be as pure as we would like. Your goal at this point is not that you mourn perfectly but that your grief experience be increasingly free from qualities that are indicative of bitterness.

▶ **Read Hebrews 12:15.** Bitterness is such an awkward subject because it resides at the intersection of sin and suffering. The event(s) that have the potential to make us bitter are painful and wrong. When we experience these events, we are sufferers. But suffering carries with it the temptation to become bitter. The similarity of mourning (a necessary part of the healing process) and bitterness make it seemingly impossible to flee the vicinity of this temptation. It would be easy to read this section on bitterness and the biblical instruction from Hebrews 12 as heavy words of condemnation. We feel that way when we interpret this verse as saying, "You shouldn't be hurt. Just move on." That's not God's heart in cautioning against bitterness. Take this verse as God saying, "Pain is real, and bitterness is corrosive. As you process your pain, be careful that bitterness does not become a pain multiplier."

> Bitterness is such an awkward subject because it resides at the intersection of sin and suffering.

FIVE DIFFERENCES BETWEEN MOURNING AND BITTERNESS

If you think of mourning and bitterness as having a relationship like overlapping circles in a Venn diagram, what we just covered shows where the two experiences overlap. Now we are going to try to define the parts of each experience that are distinct. We will consider five ways mourning and bitterness are different. With each distinction, we'll provide a reflection question to help you discern how to allow your emotional experience to migrate away from bitterness and toward healthy mourning.

1. **Bitterness depletes strength while mourning replenishes strength**. Bitterness is a form of anger, and anger requires a great deal of energy. Anger feels strong, but that is because it is pulling from your bodily reserves to artificially amp up your emotional and physical stamina. The result is an inevitable crash. Bitterness is the equivalent of an emotional parasite that feeds off time and energy that were meant for another purpose. The longer bitterness resides in our life, the more depleted we become.

   Mourning, by contrast, is a form of rest. When we mourn, we quit fighting to control a pain that we did not cause and which resides in a time zone we cannot touch (the past). We surrender, not to the evil in our past but to living in the present. As we mourn, we focus increasingly on the ways we can influence our current life. As we begin to focus more on the present and future than the past, we become freer from anger. Instead, we increasingly focus on pursuing a God-honoring, satisfying life.

> ▶ **Reflection:** As you mourn the impact of your marital disruption, are you more at peace with focusing on the aspects of your life that you can control and want to pursue?

2. **Bitterness deteriorates relationships while mourning shows value for relationships**. Bitterness exacerbates the corrosive effect of your spouse's sin, either by trying to get even for the pain caused or by surrendering to the idea of this is how things will always be. Either way, there is further deterioration in your marriage.

   As we mourn, we accept how things are so that we can begin to pursue a God-honoring, satisfying future. By this point in your *True Betrayal* journey, you have a good gauge for how much your spouse is going to participate in their *False Love* journey. Based on that, you are gaining a sense for the type and degree of changes that would be necessary and appropriate in your marriage. These changes, even if your spouse dislikes them, honor what God intends a marriage to be and calls your spouse to be the person God wants them to be. Mourning honors your spouse's freedom to choose and is willing to make the requisite choices in light of their choice.

   > ▶ **Reflection:** As you mourn the impact of your marital disruption, are you willing to begin to make choices that call your marriage and your spouse to align with God's design?

3. **Bitterness undermines long-term peace while mourning makes peace possible again**. Bitterness chooses counteraggressive tactics. Bitterness gives way to the mindset, If you [blank], then I should be able to [blank] to excuse choices we know are unproductive. When we are bitter, we are so overwhelmed by the wrongs done against us that we become blind to the wrongness or folly of our own choices. In this mindset, peace withers.

Mourning accepts the impact of wrongs done against you (Step 3) as parts of our history that cannot be undone. Grief accepts that sad and bad things are true. This acceptance frees you to think and respond differently. Mourning allows you to ask, "Given the reality of what has been and my spouse's response to their sin, what is the most peaceful outcome I can begin to pursue?"

▶ **Reflection:** As you mourn the impact of your marital disruption, are you feeling less compelled to react to your spouse's choices and freer to make choices that cultivate a greater sense of inner peace?

4. **Bitterness distracts focus while mourning restores focus.** Bitterness cannot think of anything for long without returning to the offense that ignited it. Every subject feels like a derivative of our pain: a song on the radio, the phrase someone uses, or the uncertainty you feel in a meeting at work. When we're bitter, our pain feels relevant to everything, and when our pain is relevant, it disrupts our ability to focus on anything else.

Mourning is the process that allows current events to stand on their own. Prompts in our surroundings may cause us to remember painful aspects of our marriage, but we don't lose the ability to be present in that moment. Think of this like the experience of losing a close loved one. Initially, everything reminds you of them. As you grieve, you still remember them, but you can engage fully in life without losing focus.

▶ **Reflection:** As you mourn the impact of your marital disruption, are you able to remain more present in the moment when painful memories arise?

5. **Bitterness requires God's forgiveness while mourning receives God's comfort.** Bitterness is a sin. Like every other sin, it displeases God and creates distance in our relationship with him. At a time when we are already feeling distance from our spouse, this can be particularly hard to accept. Even if you are struggling with bitterness, rest in the reality that God is eager to forgive.

However, God has a different response to mourning. God offers comfort rather than forgiveness. Our resistance to mourning can be captured in the adage, "It is easier to be angry than hurt." When we embrace the vulnerability to mourn, our courage allows us to experience a greater felt sense of God's compassion and comfort. While mourning may not feel like faith, amid suffering it can be the essence of faith.

> While mourning may not feel like faith, amid suffering it can be the essence of faith.

▶ **Reflection:** As you mourn the impact your marital disruption, are you more able embrace God's comfort rather than fearing God is displeased with your unpleasant emotions?

▶ **Read Lamentations.** This is a book about mourning. It is only five chapters in length. As you read, notice the rise and fall of unpleasant emotions. Jeremiah, the author of Lamentations, goes from hot (angry) to cold (numb), from trusting to guarded, from reverent to raw, and from hopeful to despairing many times in these few chapters. Realize that God invites you to be this honest and all over the place with him. Jeremiah's ministry was one marked by rejection. He is known as "the weeping prophet" because it broke his heart that God's people consistently rejected God's message. In that sense, Jeremiah was in a long-term dysfunctional relationship with God's people, and Lamentations is Jeremiah's memoir pouring his heart out to God about it.

CONCLUSION

This part of Step 5 is a good time to remember that our primary goal in the G4 journey is not merely to understand what is being said but to incorporate what we're learning. You may have read these pages and thought, *I'm just not there yet.* Don't feel rushed.[1]

In that case, these five points become matters of prayer:

Father,

As I am understanding how my spouse's sin has impacted me, I realize I am still raw and a bit bitter. I am growing in my ability to discern what I can and cannot control. I feel less guilt and shame over the things that happen to me and know you want to comfort me regarding those painful experiences.

I need to admit that I feel stuck in bitterness. I want to move toward a healthier and more pure grief regarding these experiences. Because of that, I am asking that you would help me with the following:

1. Help me to grieve in a way that restores my strength by relinquishing my desire to control things I can't.

2. Help me to grieve in a way that recognizes that expecting my spouse to live according to God's design honors our marriage, instead of allowing their displeasure with my choices to cause me to get lost in second-guessing myself.

3. Help me to grieve in a way that allows me to be less reactive to my loved one's actions. I want the freedom that comes from being content with knowing you are pleased with my choices.

4. Help me to grieve in a way that allows me to be fully present in each moment, rather than emotionally engulfed by each event that reminds me of my spouse's sin.

5. Help me to grieve in a way that rests in your comfort. When I fear you disapprove of my choices, I get defensive, and it tempts me to drift back toward bitterness.

It may be that only one or two of these need to be your focal point in prayer. Ask your fellow G4 group members and those in your social support circle to pray for these things. As we'll see in the next part of Step 5, grief isn't something we volitionally do (e.g., like opening our hand or blinking our eyes). Instead, it is something we prompt by making indirect choices (e.g., like lowering our cholesterol by changing our eating and exercise habits). Your G4 journey is infused with these choices. Be patient with yourself as you continue the journey. Rest in God's promise to faithfully complete the work (Philippians 1:6).

G4 GROUP DISCUSSION: STEP 5, PART TWO

As you discuss this material in G4 group, these questions are meant to facilitate a more honest and beneficial dialogue about this material. Anyone is free to respond to whichever questions they choose.

Experienced Members

- How have you grown to appreciate that "bitterness resides at the intersection of sin and suffering"?
- How have you learned to respond to those who think the emotional freedom of healthy grief is an expression of bitterness or indifference?

New Members

- How hard was it for you to see the overlap in mourning and bitterness?
- As you read Lamentations, what did you learn about the experience of mourning?
- How can we pray for you?

Everyone

- In your own words, describe the difference between healthy mourning and bitterness.
- Which of the five distinctions between mourning and bitterness are you currently praying God will work on in your life?
- Do we need to discuss any safety-level concerns from the past week??

STEP 5
PART THREE

HOW DO WE MOURN?

The video for this part of Step 5 can be found at: bradhambrick.com/truebetrayal5p3.

W hat is a cake? A cake is a mixture of flour, eggs, milk, and other ingredients baked in an oven. It is easy enough to move from a definition of cake to a recipe for a cake. With a little trial and error, we can figure out how much of each ingredient is needed.

What is grief? Grief is the emotional process of accepting the absence of someone you love or the reality of an adverse circumstance. Unfortunately, it is not as easy to move from a definition to a recipe when we're talking about grief. Baking a cake is procedural. Mourning is a process. Baking a cake is universal (everyone does it basically the same). Grief can be unique to each individual, culture, or loss. For these reasons, our question for this part of Step 5 will not be as straightforward as we would like.

We put mourning at Step 5 in our journey because it represents a pivot in our focus from looking back to looking ahead. *That's how grief works. It occurs at the pivotal points of life and represents a change of focus.* This is why there are elements of grief in positive experiences (e.g., weddings and graduations) as well as unpleasant experiences (e.g., death and betrayal in a close relationship). Both are pivotal points in life where our focus changes.

You will be completing Step 5 as your focus shifts from feeling shocked or overwhelmed to pursuing a life that can be God-honoring and satisfying. When we look backward while moving forward, we tend to run into things. In Steps 1 through 4, we've taken the time to assess and learn from the past. In the steps to come, we will shift to a future orientation. As you feel your emotions embracing this shift, you are bringing resolution to the grieving process.

HOW DO WE MOURN?

Oh, we wish we could answer this question with simple steps like this:

1. Write down a summary of your work in Steps 2 and 3 on a piece of paper.
2. Recite the destructive messages you identified in Step 4 and yell, "Lies!"
3. Go into a forest at sunset to burn the piece of paper next to a flowing stream.
4. Wear dark clothing and take a vow of silence for two weeks.
5. Wake up on the fifteenth day before sunrise and whisper, "I'm ready for what's next," as the sun breaks the horizon.

This fictional process may be cumbersome, but if it worked, we would do it. When we're stuck in grief, we become desperate to find a way to move on with our lives. If a loved one dies, funeral rituals provide some structure and social support to the process. But when we're grieving the impact of a major marital disruption, we feel even more alone and directionless.

While mourning is not as voluntary as we want it to be, that doesn't mean you must passively wait and just hope it happens. The five points below may not be as action oriented as you would like. But they represent ways that you can cooperate with the grieving process.

1. **Realize mourning is not an activity you can put on your calendar.** We wish we could block time on our calendar to grieve and get it over with. It may help you to realize you have been engaged in the mourning process during the first four steps of your journey. Accepting what really happened and understanding its impact was an essential part of processing those experiences. Steps 6 through 9 will continue the grieving process as you pursue a God-honoring, satisfying future.

2. **Do not feel rushed and don't grow impatient with yourself.** To use a sports metaphor, grief is more like a gymnastics floor routine than a sprinting race. Sprinting is all about making your

time as brief as possible. The person who finishes quickest wins. Gymnastics has to do with how well you perform your allotted task. It is the quality of your work, not the brevity of time in which you complete your tasks, that matters.

If the gymnast rushes, there is no advantage (likely a detriment) to her final score. Similarly, when we try to accelerate the grieving process, we deter it. We feel guilty for being behind. We feel insecure because we're sure others are doing it better. However, when we focus upon being as healthy as possible in the process, we experience healthy outcomes that honor God and result in our flourishing.

3. **Rest in God's care before the next stage of the journey.** One way to prevent the tendency to feel rushed is to realize that God doesn't just love you at the finish line but throughout the entire race. At the point in the race where you feel exhausted and want to quit, God loves you. At the point in the race where you stumble and fall, God loves you. At the point in the race where you lose your way and regress, God loves you.

    Remember, healthy mourning is a form of rest. Grief is not primarily about moving forward. It is about the readiness to move forward. When we lose a loved one to death and grief is intense, we resist moving forward. We want to remain bound to the past. As we grieve, we become free to embrace new possibilities. Grief isn't about where we go. It is about the freedom to begin moving forward again.

    This is why we have a bit more work to do before we engage Step 7, a highly forward-oriented step. In Step 6, we will revisit many of the questions we engaged in Step 4. We will cement the freedom that grief provides in the redemptive narrative of the gospel before we begin making difficult choices in that freedom.

4. **Assimilate Steps 1–3 without the contamination of Step 4.** This is as close as we get to a "formula" for grief. The things you learned in Steps 1–3 are real. The things you articulated in Step 4 are not true. When you can emotionally embrace both realities and face the future with hope, you have grieved your losses.

    You may realize something about this formula. The destructive scripts from Step 4 have not been replaced yet. This means that, while you do the work of Step 5, you may feel like a person without a story. Partly, that is how grief works. When we lose someone, we accept their absence before we know what our life ahead entails. But in this G4 journey, your grief does not need to be that open-ended. In Step 6, we will revisit the themes from Step 4 and begin to piece together a redemptive narrative around your hardships.

5. **Realize sadness is not the final chapter.** Notice we are on Step 5 of 9. This is not the end of your story. There is as much of your story ahead of you as there is behind you. Fear, betrayal, hurt, pain, shame, sadness, and uncertainty do not get the last word in your life.

> God doesn't just love you at the finish line but throughout the entire race.

Since you learned of your spouse's sin, perhaps before, these emotions have reigned in your life. There are many choices in front you—continue working toward restoration, separate due to non-cooperation, or consider divorce—that will be highly influenced by how your spouse is or is not engaging in their *False Love* journey. Those choices are yours; as such, you will no longer be surrendering but choosing.

This is a choice you'll seek to make in a way that honors biblical principles. But honoring biblical principles doesn't mean choosing one biblical principle and elevating it above all others. Instead, it means valuing the host of biblical principles relevant to your situation and prayerfully deciding between your available options. You may dread hearing someone say "honor biblical principles" because that phrase has been leveraged against you to unduly narrow your options. Hopefully, this G4 journey has helped alleviate those fears.

Here are some of the biblical principles you should weigh in the decisions ahead of you:

- You are loved as a precious child (Ephesians 5:1).
- Adultery is biblical grounds for divorce (Matthew 19:9).
- Limiting sinful and relationally offensive patterns is godly (the whole book of Proverbs is about avoiding foolish patterns).
- Restoration is possible (I Corinthians 6:11).

- People do not always make the choices that turn possible restoration into actual restoration (Matthew 18:17; I Corinthians 7:15).
- Believers can disagree about what ought to happen over important choices (Acts 15:36–41).
- God hates people misusing the Bible to control or manipulate others (Matthew 23:1–36).
- All decisions—even those prayerfully made based on biblical principles—are made with uncertainty (Philippians 1:22–23).

> Fear, betrayal, hurt, pain, shame, sadness, and uncertainty do not get the last word in your life.

However you choose to enact these principles, mourning means you embrace the road ahead. When we lose a loved one, for a season we want to put life on hold because it's overwhelming. Eventually, as we progress in grief, we begin to embrace the life we have left to live. That is what Step 5 has been about. Many losses that come with a major marital disruption get overlooked. Step 5 has been a sort of funeral for those. Now, as we conclude Step 5, we are regrouping to embrace the life in front of us.

▶ **Read Philippians 3:12–15.** Our work in this step should give you a better appreciation for what Paul did and didn't mean when he said, "Forgetting what is behind." Even in the book of Philippians, Paul frequently mentioned aspects of his past—both pleasant and unpleasant. So it's obvious that Paul didn't mean "lose all memory of the past" when he said this. He did mean, in effect, *Don't let the road behind you (hardships) distract you from your ability to pursue the road ahead of you (a satisfying and purposeful future).* That is what Step 5 has been all about. When our hurtful past is understood with the destructive messages of Step 4, we ruminate, get lost in insecurities, and become paralyzed by how impossible life seems. As we mourn, we don't pretend that life is any less hard than it is. But we do begin to embrace the road ahead of us and refuse to allow what has happened in the past to prevent us from pursuing what is ahead.

CONCLUSION

Realize that God is not rushing you on your journey. If anything, we are often disappointed by God's patience. We want God to push us through the process faster. But God is the ultimate gentleman, honoring us at every stage of our journey.

There is no added merit in a slow or fast journey. All God desires of us is faithfulness. This step has been intended to help you embrace this truth. As you take the remaining steps, do so with the full assurance that God agrees with your tears when you cry out "this is hard." You do not have to argue with one who is well acquainted with grief (Isaiah 53:3). He is the Good Shepherd who is willing to tenderly walk at the pace of his sheep.

G4 GROUP DISCUSSION: STEP 5, PART THREE

As you discuss this material in G4 group, these questions are meant to facilitate a more honest and beneficial dialogue about this material. Anyone is free to respond to whichever questions they choose.

Experienced Members

- What indicators helped you realized you completed Step 5 in your personal journey?
- When did you realize that your future was becoming more interesting to you than your past?

New Members

- Do you feel more rushed in your grief by others or yourself? How so?
- Does it seem possible for sadness not to be the final chapter in your story? Why or why not?
- How can we pray for you?

Everyone

- How did the devotional on Philippians 2 help you reenvision how you relate to your past?
- What does it feel like to grieve the reality of Steps 1–3 without the contamination of Step 4?
- Do we need to discuss any safety-level concerns from the past week?

STEP 6
LEARN MY GOSPEL STORY,
by which God gives meaning
to my experience.

At the end of this step, I want to be able to say . . .

"I have already told you the false narrative I drew
from my past [review Step 4]. Letting go of that story,
identity, and set of beliefs left me with only God
and the trusted friends I've invited on this journey
with me. It was good (and scary) to begin rebuilding
my life from that foundation.
Now I am beginning to understand my hardships
and my future in light of the hope the gospel brings
[examples of life lessons from Step 6]."

STEP 6
PART ONE

WHO AM I *NOW*? WHO IS MY SPOUSE *NOW*?

The video for this part of Step 6 can be found at: bradhambrick.com/truebetrayal6p1.

In Step 4, we said you might disagree with everything you wrote. In Step 6, you may have a hard time embracing the things you write. In Step 4, while you disagreed with what you wrote, most of it seemed to fit your life experience. In Step 6, you'll likely assent to the truthfulness of the things you write, but wrestle with believing that they are true for you.

At this stage in your journey, you will seek to understand yourself, God, your spouse, your setting, and your future in a way that sets you up for stable and healthy living. We will help do this by walking you through seven questions that help you identify ways God would have you understand your experience.

1. Who am I *now*?
2. Who is my spouse *now*?
3. Who and where is God?
4. What is sin?
5. Where am I?
6. Is love worth vulnerability?
7. What am I living for?

WHO AM I *NOW*?

There's a good chance you have believed the most lies about yourself. That is why we start with the question, Who am I? It is natural to ask, What does my spouse's sin say about me? Even after you embrace the reality that you are not responsible for your spouse's sin, that does not silence all of your identity questions.

The shock of a spouse's sexual sin can rattle your sense of self even without the conclusion "This was my fault." You may still wonder, *Will I ever be the same? Am I degrading myself by forgiving? Am I a fool? Am I blind to other important things?* These kinds of questions affect your ability to embrace the gospel story as the major theme in your life story.

We want to help you find a way to make meaning of your experiences that honors (without surrendering to) your past, while laying the foundation for the pursuit of a healthy, God-honoring future. To do that, we'll consider four ways to think about your personal identity.

I Am Changed and Unchanged

You are living in a legitimate tension. You are the same person you have always been. But life is different from it would have been, and this experience has impacted you in a variety of ways (see Step 3). Both realities must be reckoned with to make sense of your experience in a healthy way.

First, there is only one you, living a continuous story for the duration of your life. There is not a new you after your spouse's sin that could write a letter to the old you (or vice versa), which could be read by two different people. When you think of yourself as a fundamentally different person, you give your marital hardships the same significance as your birth and conversion (new birth). It is important for you to remember that there is a "you" that transcends these painful events.

Second, you are less naive or innocent than you were. You've experienced things that cannot be unlearned. You may begin marking time as before or after these events. This is appropriate for any major life event—graduation, marriage, having children, the loss of a parent, retirement, etc. Certain actions, words, places, or emotions may not be experienced the same way again. Acknowledging these realities is not defining your life by these events but merely understanding their impact.

▶ **Read Galatians 2:20.** In this verse we see Paul wrestling with the changed and unchanged dynamic. *Paul is changed*—"It is no longer I who live, but Christ who lives in me." *Paul is* *unchanged*—"The life I now live in the flesh I live by faith." Paul wanted the Galatians to understand the importance of this tension. He used salvation as his example (an intensely positive experience). A similar tension exists in a marital betrayal (an intensely negative experience). At salvation we become a new creation (2 Corinthians 5:17). But we are a new creation with a history (Philippians 3:5–6). There is a continuity of our personhood that transcends our salvation experience. In the same way, while your marital hardships have impacted your life in significant ways, it does not change the person God made you to be (Psalm 139:14–16; Ephesians 2:10). Living in the freedom this brings does not downplay that impact of your suffering; it merely embraces that the person God created you to be transcends these experiences.

▶ **Reflection:** Are you more prone to emphasize how your marital disruption impacted you (changed) or to resist acknowledging that impact (unchanged)? When you overemphasize how you have changed, how are you limiting your voice and agency? When you overemphasize how you are unchanged, what are you expecting of yourself that is beyond your control or capacity?

I Am Strong Enough to Be Weak

Hopefully, one of the primary things you've gained from your G4 journey is the strength to acknowledge weakness. Few things make us crumble like the perceived need to be stronger than we are. Conversely, nothing maximizes the strength God gives us like the freedom to acknowledge our need for grace, help, and encouragement.

We want G4 to provide you with language to describe your experience and to gain support from others. These things build the social strength to acknowledge our weakness. Knowing that God understands your experience and is compassionate toward suffering should give you the spiritual strength to be weak. Also, realizing that weak is not a derogatory social class under the strong removes the shame associated with being weak.

▶ **Read Matthew 5:3–6.** The Beatitudes are the epitome of being strong enough to be weak. In each Beatitude, Jesus describes as "blessed" a state of being that we would find undesirable and weak. Yet, with a little reflection, we realize attempting to be strong exhausts us. When we acknowledge that we are poor in spirit, meek, hungry, and thirsty, we find that life is better. We find there is more strength in willful God-dependency than insisting on a veneer of self-sufficiency.

> Hopefully, one of the primary things you've gained from your G4 journey is the strength to acknowledge weakness.

▶ **Reflection:** Think about your G4 journey to this point. How have you grown in your willingness to be strong enough to be weak? What freedom and opportunities emerge when you're willing to say, "I'm hurting. I need help. I'm not sure what to do"? How has acknowledging weakness (limitations) made you stronger?

I Am Free to Choose

When the choices you want most are unavailable (e.g., to stop the pain, to unwrite history, to make the healing process move faster), it can quickly feel like you have no choices or freedom at all. Throw on top of that the moral weight associated with what people think you "should" do (e.g., you *should* restore your marriage, you *should* be over it by now), and it feels like even more of your freedom is taken from you.

It is easy for this to create a sense of resentment. The natural response is, "My spouse was free to choose to sin and I am left with no freedom to choose in my suffering? That's not fair. I think it stinks and I'm angry. I should be most free, not least free." We want to avoid getting caught in the binary mindset that anger creates, which also reduces our freedom by limiting our perceived options.

In this regard, it is better to think of there being "right directions" rather than "right responses" or "right answers." Even the highly structured nature of this study cannot give the right response or universal answer to your situation. Part of your freedom is that you are walking in a direction that requires improvisation and pacing. General directions (e.g., north, south, or toward God) don't define the pace at which we travel. God is patient as he travels with us and knows many paths through the valley of the shadow of death (Psalm 23:4).

By way of giving some general direction, consider the following points of freedom in the direction of hope:

- You are free to choose whether to reconcile with an unfaithful spouse.
- You are free to choose not to say that pornography is okay or accept its presence in your home.
- You are free to choose not to accept an emotional affair as a morally viable friendship.
- You are free to involve the support of Christian friends and church leaders.
- You are free to choose the pace at which you can walk through these nine steps.

▶ **Read I Corinthians 7:12–16.** This passage captures the freedom-in-a-direction dynamic. On freedom, Paul says the believing spouse is not to be "enslaved" (v. 15) to a spouse's willful sin. In this case, Paul is talking about abandonment as grounds for divorce. The principle of not being enslaved (i.e., obligated to an unwanted outcome or morally bound to acquiesce by silence) to a spouse's sin is a God-given freedom. On direction, Paul says our goal should involve seeing our spouse's soul restored to God (v. 16). *False Love* provides the structure and support for that journey, so you don't feel enslaved to facilitating that process for your spouse.

▶ **Reflection:** Do you see yourself as "free in a general direction"? If not, what hinders that? What freedoms do you ignore because of the pressure from others? What freedoms listed above are you unsure whether God truly intends for you to have?

I Am Loved by God

A crisis has a way of defining everything it touches. After a burglary, it can be hard not to think of your home as a crime scene or a window as an entry point. After the sexual sin of your spouse, it can be hard not to think of yourself as forsaken or unloved. When we do this, we make sexual sin the defining center of our life, marriage, and identity.

In an indirect way, the sin of your spouse takes the place of God in your life. Usually, God is replaced by the pleasure of sin. In this case, God is replaced by the life-defining impact of suffering. Part of embracing the gospel story is allowing God's love to be more central to your life and identity than your spouse's failure.

It would be inaccurate to call our struggle to centralize God's love idolatry. You are not worshipping your spouse's sin. But you do want to decentralize your spouse's sin from your identity and story. You do not want to give final say over your worth and value to your spouse's choices. As we learn to resist this tendency, we are submitting to Jesus's lordship over our lives amid suffering (by giving God the final word instead of shame) as much as we do with our sin (by obeying God's ways instead of our desires).

▶ **Read Romans 8:35–39.** Put your fears about what your spouse might say about you into this passage. Put the arguments you use to convince yourself you are unloved into these verses. Read the passage out loud with your "junk" in the list with "death nor life, nor angels nor rulers, nor things present nor things to come, etc." That is what it means to allow God's love to be the definitive word over your life. Allow this to become a secure foundation for your identity.

▶ **Reflection:** Do you believe you are loved by God? When are you prone to allow the pain from feeling rejected by your spouse to usurp a felt sense of being loved by God? When this happens, it is easy to feel desperate and hopeless. When do these emotions begin to shape what you expect and how you relate to your spouse and others?

▶ **Summary: Who Am I *Now*?** Don't limit yourself to the four questions in this "Who Am I *Now*?" section. Write a statement about who you are. Include your value to God as one of his children. Include the gifts, talents, and passions God gave you. Include the role you play in the lives of healthy relationships you value. Consider reading this statement at an upcoming G4 meeting. Update this statement as you continue your G4 journey. When you feel discouraged or insecure, read this statement.

WHO IS MY SPOUSE *NOW?*

Every story has good guys and bad guys ("guys" meant to be gender-inclusive). Our lives are no different. When you got married, your spouse was one of the good guys in your story. After betrayal, it is easy to permanently label your spouse one of the "bad guys."

The label "bad guy" doesn't have to be permanent. The gospel gives us hope that anyone can change. But trusting that God is a faithful and accurate judge also means we do not have to mistake good intentions or tears for a changed life. To help us navigate this tension, we will explore three ways to think about your spouse.

Your Spouse Is a Person, Not an Action

In our current cultural moment, we have a strong tendency to label people by their weaknesses and failures. We use the terms *addict*, *abuser*, and *narcissist* frequently. On the *False Love* and *True Betrayal* journey, we might be prone to use the terms *cheater* or *sex addict* as the defining quality of our spouse. When accurate, there is nothing wrong with these assessments; they describe actions, not identities. These things may be what our loved one did but not who they are.

This doesn't minimize the impact of your spouse's actions. Rather, it increases the weight and importance of their actions. These are your spouse's choices, not a condition (like cancer). As such, your spouse is not the victim of their own choices, and their choices cannot be dismissed as something that "just happened." Calling sin "sin" honors the dignity of your spouse, even it if offends them. Scripturally, every time your loved one sins, they are making a choice to do so. It is wrong, and they are responsible. It is unbiblical, unloving, and dehumanizing to narrate their life otherwise.

On the receiving end of their sin, we face twin temptations. Either we reduce our loved one to a label and begin to view change as impossible (more on that in a moment), or we minimize their actions as being less wrong because we medicalize their behaviors. Even when our loved one has a condition, like diabetes, they are responsible to apply the appropriate remedy, like insulin, exercise, and eating habits. If they don't, we don't honor them by making excuses for their inaction or blaming their disease for their refusal to engage the appropriate care.

To gain an image of what we're saying, remember the movie *Bambi* and the scene when the little deer is learning to talk and sees the baby skunk? Bambi says, "Flower." Everyone laughs and the skunk says, "You can call me flower if you want to." When you look at the person who hurt you, you will identify them in some way. They are a person, and as we will see, they are bearing fruit and capable of change. We honor reality and our loved one by calling their actions by the right name.

> ▶ **Read 1 Corinthians 6:9–11.** Paul is speaking to a church that was filled with people who could be labeled as many things (e.g., sex addicts, kleptomaniacs, pathological liars). Paul doesn't downplay the frequency, duration, or impact of these sins. But, in verse 11, he says, "Such were some of you." Paul honored their humanity by not reducing them to their struggle and believing they, by God's grace, could make different choices. Paul advised the church to create the appropriate distance from those who would not change (2 Corinthians 6:17 and Ephesians 5:11). Likewise, as you think about your spouse, honor them by refusing to allow a label to minimize the significance of their choices. Love them enough to allow them to see the consequence of their choices in how you respond to them.

> ▶ **Reflection:** Are you prone to minimize your loved one's actions because of a label? If a diagnosis accurately fits your loved one, are they engaging in the appropriate care and treatment? Are you excusing their actions because of a condition for which they refuse to seek help? How does honoring your loved one's humanity give you greater emotional freedom to make choices in response to what they will or will not do?

Your Spouse Is a Fruit-Bearer

Your spouse will bear fruit that reveals the condition of their heart, whether for better (e.g., repentance, other mindedness, engaging counseling, seeking accountability) or worse (e.g., continued sin, self-pity, selfishness, isolation, defensiveness). If your question in the previous section was, "Well, what do I call them then?" The answer would be, "Their present fruit."

You are on Step 6. That means you have been working through *True Betrayal* for several months since you learned of your spouse's sin. That duration of time allows you to have a good read on the type of fruit your spouse is going to bear.

- If your spouse continues to have contact with their adultery partner and hides their means of communication, they are not committed to the marriage; at least, they are as committed to their adultery partner as they are to you. At this point in your *True Betrayal* journey, that means it is unwise to make choices that assume your spouse's fidelity.

> Paul honored their humanity by not reducing them to their struggle and believing they, by God's grace, could make different choices.

- If your spouse continues to view pornography and act out in other sexually immoral ways, that means the current consequences within the marriage are inadequate to make change "worth it" in your spouse's mind. At this point in your *True Betrayal* journey, that means it is unwise to make choices that assume your spouse's fidelity.

You don't need a label to make that assessment. Not mentioning a label may be in your best interest. Too many situations go from bad to worse in an "I'm not a sex addict" argument. You don't need to win that argument about a term to conclude that the fruit of your loved one's life does not merit trust.

In *False Love*, by the time your spouse reaches Steps 5 and 6, they are being directed to live with a level of transparency and integrity that would give you reasonable certainty (the most life offers) that they are prioritizing a God-honoring marriage. *False Love* also asks your spouse to engage in accountability relationships, sparing you from having to evaluate the sincerity of their fruit on your own.

▶ **Read Matthew 12:33–37.** The summary phrase of this passage is we are "known by [our] fruit (v. 33)." Unlike trees, people can change fruit when we are grafted into the trunk of submission to God (Romans 11:11–24). However, like fruit from trees, personal character takes time to produce. The fruit discussed above does not show up in the hours, days, or couple of weeks after sin is acknowledged. But fruit can be discerned in the weeks and months that follow. A key marker of a genuine commitment to change is perseverance, that is, a commitment to change that endures long enough to validate the genuineness of that commitment.

▶ **Reflection:** What fruit do you see in your loved one's life? Is that fruit stable and consistent enough to be considered fruit of a changing heart or merely having a good day? What fruit do trusted friends, an accountability partner, or counselor see in your spouse's life? Is your spouse pressuring you to make choices that assume recent changes will be permanent?

Your Spouse Is Capable of Change

Whatever change your spouse does or does not express is the direct result of their choice to actively rely on God's grace and engage with the appropriate forms of care. There is nothing you will or will not do that will determine whether your spouse makes these choices. That is between them and God.

Often, we tell ourselves that our spouse is too far gone, and we give up on them. Then we vacillate on how far gone is too far gone. The subjective measure results in us perpetually second-guessing ourselves.

- You hear a sermon on God's power to do anything, and you second-guess yourself.
- Your spouse is nice or caring, and you second-guess yourself.
- You get a question about your spouse in a social setting, and you second-guess yourself.
- You feel lonely, and you second-guess yourself.

The list can go on and on . . . Your spouse can change, and you are facing some difficult decisions. These two things are not mutually exclusive. As you move toward Steps 7 and Step 8, you will begin to make choices about the future of your marriage. Consider the following list:

- You may see positive fruit that is encouraging and feel excited to make restorative choices.
- You may see genuine effort with inconsistent results and make more cautious choices.
- You may see negative fruit and choose to pursue a more formal or prolonged separation.
- Your spouse may have seen the cost of what godly change entails and abandoned the marriage, and your choices are focused on how you'll respond to this new reality.

▶ **Read 1 Corinthians 1:18–31.** Paul is writing to a highly fractured church. Paul discusses what makes change possible. The Greeks thought change would come from wisdom and deep insight, while the Jews thought change would come from power and bringing outside forces to bear on the situation (v. 22). Christians, however, didn't fit in either camp and were mocked by both. Christians knew that neither personal insight nor powerful experiences were sufficient, in and of themselves, to change the human heart. Paul says only the gospel has the power to change people (vv. 23–25). Paul invites these believers to reflect on their own testimony to verify his claim (vv. 26–31). But don't reflect on this passage by itself. Realize that Paul wrote a second letter to the Corinthians—actually, he wrote four but only two made it into the Bible.[1] Paul had to keep writing to the same group of believers. This helps us avoid making poor choices based on an exaggerated sense of what we believe love or loyalty require. Change is possible, but that doesn't mean people will cooperate with the gospel's power. When the gospel has changed someone, the evidence of that change will be clear and tangible (Galatians 5:22–24).

▶ **Reflection:** What phrases do you tell yourself that make you believe change is impossible for your spouse? What prompts you to second-guess yourself? What changes in your marriage have you tried to make in the past but after second-guessing yourself gave up trying to make?

▶ **Summary: Who Is My Spouse *Now*?** Don't limit yourself to the three questions in this section. While your spouse may have been through many hard things and may have many admirable qualities, these are not the focal point of the decisions you are making. As you weigh the choices you are willing to enact in the steps ahead, don't get lost in trying to save your spouse from their hardships or in mourning their unrealized potential. Instead, your focus is on making the wisest choices considering the impact (i.e., fruit) of their life on your life.

CONCLUSION

As we've sought to build a redemptive narrative to make sense of your marital experience, we've tried to answer common questions about you and your spouse. We've been honest about the impact of this relationship on you. We've been equally honest about your ability to make choices (which is true, even when you doubt it). We've been no less honest about your spouse's responsibility for their actions and potential to change (which is true, even when it's easier to think it's impossible).

Our goal hasn't been to craft a simple narrative to enact quick change. That is a recipe for regret. Our goal has been to craft an accurate, redemptive narrative. One that is sturdy enough to support the ups and downs, disappointments and setbacks, good days and bad days that are inevitably ahead of us. We're not done developing that narrative. We've explored two questions of seven.

But it is wise for us to take a break. Part of God's redemptive narrative for our suffering is his willingness to give us rest, allow us to catch our breath, and regain our strength for the next leg of our journey. Even as you inevitably have many lingering questions, assimilate what you've learned in this part of Step 6 and then accept God's invitation to rest before continuing your G4 journey.

G4 GROUP DISCUSSION: STEP 6, PART ONE

As you discuss this material in G4 group, these questions are meant to facilitate a more honest and beneficial dialogue about this material. Anyone is free to respond to whichever questions they choose.

Experienced Members

- In your G4 journey, how have you come to understand that a redemptive story for your suffering isn't a falsely positive or a story that answers every question?
- How has G4 helped you become strong enough to be weak?

New Members

- What influential choices do you wonder if you are strong enough to make?
- Which of the three statements in the "Who Is My Spouse *Now*?" section was least clear for you and would be helpful to hear from other members on?
- How can we pray for you?

Everyone

- What were the most important things for you to re-narrate about you or your spouse?
- Would anyone who has recently completed the "Who Am I *Now*" summary reflection like to share it with the group?
- Do we need to discuss any safety-level concerns from the past week?

STEP 6
PART TWO

WHO AND WHERE IS GOD? WHAT IS SIN?

The video for this part of Step 6 can be found at: bradhambrick.com/truebetrayal6p2.

We started our work on a redemptive narrative for our suffering by focusing on you and the person who hurt you—that is, the two people most obviously present and active in these painful moments. But, in this part of Step 6, we're turning our attention to God and sin. How does God relate to our pain? How do we understand the actions that hurt us? As we seek to make sense of our suffering, these are not small questions.

Like we did in the first part of Step 6, we'll introduce each question and then break it down into smaller pieces that allow us to wrestle with the common points of confusion.

WHO AND WHERE IS GOD?

When we engage questions about God amid suffering, we often feel like our Christian friends act as God's defense attorneys more than ambassadors of God's care for us. That's one reason we begin to hide our suffering and honest questions. We don't want another conversation that devolves into a theological defense of why God is still good even when life is hard. Theological considerations like that are important. You wouldn't be this far into a G4 curriculum if you didn't believe that. But our primary focus is on processing pain and finding direction.

With these things in mind, let's begin to consider some of the redemptive scripts that can clarify the distortions we began to identify in Step 4.

God Is Near to Those Who Are Suffering

A danger emerges when we read our Bible in search for God's answer to our pain. We begin to think there is an answer that will fix our pain. We read our Bible like a letter, written from an absent father. A letter would mean that God cared and that he was far away. This would be both encouraging and disheartening; God's words would seem sincere but distant. This is why we must pay careful attention to the thing God most repeats and the thing we most overlook.

▶ **Read I Peter 5:6–9 and Philippians 4:5–9.** Both passages are famous for saying some version of "do not be anxious." But the most neglected aspect of these passages is their emphasis on the nearness of God. We come to these passages seeking God's answer for the things that cause us to be afraid and overwhelmed. As we search for principles and practical steps, we miss that the first and main thing God offers is himself. Yes, God does offer us strategies and truths to combat the effects of relational hardships, but these are not the first and most important things he offers. The main thing God wants you to know when these passages feel relevant is that you are not alone. *God draws near to us when we suffer.*

Think of a child who is scared—maybe they woke up from a bad dream or loud thunder. When a caring parent enters the room, what is the most impactful thing they do? They sit on the bed, draw their child near, and stay with them for a while to calm the child's racing thoughts. Being near provides more comfort than any explanation of why dreams aren't real or why thunderstorms aren't dangerous. *Presence is more powerful than answers at calming fear.* That's why God emphasizes his nearness in this and other "I will never leave you or forsake you" passages throughout the Bible.

▶ **Reflection:** How can you remind yourself of God's nearness in hard times? What moments of God's care and provision allowed you to get to this G4 group? How have the people in this group been ambassadors of God's nearness to you? What options are opening to you as you lean more on God's care?

God Is Faithful

When we are betrayed by a spouse, we can begin to wonder if anyone is faithful. Can anyone be trusted? It is easy to interpret the unfaithfulness of a spouse to mean that we are completely on our own. In this way, we begin to redefine God based on our experience in marriage. This multiplies the pain and fear we feel.

But God promises more than to never leave. God also promises to never forsake us. God doesn't just promise to be near but also to be faithful. God will forever and always be actively for us. God will act in our best interest, even when it is at great personal cost—we see that in the sacrifice of Jesus. We will never have to ask questions about God like we have had to ask about our spouse.

> ▶ **Read Deuteronomy 31:6–8; Joshua 1:5; 1 Chronicles 28:20; and Hebrews 13:5.** This promise, "I will never leave you or forsake you," shows up throughout Scripture. God knows our tendency to view him as absent or unconcerned and, therefore, makes this one of the most repeated promises in the Bible. It stands to reason that God is repetitious with his promises because we are repetitious in our fears. What we say to ourselves most frequently we tend to believe most innately. God repeats his promise as an invitation and example of how we are to cling to it—by repeating it.

> ▶ **Reflection:** How have you already seen God's faithfulness to this point in your G4 journey? When are you prone to doubt God's faithfulness (e.g., times of day, before/after certain events, with particular emotions, etc.)? For you, what are the best reminders of God's faithfulness?

God Is Our Pioneer

We want to know that someone has been where we are and has come out on the other side. Has anyone known this level of betrayal, pain, neglect, and rejection? If so, can I learn from their example? Even better, could I draw from their strength and find a way to be infused with their victory? These kinds of questions are generally met with an awkward smirk that communicates "wouldn't it be nice." But the answer to these questions is, Yes! The answer to these questions is, That is what the gospel is all about.

[Jesus] is a Man of Sorrows and intimate with grief. He was left alone, regarded with contempt. He is scarred for all eternity. His suffering has left its tracks across his face. His hands and feet carry marks of the violence done to him. He was afflicted, struck, crushed, stripped, and oppressed. Suffering does that, you know; it leaves its mark over those who must endure. . . . Jesus was storming the gates of hell even while he bowed himself to our finitude and brokenness. —Diane Langberg[1]

God pioneered the road you are traveling. Jesus walked it first. It was an impossible road before his God-man feet cleared the path you are struggling to walk. As you find yourself wanting to give up or wondering if it's possible, reflect on what it was like to walk this road with no forerunner carrying the weight. Don't use that image to discount your struggle but to grow in appreciation for Jesus's sacrifice. Your

> God repeats his promise as an invitation and example of how we are to cling to it—by repeating it.

experience should magnify your understanding of what Jesus did. What Jesus did doesn't minimize what you're going through.

▶ **Read Hebrews 12:1–3.** Notice it says to "consider" Christ "so that you may not grow weary or fainthearted" (v. 3). What does it say you should consider to gain this encouragement? Part of the reflection is that Jesus walked "despising the shame" (v. 2) of his journey. Jesus really did walk a road like yours. He knew shame and rejection. He offers to share your load with you (Mathew 11:28–30). Your road is hard. Jesus found it hard too. Pharisees tried to manipulate Jesus. Judas betrayed him. Other disciples abandoned him. Even his closest friends fell asleep when he asked for their support at a pivotal moment. Strangers beat and stripped Jesus at the cross. Political leaders abused their power to silence him. Whatever parts of these experiences align with your own, you can know that when you pray, you are talking to someone who gets what you're going through.

▶ **Reflection:** What encouragement do you take from knowing that Jesus pioneered the difficult road you are on? How does it impact you to read the painful parts of Jesus's life that mirror your own and realize "me too"? How does it feel to have a definitive yes answer to the question, Can anyone, even God, understand what I'm going through?

God Is Capable of Transforming Suffering

We often equate transformation with elimination. We want the transformation of our hardships to result in the elimination of the hardship and its aftermath. This is not a bad desire, but it would require removing these experiences from our story (the impossibility of rewriting history) rather than redeeming the presence of these hardships within our story.

We think of the elimination model of transformation because it is most common in our experience. We see it when a water droplet is transformed to vapor; the droplet no longer exists. But God's transformation of suffering is usually much more like the change in our memories of a loved one during grief. These memories aren't eliminated. Instead, our experience of these memories is transformed. Initially, we feel like we're drowning when we remember our departed loved one. Over time, that memory is transformed, and while it still may make us sad, it doesn't overpower our ability to function.

In this G4 journey, we are dealing with both memories (past hardships) and present hardships (painful situations and decisions we wish we didn't have to make). What we are gaining from this reflection is an understanding that transformation is not elimination. Grief gives us an example of a painful experience that can be transformed without erasing it. This helps us remember that the presence of pain does not mean the absence of God's redemptive work in our suffering.

▶ **Read John 4:1–42.** Because this woman gets saved and revival breaks out in Samaria (vv. 39–42), we often miss her pain. She has been married five times. Her current living arrangement provides her with no long-term security. She feels immense shame; hence she comes to the well at the hottest part of the day to avoid being seen or scorned by others (v. 6). We don't know the pain that connects these dots of information about her life, but it's safe to assume that some variety of betrayal, abandonment, or other major dysfunction marked her marriages. She didn't return to her parents or go to a sibling, so it is likely these relationships were unhealthy or absent as well. Notice that Jesus transforms but doesn't erase her painful history. What once brought her shame became part of her testimony (v. 39). She no longer feels the need to hide from people. This is the same Jesus we are inviting into our story and the kind of work we are asking him to do.

▶ **Reflection:** How does the idea of transformation rather than elimination change your expectations of what it would mean for God to work redemptively in your experience? How have you already seen this work begun during your time at G4? When has the transformation been slower than you would like? When has the transformation been faster than you expected, or even faster than you were comfortable with?

▶ **Summary: Who and Where Is God?** Don't limit yourself to the four questions in this section. Also consider the destructive scripts about God that were sticky for you as you worked Step 4. Summarize the things you have come to value and trust about God to this point on your G4 journey. What have you learned about God that is meaningful? What have you unlearned about God that is freeing? Don't rush past these truths. Savor these truths in a way that deepens your relationship with God. Pray prayers of appreciation and praise about these truths.

WHAT IS SIN?

For many of us, at this stage on our *True Betrayal* journey, *sin* probably seems like a much more significant word than it did when we were unaware of our spouse's sin. Before our life felt ravaged by our spouse's actions, a simple definition like "sin is the bad things that we do" seemed adequate. Now that feels like referring to the events of 9/11 as "an air traffic control problem." While in some ways accurate, it's not adequate or complete.

Sin is a destructive force that, once unleashed, takes on a life of its own. Dealing with sin requires more than uttering the tender words "I forgive you." It requires something to die. The thought of Jesus having to die on the cross for sin probably seems like less of an exaggeration to you now.

In this section, we will look at three aspects of sin that are important to help you continue to build a gospel narrative for your experience.

Sin Is Spiritual Adultery

We don't want to use the phrase "spiritual adultery" as a flippant description for "really bad." That would trivialize the significance of the work you've done on this *True Betrayal* journey, and it would trivialize the nature of sin. We also don't want the adjective "spiritual" to carry the connotation of "less real" as if sin wasn't really a violation of our covenant relationship with God. The force of those words likely resonates with you more than they ever have.

God chose the imagery of adultery to portray why sin is so offensive and so damaging to relationships. Sin isn't just bad moral etiquette. Sin is choosing an idol as our source of pleasure, security, and identity over God. This is why God isn't primarily concerned with the behavior of sin but with the motive behind our sin. Sin is wrong because we seek in something else what God intends for us to find in him.

Your *True Betrayal* journey should allow you to marvel at the gospel in new ways. But this should not be a guilt exercise, turning the tables with, "I guess I am a spiritual adulterer too, why should I be upset with my spouse?" The first part is true, but the question about being upset distracts us from what we need to see. Your response mirrors God's. You were offended by your spouse's sin. God is offended by our sin. Therefore, God does not call you to be unmoved.

God felt what you're feeling first. God took the steps necessary to provide ultimate hope for the pain you're feeling—sending Jesus to die on the cross—so that we could have hope for the painful situations where such hope is needed. You are not praying to an aloof God who is unfamiliar with your pain. We pray to a God who "gets it" at the deepest level. You are seen, and you are understood.

▶ **Read Romans 9:22–10:4.** Romans is a letter full of deep theological truths. It could be easy to think that Romans is only for highly intellectual Christians. But Paul makes a strong emotional appeal in these verses. Paul references Gomer's adultery against the prophet Hosea to help us feel the weight of sin and appreciate God's response. As you read this passage, allow your appreciation for how much God understands your pain and sacrifice to grow. Notice that in the adultery of God's people, some chose not to repent, and God did not restore his relationship with them (9:27–29; 10:1–4). This was not failure on God's part but hard-heartedness on the part of God's people. But when God's people did repent, he was restored to them (9:30–33). You can rest knowing that being "godly" in response to adultery doesn't entail being naive toward an unrepentant spouse (Galatians 6:7).

▶ **Reflection:** How have you felt alone in your experience of betrayal? How does Romans 9 help alleviate that aloneness? Have you felt like there was one Christian response to your spouse's sin? How does Romans 9 help you see that a wise, godly response is contingent upon the choices of your spouse?

Sin Is Illogical

The "why" question just won't go away. With every significant marker of progress, we look back to see if the sin makes any more sense. It doesn't. That's disappointing. Even if we knew better, we hoped by the time we reached Step 6 and addressed sin from within a gospel narrative, it would make sense. This doesn't mean your progress isn't real. It doesn't mean you can't know important things that allow you to make wise decisions. It just means sin is illogical.

We can understand the motives for our spouse's sin; that is, the idolatry from which sin emerged. We can identify unhealthy aspects of our marriage culture that may have created an environment of elevated temptation. But these things do not add up to an explanation for why your spouse was unfaithful.

We can see the fruit of genuine repentance and be encouraged by the transparency in our spouse's life. We can appreciate the renewed closeness this allows. We can identify wise plans for a healthier marriage and grow more optimistic about the future. But these things do not add up to guarantee for safety that silences our fears.

All of this to say that we can't treat sin like a science experiment; do the right steps, in the right order, with the right measurements, and sin will vanish. The only thing that will protect a marriage is both spouses' continual, mutual dependence upon God and willing, humble care for one another. The only thing that disrupts this is "choices" not "cause." Choices are voluntary and not compelled by a formula of logic.

▶ **Read Genesis 3:1–21.** As you read this passage, notice that none of the descriptions or conversations makes sin logical. As we read the passage, we are left with the nagging question, why? I know all that happened. I heard what was said, but why did Adam and Eve think the fruit was better than what they already had with God? When our life is affected by sin, we still look back at Adam and Eve to vent our frustrations with the rhetorical question why? As we mature as Christians we learn to live without a satisfying answer because we come to understand the nature of sin as illogical. We become satisfied to pursue God (moving in the opposite direction of sin), knowing that safety is not found in an answer to our question but in active dependence upon God.

▶ **Reflection:** What would it mean for you to surrender your "why" questions? Can you be content knowing the motive for sin and wise practices in response to sin? If you struggle to be content with these two pieces of information, what are you desiring beyond that?

Sin Is a Conquered Enemy

Saying that sin is illogical can sound like surrender, and in a way, it is. But it is surrender to God's care, not surrender to the perpetual presence of sin. Sin may not submit to logic (actually, it can't because sin, by definition, is counter to God's created order), but it must submit to God. This means sin will not get the last word.

If your spouse is unrepentant, their sin will not reign wild and free, defiantly thumbing its nose at you and God for all eternity. In that case, your spouse's sin will meet a greater pain than it caused you and an equal pain to what it caused God—hell. Because God is not mocked, you can rest in knowing that the sin against you will not get the final word.

If your spouse is repentant, their sin will not get off scot-free, fading into forgetfulness as if it never happened only to live in the privacy of your memory. In that case, your spouse's sin will meet a greater pain than it caused you and an equal pain to what it caused God—the cross. You can rest in knowing that even forgiven sin is not merely erased; it is still "paid in full."

> ► **Read Revelation 20:7–15.** This is not the time to try to figure out the most accurate interpretation of the book of Revelation. Allow yourself to read the big story even if you don't understand all the details. In this passage you see the fate of your Enemy (Satan) and enemies (those who cooperate with Satan's destructive agenda). You see how clear and definitive victory is. Death and Hades are tossed around and made to obey like rag dolls. Those who mock God no longer have any voice over their destiny. Those who submit to God have no pride or secret desire for their sin. This is how conquered the sin that has disrupted your life is.

Sin will not get the last word.

> ► **Reflection:** Are you able to take comfort in the certainty of sin being a conquered enemy? How does seeing the two fates of your spouse's sin help you avoid feeling like God offers cheap grace that is insufficient for the pain your spouse's sin caused?

> ► **Summary: What Is Sin?** Don't limit yourself to the three questions in this section. Also consider the destructive scripts about God that were sticky for you as you worked Step 4. Summarize the things you have learned about sin. How does seeing sin more clearly motivate you to avoid sin in your own life? What have you unlearned about sin that made it feel like your experience was being trivialized? Don't rush past these truths. Allow them to cultivate a deeper appreciation for what God has done for us through the gospel.

CONCLUSION

In this part of Step 6, we sought to better understand our source of pain (sin) and our source of hope (God). A better understanding doesn't make painful things less painful, but it can make painful things less confusing. It is often confusion about our pain and whether there is hope that makes our pain linger.

Embracing a redemptive narrative for your life is more than simply naming lies and articulating corresponding truths. It is about resting in the new truths you've come to understand and muffling the lies that echo in our mind. Narratives build as we repeat things to ourselves. As you continue to work Step 6, look for opportunities to repeat the things you are learning about God to good friends and yourself throughout the day. Repetition is a key difference between merely passing a theology quiz and embracing a new narrative.

G4 GROUP DISCUSSION: STEP 6, PART TWO

As you discuss this material in G4 group, these questions are meant to facilitate a more honest and beneficial dialogue about this material. Anyone is free to respond to whichever questions they choose.

Experienced Members

- What are the most tangible examples of God's nearness in your suffering on your G4 journey?
- What were the most frustrating parts of accepting that "sin is illogical"?

New Members

- What fears about God did this part of Step 6 begin to assuage for you?
- Does it feel premature to think of sin this early in your journey as a conquered enemy?
- How can we pray for you?

Everyone

- In your words, what is the difference between transforming and eliminating suffering?
- What are the most important things about God and sin that you need to remember?
- Do we need to discuss any safety-level concerns from the past week?

STEP 6
PART THREE

WHERE AM I? IS LOVE WORTH VULNERABILITY?
WHAT AM I LIVING FOR?

The video for this part of Step 6 can be found at: bradhambrick.com/truebetrayal6p3.

As you've worked Step 6, you've come to realize that embracing a redemptive narrative isn't about looking for a silver lining in the dark cloud of marital betrayal. It is not about convincing yourself that what has happened is somehow good.

Instead, we're engaging with hard questions that frequently emerge during suffering. We're seeking honest, biblical, and hopeful perspectives on these questions that don't explain away our suffering. Life is hard, but we can have a satisfying purpose in that hard life. Life is hard, but God can still be good and active in a hard life.

That's been our rhythm: Life is hard (there's no point in downplaying that), but . . . (a gritty, hopeful perspective on the subject at hand). That is the rhythm we'll continue in this final part of Step 6. As you finish Step 6, seek to embrace this pattern of thought rather than merely working through the questions and reflections.

WHERE AM I?

What kind of world do we live in? That's a big question that impacts the story of our lives. If we are too optimistic, suffering crushes our naivety. If we are too pessimistic, then we lose the hope necessary to thrive. In this part of Step 6, we'll seek to acknowledge the brokenness of this world without losing hope.

As you complete this part of Step 6, you should grow in confidence in your ability to accurately name and define your world. After a major betrayal, it is easy to give into the mindset that says, "If I can't change

179

it, why acknowledge it?" The reality is, there are many things about the world we live in that we can't change. But accurately naming and assessing our environment is an important part of a thriving life.

I Live in a Dangerous World

Having a redemptive narrative does not require minimizing the dangers that exist in this fallen world. Prior to this *True Betrayal* journey, we might have thought that God's response to the fall in Genesis 3 was an overreaction. Now, we no longer have the innocence to be that naive.

The more difficult question becomes, how do we see the dangers of a fallen world and not see danger everywhere? After all, sexuality is everywhere. This can be a temptation for your spouse and a trigger for you. It would be easy to live in perpetual fear. Instead, we want to acknowledge potential dangers and gauge their severity. We do not want our pain to become the interpretive center of life. We avoid this by reestablishing more degrees on our relational safety thermometer. We can do this by asking two questions:

1. What is the actual level of concern my situation warrants?
2. What is an appropriate response to this level of concern?

Your work to this point on your G4 journey has bought you the time necessary to ask the questions. You've also developed relationships to help vet your answers to these questions. You have placed yourself in a position to better discern "safe dangers" (e.g., insecurities, anomalies in your schedule, the phrase "there's something we need to talk about") from "destructive dangers" (e.g., signs that your spouse is being unfaithful again). Be encouraged by the progress you've made.

> ▶ **Read Matthew 10:16–24.** Notice that Jesus does not minimize the dangers his disciples would experience. Reading about the environment into which Jesus sent his disciples may be unsettling for you. But Jesus did not send them out naively. Instead, Jesus told his disciples to be "wise as serpents" (v. 16). Because Jesus knew the dangers of this world, he wanted his disciples to take appropriate precautions. Yet in this vigilance, Jesus wanted

to protect them from becoming hypervigilant, so he asked them to be "innocent as doves" (v. 16). This space between being "wise as serpents" and "innocent as doves" allows us to take steps to ensure marital stability without robbing us of peace. Jesus does not call his followers to be passive toward danger or naive about danger. As you take steps to be wise as serpents and innocent as doves, you can rest knowing that you are following Jesus's instruction.

▶ **Reflection:** When and how have you been made to feel like being wise as a serpent toward your spouse's sin was wrong? When have your fears generalized to relatively safe situations that you are unsure how to categorize?

> We do not want our pain to become the interpretive center of life.

I Am Not Alone

This is worth saying out loud: "I am not alone." When home has been disrupted, it can make us feel alone for at least two reasons: (a) we don't think anyone understands so (b) we don't feel like we have anyone to talk to.

Your G4 journey is meant to counter this experience in three ways. First, we want to help you see and feel the reality of God's care for you. Second, your G4 group surrounds you with people who have a similar experience. Third, your G4 group provides a context for you to examine and talk about your experience as you gather the information you need to make decisions about the future.

The longer you are in G4, the louder you should be able to say, "I am not alone." Yes, this world is highly sexualized. Yes, it is painful and disorienting to be betrayed by a spouse. Yes, it is lonely when home is disrupted. But no, we are not alone . . . we are not the only ones . . . we do not have to be silent! You are known and you are loved.

▶ **Read Romans 12:15 and I Corinthians 12:14–26.** God does not call allowing others to care for you being a burden; instead, God views it as being part of his body, the church. God made us to live in community so that our pain could not exist without affecting others. God did this to protect his people and ensure our care in hard times. Early in your G4 journey this truth may have felt novel. We hope it's becoming redundant to the point of being borderline boring. If so, that means it has been repeated enough that you're beginning to assimilate it into how you think about life. That's what this part of Step 6 is all about.

▶ **Reflection:** When do you feel alone? What experiences still feel off-limits to share with your most trusted friends? At this point in your G4 journey, if some of your experiences feel too weighty to talk about, individual counseling might be a wise step. Your G4 group can be a place of continued support as you work through these matters.

I Am on a Journey

When our scenery is changing, it can be hard to get our bearings. Imagine you're on a road trip. You fall asleep as you're crossing the plains, and you wake up as you're passing over the mountains. The same would be true if you fell asleep during a storm and woke up with it being sunny. As you've taken this G4 journey, your relational scenery has likely begun to change. Even if your marriage is still hard, you now have support and a better understanding of what's happening.

Rarely is any journey all good or all bad. There are times of action and times of waiting; times of change and times of stagnation; times of positive anticipation and times of dread. If you have felt these conflicting emotions, that doesn't mean you're wishy-washy. Instead, it means you are on a real-life journey for which the destination is unknown. This is why even good change can feel disorienting.

▶ **Read Psalm 23.** Notice that this well-known psalm depicts a journey of a sheep with the Good Shepherd through perilous times to a place of safety. The sheep, with whom you are invited to identify, travels through barren country where skill is needed to find green pastures and water (vv. 1–3). It traverses dangerous places where the terrain is unsafe and needs a rod to protect against predators (v. 4) before coming to the place God had prepared for it to dwell (vv. 5–6). Imagine the doubt and fear the sheep experienced along the way. The hope of this sheep was not in its surroundings but in its companion.

▶ **Reflection:** How has your experience in G4 been like a journey? How many times have you had to orient yourself to changes? How many times have you had positive anticipation about where you're headed? When have you wondered if you would ever get there? How does it encourage you to realize that you are a work in progress and haven't arrived?

▶ **Summary: Where Am I?** Don't limit yourself to the three questions in this section. Describe the relational setting of your marriage. Where are you now, and how has it changed since you began G4? How have you matured during this time? Where do you still want or need to grow? Are you gaining greater clarity on the changes your marriage warrants? If so, as you think about taking the next steps in that journey, do you get more optimistic or overwhelmed? How does that reaction compare to how you felt when you took the first steps to start your G4 journey?

IS LOVE WORTH VULNERABILITY?

Don't read this question as exclusively referencing romantic love. When we get hurt in our marriage, we don't just pull away from our spouse. Our mistrust for being vulnerable easily generalizes to anyone with whom we have a meaningful relationship. But this question also applies to your marriage, if your spouse is taking steps of repentance and change that would make vulnerability in your marriage wise again.

Absolutely Yes!

Maybe you're not convinced the answer "Yes!" deserves an exclamation point. The exclamation point isn't meant to coerce enthusiasm for the answer but to communicate certainty. A life where we refuse to be vulnerable with anyone is a painful life.

To love at all is to be vulnerable. Love anything, and your heart will certainly be wrung and possibly be broken. If you want to make sure of keeping it intact, you must give your heart to no one, not even to an animal. Wrap it carefully round with hobbies and little luxuries; avoid all entanglements; lock it up safe in the casket or coffin of your selfishness. But in that casket—safe, dark, motionless—it will change. It will not be broken;

it will become unbreakable, impenetrable, irredeemable. The alternative to tragedy, or at least to the risk of tragedy, is damnation. The only place outside of Heaven where you can be perfectly safe from all the dangers and perturbations of love is Hell. —C. S. Lewis[1]

Personify trust as an old friend. You used to know and like Trust. But you and Trust had a falling out because someone pitted Trust against you. You blamed Trust for how the other person used Trust to hurt you. Now, even though you can acknowledge that your pain wasn't Trust's fault—it was how the other person manipulated Trust— you are still hesitant. Our goal is to trust Trust again.

How does this happen? It happens like it does in any other relationship. Be honest about what's hard. Ask for God's help to grow in this area. Begin to allow yourself to trust in small areas of your life with safe people and stretch yourself to trust in increasingly more vulnerable and uncertain areas of your life. Realize that God is willing to take this journey to restored trust with you at whatever pace you can bear. Be encouraged by progress rather than beating yourself up for not being at the desired destination.

Notice how we're approaching this narrative element. We're intentionally not allowing it to get sucked into an all-or-nothing mentality. We can say yes to the question, Is love worth vulnerability? We can even say it emphatically without rushing ourselves to give blind trust. On this journey, you are not just learning to pursue good things, you are learning to pursue good things in healthy ways that honor the pain of your past without being paralyzed by it.

> ▶ **Read Romans 5:1–5.** Read this passage patiently; meaning, don't feel rushed by this passage. This passage contains a journey: we move from endurance (we don't think we can make it) to character (a growing confidence in God's faithfulness) to hope (a confidence in God's faithfulness that can become contagious to others) to the removal of shame (our fear and despair no longer carry a sense of stigma). You may not be at the end of this journey yet. That's okay. God didn't map this journey as a racetrack. God mapped this journey as a trail we take with the Good Shepherd by our side. As such, this passage represents a promise

that you will reach the destination because God is faithful. In the moments you feel weak, acknowledge them with God and trusted friends. It is part of being vulnerable. You'll find it makes your journey easier (not easy) and better.

▶ **Reflection:** What areas of weakness and uncertainty are you tempted to hide from those closest to you? From this list, what are the smaller (i.e., less consequential) items you could begin to confide in others? Look at your full list. How much lighter would your journey be if you realized you didn't need to hide these secrets you had to hide anymore?

But It's Okay to Doubt and Believe

Belief and doubt are not mutually exclusive. Like the person who is shoveling their driveway after an ice storm can sweat, so can a person with assurance that love is worth the possibility of pain still have doubt. The dominant experience of cold does not prevent the temporal experience of heat; likewise, the dominant theme of trust does not preclude moments of doubt.

It might be easy in step-work material like this to think that life should be a steady, uninterrupted progression toward trust and hope. If that is your expectation, then each intrusion of fear will feel like a relapse (borrowing from addiction language). That's not true. That is an impossibly high expectation.

What does this mean at a practical level? It means you can listen to your doubts. It means you can learn from your doubts without feeling like you've let God down. It means you can doubt your doubts, seeing them as a subplot of your story instead of the main plotline, without being a hypocrite. It means doubt does not have to be as dangerous as it feels; instead you can handle it in the overarching story of God's care for you.

▶ **Read Mark 9:14–29.** As you read, let verse 24 be the apex of the story—where the father says to Jesus, "I believe; help my unbelief!" Notice there is no rebuke from Jesus toward the father. His belief-with-acknowledged-doubt was enough. As you seek to cling to these themes of a gospel narrative against the suffering scripts you articulated in Step 4, this prayer is all God expects of you as well. Rest in the fact that you don't need perfect faith but merely honest faith that clings to God even during times of doubt.

▶ **Reflection:** What are your lingering doubts about whether you can have a healthy marriage? When do these doubts emerge? What good things do these doubts teach you about where you are on your journey? What would it look like to trust God with these doubts?

▶ **Summary: Is Love Worth Vulnerability?** Don't limit yourself to the two questions in this section. Whether we are open to being wisely vulnerable again is a big question. Other questions we've considered may be more central to your life story, but none is likely to be more emotionally impactful. How do you respond to words like *trust*, *honesty*, and *vulnerability*? How do you feel when people ask you meaningful questions? Is your sense of trust for others steady, or does it vacillate between suspicion and blind trust? As you acclimate to more healthy trust in your life, remember that healthy trust is proportional to how well you know someone and the quality of their character.

WHAT AM I LIVING FOR?

Whenever a struggle is prolonged, it can begin to define our life. Often, we don't even notice it happening. We used to dream about what we wanted the future to be like. Then, somehow, at some point, our definition of a good day quietly morphed into, "I didn't fall apart today," or "No new, bad news was discovered today."

That may not seem like a big deal. But it can be one of the most pernicious effects of marital betrayal. Domestic violence may be more painful and living with an addict might be scarier, but like these other two examples, life after unfaithfulness can become so focused on survival that all sense of purpose evaporates.

In this question, we want to counteract this effect. It may be Step 9 before you begin to fully pursue these dreams, but our goal at this point is to reintroduce the idea of living with purpose. The main outcome for this question is not to come up with satisfying answers but simply to give yourself permission to ask the question.

I May Live for the Same Things Differently

Living for the same things differently is an extension of the you-as-unchanged theme. As you think about living a life with purpose and dreams, realize that anything that was once important or enjoyable to you before is still viable. What talents did you enjoy expressing? What causes brought you joy to advance? What activities added energy and vitality to your life?

Now, you may enjoy these things differently. The poet may find new themes emerging in his poetry. The runner may find new significance in the endurance required in a long run. The caretaker may see those she cares for with new eyes. The leader may have new appreciation for the challenges of those being led.

> Belief and doubt are not mutually exclusive.

Here's the point: *The experience of marital betrayal doesn't have to change everything about you.* That's important for you to hear. It is not bad if the passing of time has changed your interests. That's normal. But don't attribute the changes that occur with maturation and entering new seasons of life to the impact of your spouse's sin.

To avoid this, we start by exploring old interests and surveying for dreams we might want to rekindle. What did you use to enjoy filling free time with? What did you use to motivate yourself when completing a mundane task? What do you know more about than the average person because you spent a season of your life highly invested in that activity or cause? These kinds of questions help you identify old interests that you might enjoy differently in this season of life.

▶ **Read Philippians 3:1–11.** This may seem like an odd passage for this point. But notice that both before and after his conversion Paul was a leader. After the Damascus road experience, Paul's disposition and skills didn't change. Paul's drive to make whatever cause he was a part of succeed did not change. When God knit us in our mother's womb and endowed us with abilities and passions that matched his purpose for us, he knew what we would go through in life. The same is also true for unpleasant life experiences—like recent events in your marriage. God takes you, with the same personality, passions, and skill sets he gave you at conception, and intends to use them. In the same way that no one would have been surprised to see Paul as a leader in the early church, it is not surprising for God to rekindle some of your old interests.

> ▶ **Reflection:** What are you naturally good at (i.e., God-endowed skills)? What things used to make you happy or passionate? What did you enjoy about them? If you were to enjoy those things again now, what would be the same? What would be different? Don't talk yourself out of exploring these interests.

I May Live for Some New Things

The idea that you may live for some new things is an extension of the you-as-changed theme. If you felt like the previous point was incomplete, you were right. This is the other half.

Persevering through major life challenges has a way of showing us what really matters. Petty interests fade away as we realize what is too trivial to invest our life in. Substantive interests often become less intimidating. After all, we've proven to ourselves that we could endure and overcome more than we ever thought possible. Simple time with people we care about becomes more valuable as we grow to appreciate the value of healthy relationships.

Unlike most of the other changes experienced on this journey, these changes are almost universally considered good. We become mature enough to identify the more important thing we want to invest our time in. The hard things we've endured give us greater confidence that our assessment of what is important and meaningful is accurate.

> ▶ **Read 2 Corinthians 1:3–5.** Focus on the phrase "in *any* affliction" (v. 4, emphasis added). One of the fruits of God's comfort is that we grow in our ability to care for others. What we learn about God and his care in our affliction is not limited to only similar afflictions. As you begin to consider what the next stage of life holds, do not allow your marital disruption to be a limiting factor in what you consider. The word *any* in verse 4 means you don't have to limit yourself that way. You may choose to make helping people facing comparable marital challenges part of your life calling (e.g., coleading in this G4 group), but if you

do, don't make that choice because you think it is all you can do. That would give this hardship too much limiting power over your life story.

▶ **Reflection:** How have you seen your interests and passions change because of your marital disruption? How have your values, dreams, and interests matured? What new interests or priorities have emerged? What would you want to invest the next season of your life in?

▶ **Summary: What Am I Living For?** Don't limit yourself to the two questions in this section. Remember, this question is a precursor to Step 9. If some of these dreams you've listed feel far off, that's not all bad. You still have significant work to do before you finish your G4 journey. But if the dreams are appealing, allow that vigor to motivate you to complete this journey even as you face some of the hard choices that emerge in Step 7.

CONCLUSION

Concluding Step 6 brings you to another pivot point in your G4 journey. Steps 4, 5, and 6 have focused on narrative; that is, the story we draw from and use to make sense of painful experiences. We didn't want to begin the work of Step 7 on a foundation of lies. That's why we devoted this time to rooting out and replacing those destructive suffering scripts with a redemptive narrative to make sense of our suffering.

A fitting conclusion to your work in Step 6 is the work of Miroslav Volf, a political prisoner of war in former Yugoslavia, who grappled with the question, "What do I do with the memories of my interrogation and imprisonment since I cannot simply forget these years of my life?" As a Christian, Volf was seeking to remember redemptively things he could not forget. Here are several excerpts from his book *The End of Memory* that encapsulate your Step 6 work:

> We're more than what we have suffered, and that is the reason we can do something with our memory of it—integrated into our life story, turn it into a junction from which we set out on new paths, for instance. . . . All three elements of the healing of memories—a new identity, new possibilities, and an integrated

life story—drew their basic content from the memory of the Passion understood as a new Exodus, a new deliverance. . . .

Wrongdoing does not have the last word. If we remember a wrongdoing—no matter how horrendous—through the lens of remembering the Exodus, we will remember that wrongdoing as a moment in the history of those who are already on their way to deliverance. . . .

We do not need for all of our life to be gathered and rendered meaningful in order to be truly and finally redeemed. . . . No need to take all of our experiences, distinct in time and bind them together in a single volume so that each experience draws meaning from the whole as well as contributes meaning to the whole. It suffices to leave some experiences untouched (say, that daily walk I took to school in the second grade), treat others with the care of a healing hand and then abandon them to the darkness of non-remembrance (say, the interrogations by Captain G.), and gather and reframe the rest (say, the joy in the struggle of writing this book). —Miroslav Volf[2]

These words demonstrate the significant power of the work you've done in Step 6. Now, as you prepare to start Step 7, you are entering a "junction from which we set out on new paths." Before you do, take a moment to celebrate with God in prayer for all the work he has done to bring you to this junction.

G4 GROUP DISCUSSION: STEP 6, PART THREE

As you discuss this material in G4 group, these questions are meant to facilitate a more honest and beneficial dialogue about this material. Anyone is free to respond to whichever questions they choose.

Experienced Members

- How have you made peace with the idea that we live in a dangerous world and kept your hope?
- How have you navigated the question, Is love worth being vulnerable? on your G4 journey?

New Members

- What are your "I believe; help my unbelief" truths at this early stage of your G4 journey?
- When do you feel most alone and like no one understands?
- How can we pray for you?

Everyone

- What does being wise as a serpent and innocent as a dove look like in your current situation?
- Using the personification of trust exercise described in this section, how is your current relationship with trust?
- Do we need to discuss any safety-level concerns from the past week?

Which Way Is Forward
and How Do I Go That Way?

STEP 7
IDENTIFY GOALS that allow me to combat the impact of my suffering.

At the end of this step, I want to be able to say . . .

**"I can now see that innocence and powerlessness
are not the same thing. I used to think 'it was not
my fault' meant 'there is nothing I can do.' I now
recognize that it honors God to take active steps to
counter the impact of my suffering. There is nothing
about my identity as a follower of Christ that requires
me to be passive in response to my spouse's sin.
As I have assessed my life and relationships, I have
decided to make the following changes [describe].
Because of the freedom the gospel provides,
I can make these changes without a sense of
condemnation [describe why]."**

STEP 7

PART ONE

THINKING WELL ABOUT FORGIVENESS

The video for this part of Step 7 can be found at: bradhambrick.com/truebetrayal7p1.

A key theme for Step 7 is that innocence doesn't mean powerlessness; that is, just because suffering isn't your fault doesn't mean there are no wise responses to your suffering or that you need to be passive.

But admittedly, to this point we have emphasized *knowing* facts, *understanding* impact, and *processing* pain over *doing* or *responding*. If we stopped our *True Betrayal* journey at Step 6, we could rightly be accused of being passive. However, if we started our *True Betrayal* journey at Step 7, it is unlikely that our responses would have either the information necessary to be wise or the emotional stability necessary to be implemented consistently.

By the time you arrive at Step 7, you are in a better place and you have greater clarity about how your spouse will or will not respond to their sin. Unfortunately, these assets will not make the choices in front of you easy. Identifying choices of this emotional weight inevitably gives us pause. But it does mean you have the information you need, at least as much information as is going to be available, to make the choices ahead.

In Step 7, you will be equipped to make choices for how to respond to the impact of your spouse's sin in four areas.

1. Discerning what forgiveness is and is not
2. Realizing trust is not a blind leap
3. Communicating about the marriage: past, present, and future
4. Facing the divorce decision

DISCERNING WHAT FORGIVENESS IS AND IS NOT

What is the first thing you need to "do" with all you have learned, understood, and processed to this point? Forgive. But that succinct answer doesn't have to be as intimidating or overwhelming as it initially seems. Forgiveness may only be a matter of gaining emotional freedom from the pain that has been created, or it may result in marital restoration. Forgiveness is not a one-size-fits-all response that always results in the same outcome.

Before Step 7, forgiveness would likely have been only a well-intentioned promise. When we forgive, we absorb the cost of someone else's sin. Forgiveness is forgoing a debt.[1] Until we know what that debt is, we are not in a position to forgive wisely. In that sense, understanding the offense (Step 2) and impact (Step 3) have been steps in pre-forgiveness. Jesus knew the cost of saying the words "Your sins are forgiven" (Luke 7:48) and "Neither do I condemn you" (John 8:11). Wise forgiveness, especially when it potentially leads to restoration, knows the cost of the check it writes.

> ▶ **Read Matthew 18:21–35.** Notice that precise amounts are given for what is forgiven. Part of the benefit of Steps 2–4 was ensuring you understood what you are forgiving. Too often a passage like this is used to imply that because the offenses against us are small compared to our offenses against God (which is true) that all offenses against us are small (which is false). In reaction to that logic, we often resist forgiveness because the act of forgiving minimizes the offense. The act of saying, "I forgive you" assumes the statement, "You wronged me in a way that should not be overlooked or minimized." It should also include the assumption, "I am only able to assume the debt of your sin against me because God has assumed my debt against him and promised to cover whatever losses I incur by forgiving others."

> The fact is, what your spouse has done against you and God may be inexcusable, but it is not unforgivable. — Mike Summers[2]

So, what is forgiveness? Forgiveness is the choice to no longer require someone to receive the punishment that their sin deserves.

Forgiveness is an act of faith that trusts that the penalty for their sin was paid by Christ on the cross or will be paid by the sinner in hell. Forgiveness is a commitment to treat the offender as gracious wisdom would allow, given the offender's response to their sin.

Forgiveness vs. Restoration

Forgiveness and restoration are distinct but have significant overlap. You might remember our discussion that paralleled the relationship of forgiveness and restoration with the geometric relationship between squares and rectangles. All squares are rectangles, but not all rectangles are squares.

We can say that all restoration is built on forgiveness, but not all forgiveness results in restoration. We can forgive whether our spouse is repentant or not. God calls us to do so. It is good for our emotional freedom to forgive; otherwise, past pain remains too central in our life story. However, wise restoration requires that your spouse be repentant and cooperates with a restoration process.

In the discussion below, we will clarify five important misconceptions about forgiveness. As we do so, the tone of the discussion assumes movement toward restoration. However, if your spouse is unrepentant, then your personal recovery may involve applying these principles without the applications made toward restoration.

As you read through these misconceptions, allow them to calm your fear that you could never forgive because . . . . You will likely find that forgiveness doesn't require many of the things you say you could not do.

Forgiveness Is Not Ignoring Hurt

If we think forgiveness is ignoring hurt, then forgiveness becomes a synonym for being fake. Forgiveness becomes a form of self-imposed silence rather than an other-minded expression of grace. With this bad definition of forgiveness, we resist godly self-control in the name of resisting hypocritical forgiveness.

Forgiveness is what allows us to express hurt as hurt rather than hurt as anger. Even after forgiveness, hurt still hurts. However, after forgiveness, the penalty for that hurt is absorbed by the forgiver. When you forgive, you are not making a commitment not to hurt; you are making a commitment about what you will do with hurt when it flares.

Forgiveness Is Not Letting Your Spouse Off the Hook

Forgiveness is the opposite of saying, "That's okay." If the action being forgiven were okay, then no forgiveness would be needed. Forgiveness is not saying, "This is finished. Nothing more needs to be said about this." Forgiveness is the start of restoration, not the culmination. When God forgives us, he does not assume we are a finished product. God remains active in our life to remove the sin he forgave. Similarly, when you forgive your spouse, it is the beginning of restoring your marriage. This is why you and your spouse will continue dealing with the fallout of their sin as you complete your *False Love* and *True Betrayal* journeys.

> Forgiveness is what allows us to express hurt as hurt rather than hurt as anger.

Forgiveness is an important part of recovering from adultery, but forgiveness isn't God's way of "dropping the subject." —Winston Smith[3]

Forgiveness Is Not Excusing Sin

Forgiveness does not reclassify the offense from a sin to a mistake. Mistakes are excused. Sins are forgiven. Sometimes we resist forgiving because we do not want to ratify this perceived downgrade. Forgiveness inherently classifies an offense at the top level of wrongness. We can translate, "I forgive you," as, "I accept Jesus dying for what you did as enough." That is not a downgrade.

On the opposite side of excusing sin, is over-personalizing your spouse's sin. While your spouse's sin was absolutely *against* you, it may or may not have been *about* you. Your spouse may not have been trying to punish you. Your spouse may not have been motivated by a high degree of dissatisfaction with you. As you seek to express forgiveness, you may have to battle against validating each way your imagination personalizes your spouse's sin. You can consider this an extension of your Step 4 work.

Forgiveness Is Not a Form of Sentimental Amnesia

Forgiveness is not the culmination of a journey but a commitment to complete it. Forgiving does not require a rush of warm emotions toward your spouse that are consistently stronger than the emotions of hurt you feel about their sin. This conception would make forgiveness a state of being to achieve rather than a promise to give.

A naive-amnesia view of forgiveness implies that your spouse's struggle with lust is over and that any future offense should be responded to without reference to past, forgiven sexual sin. Any future sexual sin committed by your spouse would be the continuation of a pattern, not a fresh start. At the same time, forgiveness does mean that you will allow unclear facts to be examined before making accusations and that progress should be considered in determining how to respond to a relapse.

So what does forgiveness mean you are committing to do with your memories, fears, and imagination? Forgiveness does not add anything new to how you respond to your memories, fears, and imagination that wisdom did not already entail. The patient honesty outlined in Step 2–6 is the kind of response you should give. Forgiveness is not a commitment to be emotional Teflon. Instead, forgiveness is a commitment to honor your spouse even when you feel hurt by them, or uncertainty makes you fear being hurt by them.

> ▶ **Read 2 Corinthians 5:10.** Paul is writing this passage to Christians. In this passage, we learn that when we get to heaven, we will stand before God and give an account for our life. We will give an account both for our good, holy actions and our bad, sinful actions. Often, we feel pressured to "forgive and forget" because that is what we believe it means to forgive like Jesus forgave us (Ephesians 4:32). But an omniscient (i.e., all-knowing) God does not forget. God always knows history. When God forgives, he chooses not to view us through the lens of our sin and failure. Instead, he sees us as his children. God does this perfectly. When we forgive, we strive to grow in not seeing our spouse through the lens of their sin. We can't forget the months or years of their betrayal (as much as we sometimes wish we could), but we can view our spouse through a different primary lens.

Forgiveness Is Not (Necessarily) Trust or Reconciliation

Step 7 Part Two will talk about the process of restoring trust. But, for the moment, know that forgiving and trusting or forgiving and saying things are back to normal are not the same thing. If you believe you must be there to forgive, this belief will impair your ability to allow wise trust to grow toward your spouse.

> ▶ **Read Ephesians 4:31–32.** This passage describes where you should be at this stage in the process. There should be a commitment to put away "all bitterness and wrath and anger and clamor and slander" (v. 31). Forgiveness is making this commitment, not declaring the commitment has been completely fulfilled. You learn to fulfill this commitment the way you walk out the rest of your sanctification (i.e., process of becoming more like Jesus). You do it bit by bit, a little better every day.

> We can't forget the months or years of their betrayal, but we can view our spouse through a different primary lens.

CONCLUSION

As you complete this part of Step 7, you should begin to experience more emotional freedom. If your spouse is repentant and cooperative with their *False Love* journey, that emotional freedom can provide the foundation for trust and closeness to reemerge in your marriage. If your spouse is not repentant and unwilling to cooperate with a restoration process, then that emotional freedom should allow you to take the next steps you choose without fear of those steps being an expression of bitterness.

As you reach this point in your journey, you may need to remind yourself that you are not responsible for your spouse's choices. Their choices are between them and God. You are responsible to make wise, God-honoring choices in light of what your spouse is or is not willing to do. When you have done that, you have done all that is in your power to do. If the result of those choices is less restoration than you hoped for, the unpleasant emotions that accompany that disappointment are best categorized as regret (a form of grief), not guilt (an indication that God is displeased with you).

G4 GROUP DISCUSSION: STEP 7, PART ONE

As you discuss this material in G4 group, these questions are meant to facilitate a more honest and beneficial dialogue about this material. Anyone is free to respond to whichever questions they choose.

Experienced Members

- Which of the five misconceptions about forgiveness were most impactful for your G4 journey?
- How did the Ephesians 4 devotional help you understand the difference between forgiveness as a commitment versus a completed action?

New Members

- What fears do you have when you anticipate a discussion about forgiveness?
- If you are not yet at Step 7, how does it help you to understand that your current work is pre-forgiveness work?
- How can we pray for you?

Everyone

- In what areas do you still need forgiveness to provide more emotional freedom?
- What is your response to the statement, "Forgiveness is what allows us to express hurt as hurt rather than hurt as anger"?
- Do we need to discuss any safety-level concerns from the past week?

STEP 7
PART TWO

REALIZING TRUST IS NOT A BLIND LEAP

The video for this part of Step 7 can be found at: bradhambrick.com/truebetrayal7p2.

There may be no subject that is more practical or more difficult after a betrayal than trust. We know we can't just mistrust for the rest of our life. Yet we also desperately don't want to be hurt again. If we're not careful, we fall into the trap of thinking about trust in an all-or-nothing mindset. When we do that, we vacillate between naive and suspicious.

Unless we develop a healthier approach to trust, all our relationships will suffer, not just our marriage. When mistrust generalizes to other relationships, friendships become strained and superficial. It also means that even appropriate steps toward restoration begin to feel like a threat. A proportional sense of trust is essential to healthy relationships like a functional fuel gauge is necessary for operating a vehicle. That is why we're taking the time to help you develop a more robust understanding of wise trust.

TEN STAGES OF WISE TRUST

You may have heard "Either you trust me, or you don't" from your spouse. Those are not your only two options. Trust is not binary. Trust exists on a spectrum, in the same way that trustworthiness exists on a spectrum. This is why *trust is a proportional virtue. Trust is good when it matches (i.e., is proportional to) the trustworthiness of the other person.* That is what we want to help you identify. We want you to have confidence—and thereby a growing sense of emotional strength—that your level of trust is proportional to your spouse's trustworthiness.[1]

Metaphorically speaking, there are degrees on the thermometer of trust. Below we offer a proposal for what those degree markers might be. We will begin with trust at its most broken point. As you read through this progression, there are two key questions to ask: (1) When things were at their worst, what stage of wise trust was warranted? and (2) What does wise trust look like now? Your goal is not to get to Stage 10. Your goal is to respond proportionately to your spouse's current level of trustworthiness.

Movement through this progression can be compared to a dance between your spouse's efforts at change and your willingness to take relational risks. If your spouse isn't making changes, your trust shouldn't be increasing. The mere passing of time doesn't make trust wiser. You're not punishing your spouse if your trust stalls where their trustworthiness stalls.

> Trust is a proportional virtue. Trust is good when it matches the trustworthiness of the other person.

Stage 1: Third-Party Mediation

At Stage 1 level of broken trust, you do not feel safe, at least emotionally, to be with your spouse without someone else present. At this stage, trust is built as you hear your spouse being honest about their sin with someone you trust (perhaps a counselor, pastor, or mutual friend) and being willing to receive correction or instruction from that person. Having a third party there gives you the sense of security to be honest about your perspective. As your spouse cooperates, you begin to trust them vicariously through the trust that you have for the third party.

Stage 2: Listen and Validate

At Stage 2, you are willing to have a one-on-one conversation with your spouse, but you are skeptical of most everything they say. You don't believe them, you believe facts. If they have facts to back up what they say, you will trust that much and little more. This is a tedious way to communicate, but the inconvenience feels necessary to avoid pain. Any statement that is not factual (e.g., a future promise, an interpretation of an event, an expression of emotion) is viewed as deceptive, manipulative, or insulting. As a pattern of validated facts emerges, you begin to trust that there is a commitment to honesty and transparency.

Stage 3: Listen and Require Less Validation

Listening to your spouse during Stage 3 feels less like work. The rate at which you are searching for questions and processing information is decreasing. Giving the benefit of the doubt for things you are uncertain about may still feel unsettling. Any statement that is incomplete or slanted too positively is often assumed to be intentional deceit and creates a trust regression. As your spouse's statements prove to be accurate, the practical necessities of life create an increasing reliance upon them. Each time you notice trust increasing you may still feel cautious.

Stage 4. Rely on the Other Person Functionally

At Stage 4, you begin to do life together again. Life tasks (e.g., scheduling, managing projects, going to social events) begin to be reinstituted. But the tone of these engagements is primarily functional. The dissatisfying nature of this arrangement can often discourage continued growth (e.g., "I don't want to work this hard at trusting out of a sense of duty"), but this discouragement can be alleviated by understanding where it falls in the process of trust restoration. This is only Stage 4 of ten.

Stage 5: Share Facts

As you functionally do life with your spouse, there is the opportunity for you to begin to share in Stage 5. To this point you have been receiving information more than giving information. Now you begin the process of giving yourself again. You allow yourself to be known at a factual level. Questions from the other person that start with "why?" or "how come?" are still met with defensiveness. Questions that start with "would you?" become more comfortable as you allow your spouse to influence the facts (e.g., schedule) of your life again.

Stage 6: Share Beliefs

Becoming more comfortable sharing facts again naturally leads to Stage 6 and sharing what you think about those facts. Conversations become more meaningful as you share more of what you like, dislike, agree with, disagree with, and want from the events of life. You can now talk about the way you believe things should be without a tone of judgment, sadness, or guilt overpowering the conversation. As you share your beliefs, you feel more understood. At this stage, you and your spouse may have to learn or relearn how to have different opinions or perspectives without getting defensive.

Stage 7: Share Feelings

Up until this point in the process, emotions have likely been "thrust at" (shared in emphatic language as a demonstration of the intensity of your hurt) or "shown to" (cautiously shared in way that maintains control of the conversation) more than shared with your spouse. At Stage level of trust, you are willing to receive support, encouragement, or empathy toward your emotions. You are beginning to experience your burdens being reduced and your joys multiplied as you share them with your spouse. Your marriage, if it reaches this point, is beginning to feel like a blessing again.

Stage 8. Rely on Your Loved One Emotionally

In Stage 8, you can believe your spouse is being transparent and sincere when they tell you about their day or share their feelings with you. It is now the exception to the rule when suspicions arise about your spouse's motives. Most interactions with your spouse are now an emotional net win; that is, you feel better because of the interaction.

Stage 9. Allow Your Loved One to Care for You

In Stage 9, allowing your spouse to be kind has lost any sense of being unsafe, unwanted, or manipulative. When your spouse wants to serve you, you no longer think they are doing an act of penance or setting you up for a request. How your spouse hurt you is no longer the interpretative center point of the marriage. Their efforts to bless you can be received as blessings rather than being treated as riddles to be solved.

Stage 10. Relax and Feel Safe with Your Loved One

In Stage 10, trust is restored when you can relax and feel safe with your loved one. Your spouse's presence has become a source of security rather than a pull toward insecurity. Their presence reduces stress in troubling circumstances. You find yourself instinctively drawn to them when something is difficult, upsetting, or confusing. Even when they don't have the answer, their presence is its own form of relief and comfort.

> ▶ **Reflection:** Where on this scale from Stage 1 (third-party mediation) to Stage 10 (relax and feel safe) would it currently be appropriate for you to trust your spouse? When are you tempted to be too trusting out of a sense of guilt or obligation? How does this sense of guilt or unmet obligation sap your resilience? What kind of relief does it create to identify what wise trust should currently look like?

TRUST AND TIMETABLES

There is intentionally no pacing guide for this trust progression. Remember the dance metaphor. Progress means your spouse should live with a Stage-4-level integrity before you respond with a Stage-4-level trust. Once that stabilizes, the two of you continue to move forward. You are encouraged to focus on growth markers rather than segments of time (e.g., "I'll give it three months and if we're not at Stage 7, then I don't think there's any hope").

Focusing on time segments creates a sense that you are punishing your loved one for their betrayal (e.g., "How long are you going to [expression of caution] before you treat me normal again?"). The slowness of wise trust is not punishment but a consequence. The focus of any conversation needs to be on their change, not on your acquiescing to unwarranted trust.

Remember, your goal in reading this progression is merely to gain an understanding of where you are and what is next in the development of trust. Efforts at artificially accelerating the process will ultimately do more harm than good. If you know where your marriage is and what's next, you have the information you need to gauge the next step in wise trust.

> ▶ **Read Matthew 25:14–30.** Notice that the master in this parable (representing God) is both gracious and cautious. The master graciously gives talents (i.e., sums of money) to each servant. The master is fair and proportional in his expectations. The

person who is given less isn't expected to outperform the person who was given more. But this graciousness does not blind the master to a servant who fails to steward his grace well. Our trust is a grace we give to others. We want to be fair and proportional in our expectations. This section has been intended to help you identify what fair and proportional trust looks like. But we are not being ungodly when we remove trust from those who do not steward our trust well. Being godly and gracious does not require us to be relationally foolish, naive, or place ourselves in unwise situations.

> Our trust is a grace we give to others.

TRUST AND SEX

Physical intimacy was intentionally left out of the progression of trust. By the end of the progression, your marriage should be as intimate (if not more) than it has ever been. However, the term *intimacy* is broader than sex. It includes all the closeness and trust that makes a marriage satisfying.

How and at what pace physical intimacy reemerges will be different for each couple. Being able to communicate about sex and the surrounding emotions will be one of the subjects that goes through the progression of sharing facts, sharing beliefs, sharing feelings, relying on each other emotionally, and allowing your spouse to care for you.

When trust has been severely damaged, it is common for couples to go back and forth about sex for a while. Initially, the betrayed spouse may want to feel desirable and be very invested in sex. Or the betrayed spouse may feel repulsed by sex and not even want their partner to see them changing clothes. Similarly, as sex is reengaged, the response may be both pleasure and sadness. These are normal reactions to an abnormal marital circumstance.

As you and your spouse navigate this difficult terrain, realize that restoring trust is a more important goal than enjoying sex. That means your communication about the fluctuations in your emotions is more important than your level of pleasure. If you communicate well, your enjoyment of sex will return. If you communicate about these fluctuations poorly, it will further detract from your sexual enjoyment. As contradictory as it sounds, patience is the best accelerator of restoring your enjoyment of sex.

▶ **Read James 5:7–12.** In this passage, James intertwines the subjects of patience and trust. He starts with a repeated emphasis on patience. His central illustration is that of a farmer waiting for his crops to grow (v. 7). If the farmer impatiently paws at the soil, the seed will never become a plant. The same is true of the seed of trust and the fruit of sex. Interestingly, James moves from discussing patience directly into a command to remain completely honest (v. 12). When we are not getting what we want, we are tempted to become dishonest or manipulative to get what we want. Heed James's warning as you allow the harvest of trust and intimacy to grow.

CONCLUSION

It is not uncommon for this part of Step 7 to be considered the most helpful and most disappointing part of your *True Betrayal* journey. If that is your experience, don't feel like you must choose between these two responses. Both can be valid at the same time.

Sometimes when we face contradictions like this, it is because someone is being hypocritical. After a major betrayal, that can easily become our default interpretation. Other times when our emotions have this level of dissonance, it is because we are at a major life transition (e.g., the happiness and sadness that collide at a graduation or wedding). You are currently in a major transition from hurt to trust. This is a time when emotional dissonance makes sense and doesn't need to mean that anyone is being duplicitous.

G4 GROUP DISCUSSION: STEP 7, PART TWO

As you discuss this material in G4 group, these questions are meant to facilitate a more honest and beneficial dialogue about this material. Anyone is free to respond to whichever questions they choose.

Experienced Members

- As you are/were facing the potential of active trust restoration, what is most unsettling? Exciting?

- How did the James 5 devotional help you understand the importance of patience in cultivating wise trust?

New Members

- How did the Matthew 25 devotional help you resist the fear that any trust of your spouse would be inherently naive?
- What parts of Step 7 were premature (i.e., purely foreshadowing) for you to try to apply right now?
- How can we pray for you?

Everyone

- Where are you on the progression of wise trust with your marriage?
- What is next on the progression of wise trust, and what indicators would reveal that this next level of trust would be warranted?
- Do we need to discuss any safety-level concerns from the past week?

STEP 7
PART THREE

COMMUNICATING ABOUT THE MARRIAGE: PAST, PRESENT, AND FUTURE

The video for this part of Step 7 can be found at: bradhambrick.com/truebetrayal7p3.

W e ended Part Two of Step 7 by talking about the importance of communication for the restoration of trust and intimacy. We'll pick up Part Three of Step 7 by returning to the subject of communication but with a broader focus.

For most of the seven steps, we've focused on the impact of your spouse's sin and marriage restoration. But a marriage without sexual sin is not, in and of itself, a healthy thriving marriage. There were other weaknesses and challenges in your marriage that need to be addressed. There are other good things you want to cultivate in your marriage.

Before those other things can be addressed, they need to be discussed. You and your spouse need to be able to name them, explore them without defensiveness or insecurity, prioritize which one(s) to address first, and consider approaches to addressing them. That is the process we'll help you begin in this part of Step 7.

Note: If your spouse has been noncooperative with their *False Love* work, and as you reach this point you are discouraged by their lack of engagement, this content will be less relevant for you. Metaphorically, this part of Step 7 is talking about hiking after recovering from a broken leg. It would be unwise to attempt a hike with a spouse who has not cooperated with their course of care in a way that would make it possible at this point.

COMMUNICATING ABOUT THE WHOLE MARRIAGE

It is helpful to recognize this part of Step 7 as the transition from marital restoration work to marital enrichment work. You may remember that we defined these terms earlier in this journey.

- *Marital restoration* involves addressing challenges that threaten the viability of your marriage. If marriage were a vehicle, this would be a transmission overhaul.
- *Marital enrichment* involves identifying ways to enhance your mutual enjoyment in a healthy marriage. If marriage were a vehicle, this would be oil changes and tire rotations.

Remember the marriage survey you completed in Step 2? When you initially completed this survey, you were looking for problems more significant than your spouse's betrayal (e.g., abuse or addiction). Now you are looking for things that are less significant than your spouse's betrayal but still merit attention. It is time to consider how you might grow past where you were when your marriage was at its best.

However, it would be inaccurate to think that you will engage in this growth like you would have had your marriage not needed this season of marital restoration. That would minimize the intensity and impact of the work you've done.

With that in mind, here is the phrase we will use: You and your spouse will *talk about old challenges in a new context after a prolonged strain.* Let's define the three key phrases before we explore each in more detail.

- *Old challenges*—most of what you'll name and work on from this point forward are challenges or weaknesses that were present in your marriage before your spouse's betrayal.
- *New context*—the work you and your spouse have done to arrive at this point puts your marriage in a qualitatively and quantitatively different context.
- *Prolonged strain*—while your marriage is in a distinctly different (hopefully better) context, the work necessary to arrive at this point can create relational and emotional fatigue.

Talking About Old Challenges

Review the marriage survey you completed in Step 2. Get a different color pen and remark items where you see the pre-betrayal marriage differently than you did a few weeks or months ago. With a third color pen, ask your spouse to do the same. As you do this, remember your initial goal is not agreement but conversation. You want to talk about the quality of your pre-betrayal marriage as openly as you've talked about everything else on your *True Betrayal* journey. At this point in the process, disagreement is not a threat to your marriage, but either of you being disagreeable (i.e., defensive) is. The ability to have peaceable conversations about hard things may be the best predictor of the future health of your marriage.

> Adultery is more likely to happen when a marriage is already weak. You should not take responsibility for your spouse's sin, but you may need to examine yourself and acknowledge how you contributed to weaknesses in your marriage. —Winston Smith[1]

▶ **Conversation Prompts:** Where do the two of you agree that your marriage was weak or underdeveloped? What areas of the marriage did you score differently? Did you disagree about these items "then" (i.e., when you first completed the survey) or is it only "now" that you see the history of your marriage differently? What do you appreciate about the way your spouse is talking with you about these differences? What would make a discussion of these differences more comfortable?

▶ **Exercise:** We evaluate our marriage against what we consider ideal. If I asked you, "How are you at art?" you would compare yourself against an excellent artist and grade yourself down from there. Similarly, when I ask, "How healthy was your marriage?" you compare your marriage to a thriving marriage and grade it down from there. This means, to be fair, we must evaluate both our marriage and the ideals by which we grade our marriage. To do that, consider these four question clusters:

  1. **How would you define a good marriage?** What key areas are important to you as you make this assessment (e.g., communication, life planning, romance)? How

close to "perfect" does a marriage need to be in your eyes to be "good"?

2. **Which parts of your definition are realistic?** As you look at what you wrote for question one, what parts of your definition seem most valid? What parts are reasonable standards that any healthy marriage should achieve? By contrast, which parts are above and beyond a reasonable definition of good (e.g., never arguing)?

3. **Which parts of your definition can be naturally restored?** Where your marriage is not at your standard of a good marriage, what parts will become good as you continue to live in transparency and integrity? What things just need more time of living like you're currently living to reach a satisfying level of enjoyment and trust?

> The ability to have peaceable conversations about hard things may be the best predictor of the future health of your marriage.

4. **Which parts of your definition can be achieved with help?** What areas of your marriage will require outside help—like counseling—to reach a satisfying level of health? In what areas do you and your spouse disagree on what "good" or "reasonable" would look like, which you need to talk through with a mutually trusted person?

These questions help you and your spouse create a path forward. Question 1 defines a desired destination. Question 2 vets the reasonableness of your desired destination. Question 3 identifies areas where patience is the most important factor. Question 4 identifies where you should focus your intentional efforts. Quality conversations about these questions indicate that your marriage is moving in a good direction and there is reason for significant hope.

Talking in a New Context

In the previous section, you defined what has been historically hard in your marriage. You defined the things that you and your spouse should have been working on before there was a crisis. But it would be inaccurate to believe you can work on those things as if nothing happened. That would be like the person dropping out of high school and thinking that they will go back and finish their GED—as if it would be as easy later as it could be now. The work may be just as easy or difficult as it was before, but the context is different, and that's a big deal.

Think about the differences between being seventeen years old and finishing high school versus thirty years old and studying for a GED. The older person has a full-time job, marriage, children, debts to pay, and may not have read a book in fifteen years. Algebra didn't get more difficult, and chemistry didn't change its standards, but the context of the learner is different.

> ▶ **Reflection:** As you think about enriching your marriage in ways that you should have been doing all along, what is different now? What is different for you? What is different for your spouse? When and how are you prone to use these differences as excuses? When are you prone to dismiss these differences as irrelevant?

The most important thing you and your spouse can do with the answers to these questions is talk about them. Many of these are real challenges that need to be accounted for. Many of them represent real hurts or disappointments that need to be grieved together. Some of them are enticing excuses that demoralize effort toward change and need to be acknowledged as such so they don't encumber progress.

You are not trying to fix "what was" as if restoration required time traveling. You are working on "now." However, examining your pre-betrayal marriage helps you avoid allowing old habits to reinforce old ruts. Basic habits probably haven't changed that much (e.g., household routines, scheduling patterns, laziness, control). You're the same two people you've always been. If you were uptight about dishes in the sink or the AC being set too low before, you'll probably be agitated by the same things now. If we're not careful, in moments of weakness, this makes us prone to think nothing has changed and become despondent.

> ▶ **Read Mark 2:21–22.** Both you and your spouse have been through an intensive process of allowing the gospel to transform

your struggles with sin and suffering. You are each "new" people living in an "old" marriage. Your marriage is older than your recent changes. The truths that you have embraced individually have not had the opportunity to become marital habits and culture. These new habits and culture need time to solidify. These new habits and culture are like patches on the garment Jesus spoke about in this passage. When we fail to account for this tension between old and new, we inadvertently contribute to new, unnecessary tears in the relationship.

> Examining your pre-betrayal marriage helps you avoid allowing old habits to reinforce old ruts.

▶ **Read Colossians 3:5–10.** This passage vividly portrays how God changes people. Both the "old self" and the "new self" are alive and active in us. This should be a sober reminder that the old problems will not just go away because of the work God has been doing in the two of you personally. Each of you will have to continue learning what it looks like to live out of the new work that God has been doing in you in the context of your marriage.

Talking After a Prolonged Strain

You might be able to run a 10K. Even if you can, running a 5K after you finished a 10K would be harder. You have proven you could do everything it took to arrive at this point in Step 7, even if you doubted yourself many times along the way. In the same way, the marriage enrichment activities from this point forward might seem less intense than the work you've already done, but the prolonged strain means you're tired.

Consider this example from Gary and Mona:

One habit in particular was extremely destructive. Whenever Gary felt like Mona didn't want him sexually, he would withdraw emotionally in an attempt to "give her space and an opportunity to want him." Mona would perceive his withdrawal as his not wanting her and would then withdraw herself "until he wanted her again." Of course, as time went on, we both would end up feeling increasingly unwanted by the other and hurt because of it. Every word and action seemed to underscore this belief. —Gary and Mona Shriver[2]

Both Gary and Mona were tired from their marital restoration efforts. That's probably why she wasn't as interested in sex and why he was more prone toward pouting and withdrawal. Gary and Mona help us see how the bad habits that emerge from this fatigue can easily feed off one another.

Don't feel threatened by this realization. Do allow yourself to be humbled by it, particularly in how you interpret the responses of your spouse. Our goal in this section is to interpret less and talk more; ask, don't assume. By talking more, we leave less room for inaccurate or unhelpful interpretations.

▶ **Reflection:** What unhealthy patterns of conflict have been most prevalent in you and your spouse as you've worked on this *False Love* and *True Betrayal* journey (e.g., pouting, sarcasm, shaming)? When do these patterns tend to emerge?

▶ **Reflection:** What unhealthy personal habits have emerged in you and your spouse as you've worked on this *False Love* and *True Betrayal* journey (e.g., escaping through alcohol, overworking, comfort eating)? Are you and your spouse willing to acknowledge the impact these habits would have if unaddressed?

CONCLUSION

You've worked hard to get to this point. Don't be discouraged because you've mapped out more of the journey ahead. What you've gained is a continued sense of direction, not a sense of pressure. Remember, there is no stopwatch on your G4 journey. You are not in a race. You are simply taking the next step as you are able. Rest is not regression. When rest is needed, willingness to embrace that rest is expressing grace toward yourself and your spouse.

If this part of Step 7 has been relevant for you, you and your spouse are turning a corner and beginning to draw the map for the next phase of your journey. If working through this part of Step 7 made you realize that your spouse has not joined you on this journey toward restoration, then the next part of Step 7 discusses the type of choices in front of you.

G4 GROUP DISCUSSION: STEP 7, PART THREE

As you discuss this material in G4 group, these questions are meant to facilitate a more honest and beneficial dialogue about this material. Anyone is free to respond to whichever questions they choose.

Experienced Members

- As you moved through your *True Betrayal* journey, how did the distinction between marital restoration and martial enrichment become clearer and more important to you?
- Which part of (a) old struggles, (b) new context, or (c) after a prolonged struggle was most beneficial for you?

New Members

- In what ways does it help you have more peace to know that you are at a marital restoration phase in your journey?
- What part of this material do you need to put on hold (i.e., not think about) as you focus on where you are in your journey?
- How can we pray for you?

Everyone

- In what ways are you experiencing change fatigue, and what would it look like to be more gracious toward you or your spouse?
- In what ways could you relate to the vignette from Gary and Mona's story?
- Do we need to discuss any safety-level concerns from the past week?

STEP 7
PART FOUR

FACING THE DIVORCE DECISION

The video for this part of Step 7 can be
found at: bradhambrick.com/truebetrayal7p4.

Within a G4 group, there are two types of participants arriving at this part of Step 7. First, there are those who are grappling with the decision of divorce. This material meets you where you are. Second, there are those whose spouse has cooperated with *False Love* to a degree that allows you to feel spared from needing this discussion. If you're in that second group, be supportive and encouraging to those who are facing this difficult decision.

Some Christians want to treat the question of divorce as an easy, open-and-shut case. They would say, "Malachi 2:16 says, 'God hates divorce,' so if God dislikes something, we shouldn't do it. Therefore, divorce should never be a consideration. What's so hard about that?" Even if that is the best English translation of Malachi 2, and there is debate about that, the decision is not that easy.

Jesus gave reasons why divorce would be acceptable. Adultery was one of those reasons (Matthew 5:32). Paul said that abandonment is also a legitimate reason for divorce (1 Corinthians 7:12–16). Debate exists between faithful Christians about (a) whether adultery and abandonment are the only acceptable reasons for divorce, (b) whether these passages are representative of the severity of problems for which divorce is a biblically viable option, and (c) whether actions like viewing pornography fit with the term Jesus used for adultery—the Greek word πορνεία (*porneia*).

If you are arriving at the end of Step 7 on your *True Betrayal* journey and the noncooperation of your spouse makes this section relevant, these debates can seem tedious. Why should the etymology of a

Greek term have that much influence on the present decisions of your marriage? It's not that you don't care about the Bible. You wouldn't have persevered in a study like this if you didn't. It is merely an acknowledgment of how academic discussions like this can feel when you're deciding something so personal.

Even when divorce is a legitimate option, that does not mean it is the option you *should* choose. A variety of factors will contribute to this decision. We have explored those in detail over the last seven steps. For better or worse, your spouse has shown you who they are. Their current choices reveal the character of the person you will make these decisions concerning.

If you are considering divorce, you likely realize your church may not agree with your decision. This part of Step 7 will help you arrive at a decision that (a) you believe honors God while addressing the severity of brokenness in your marriage, while also (b) communicating that decision with your church in a way that seeks to preserve social support from your church.

TRACING YOUR JOURNEY TO THIS DECISION

With that in mind, we will outline a process of decision-making regarding divorce. This process does not begin where you are now, but instead, begins with what prompted you to come to G4 and incorporates the work you've done to arrive at this point.

1. You realized your spouse was engaged in sexual sin. This is what prompted you to come to G4.
2. You sought help to think through how to respond. G4 is one place you sought this help. You may also be engaged in counseling or consulting with friends or your pastor.
3. You found words to express what was broken in your marriage. This is the work you did in Step 2.
4. You grew to understand the impact the brokenness in your marriage was having on you. This is the work you did in Step 3.
5. You sought to replace the lies you came to believe because of your spouse's unfaithfulness. This is the work you did in Steps 4, 5, and 6.

6. You identified ways you could reduce the impact of your spouse's sin on you and your marriage. This is the work you did in Step 7.

7. With those changes, you assessed where your marriage is, and you are deciding how you wish to proceed. That is where you are now.

So much time, energy, emotion, and effort are contained in those seven brief points. It is almost unfair to summarize them this succinctly. But this is an accurate summary of how you got to this point. Remember, this process has been monthslong for you, but when you have your first conversation with your church, the process will be minutes-long for them.

NAMING YOUR OPTIONS

At this juncture, you have three basic options:

- You may choose to **stay** with your spouse and seek to win them back to God through your example of godly character and selfless love (I Peter 3:1–7). *If your marriage is not safe, it is not recommended that you choose this option.*

- You may choose to **separate** from your spouse to reinforce the seriousness of their sin but not seek divorce. If this option is chosen, you should (a) be prepared for an indefinite separation, and (b) have a clear expectation for what would end the separation. If you pursue this option, we advise you also pursue counseling. Guiding you through the questions that emerge amid a prolonged separation goes beyond the scope of this curriculum.

- You may choose to pursue **divorce** as a means of alerting your spouse to the seriousness of their sin. If you pursue this option, we also advise you to pursue counseling. Remember that divorce may end a marriage, but it does not end the relationship; it only rearranges it. Guiding you through the questions that emerge amid divorce goes beyond the scope of this curriculum.

At this point, you do not have to just choose one. You might choose Option A for a while and give implementing the strategies from Step 7 more time to influence your marriage. You might choose Option B for a length of time and see if your spouse responds by owning their sin and engaging in the process of change. The point is, don't allow the presentation of options to rush you to a decision you are not ready to follow through on.

It is important that you be ready to follow through on whatever decision you make. The more you vacillate, the less seriously you will be taken by your spouse. Inadvertently, you will be teaching your spouse to just wait until you change your mind.

> Divorce may end a marriage, but it does not end the relationship; it only rearranges it.

Also, realize that making a decision is not the same thing as having a plan. Knowing where you want to go is not the same thing as knowing the turns and distance involved in getting there. Your G4 journey has helped you develop a plan for Option A. If you choose Options B or C, you will need to do comparable planning work. That is why counseling is recommended if you choose one of these options.

If you choose Options B or C, here are several recommendations to help you garner as much support as possible from your church's leadership and, thereby, maintain as much social support as possible from your church community.

- Involve your church leadership as early as possible. As we mentioned above, it took you months, maybe years, to arrive at your decision. It would be unfair to expect them to arrive at the same conclusion in one or two conversations. Allow your church leaders time to catch up to where you are.
- Share the work you've done at G4 to help them catch up to where you are. This helps demonstrate you are not being impulsive or reactive. It demonstrates that you've taken the Bible and your faith seriously as you've grappled with this decision. It helps them get to know the severity of the situation that is prompting your decision.
- You do not need anyone's permission to decide, but you do want to preserve as much social support as possible. Both separation and divorce are stressful and lonely journeys. Be careful not to magnify these effects by perceiving honest questions about your decision as attempts to change your mind.

- You are not asking for the church to be on your team and against your spouse. You are bringing a church-discipline-level concern to their attention and asking them to treat it as such.[1] If your concerns are treated as an attack on your spouse (their interpretation is outside your control), you will likely have difficulty continuing to attend that church.

- Realize that moving toward separation or divorce may result in joining another church. It is rare for a couple to divorce and both remain members of the same church. It may be because the church's leadership disagrees with your decision, or it may be because of relational drama from fellow members who have an opinion about your decision. This would be unfortunate, but it is not a failure on your part.

There is no easy way to make this decision. Challenges and hardships will exist with all three options. Other than prioritizing safety, there is no reason to rush this decision. But there is also no way to avoid this decision. Deliberating on this decision is choosing Option A, at least for the short-term. Until you know which option you want to choose long-term, that is fine. But eventually, this is a decision you need to make intentionally. You do not want to make a decision of this magnitude in reaction to a straw that broke the camel's back moment. That is a recipe for second-guessing yourself and regret.

As with every other part of this journey, prayerfully engage this decision and trust God to sustain you in both making the decision and following through on the decision that you make. Don't confuse the angst that comes with a decision of this magnitude as God's silence or God's absence.

G4 GROUP DISCUSSION: STEP 7, PART FOUR

As you discuss this material in G4 group, these questions are meant to facilitate a more honest and beneficial dialogue about this material. Anyone is free to respond to whichever questions they choose.

Experienced Members

- If you chose Option A, what did you learn from that experience?
- If you chose Options B or C, what did you learn from that experience?

New Members

- How does seeing that the early steps of your G4 journey contribute to a decision of this magnitude motivate you to engage these early steps with excellence?
- What did you take away from hearing experienced members talk about the challenges related to Options A, B, and C?
- How can we pray for you?

Everyone

- Is this a wise juncture in your journey to let the leadership at your church know about the marital challenges you are facing?
- In your own words, what is the difference between asking for the church to be on your team versus taking a church-discipline-level concern seriously?
- Do we need to discuss any safety-level concerns from the past week?

Embracing a Life Not Defined
by My Challenges

STEP 8

PERSEVERE in the new life and identity to which God has called me.

At the end of this step, I want to be able to say . . .

"Some life disruption from my spouse's sin remains [describe], but it defines me less. However, I am also experiencing more of the peace and freedom God wants for me. For a time, I doubted whether I would experience peace, freedom, and [list] again. I am learning to enjoy these good things without guilt, fear, or guardedness. I have come to realize that 'healthy' means more than the absence of pain or sorrow. I am learning to trust and enjoy God in the rise and fall of my circumstances."

STEP 8
PART ONE

MARKS OF A NEW, HEALTHIER NORMAL

The video for this part of Step 8 can be found at: bradhambrick.com/truebetrayal8p1.

As we enter Step 8, we will begin to think about life after G4. We should realize some of us are coming to Step 8 differently than others. Some of us are entering Step 8 with a focus on seeing our marriage restored, because our spouse has responded with repentance and cooperation. Others of us are beginning Step 8 with the sad realization that our spouse would not engage restorative efforts with humility, repentance, and transparency. In that sense, G4 is a place where we, "Rejoice with those who rejoice, weep with those who weep" (Romans 12:15).

Either way, we pray that G4 has been a refuge and source of strength in a season of turmoil. We also pray that G4 releases you to live a satisfying life with purpose. But G4 is not meant to be a long-term home. The church is your long-term source of care and spiritual family. G4 is a place you came to for a season to focus on learning to navigate a significant marital disruption. To prepare you for this transition, we will discuss two subjects in Step 8.

1. The marks of a new, healthier normal
2. Preparing to transition from G4

TWELVE MARKS OF A NEW, HEALTHIER NORMAL

New and *normal* are words that do not belong together. Without the effects of sin, our old normal wouldn't have needed to change. In Steps 2 to 4, you looked at ways your spouse's sin disrupted your marital normal. In Step 5, you grieved the impact of the disrupted normal that emerged. In Steps 6 and 7, you began to piece together a new, healthy normal. Now, in Step 8, you will begin to acclimate to this new normal and allow it to solidify.

Embracing a new normal is the culmination of the grief work you started in Step 5. That is why these points are modified and adapted from H. Norman Wright's book *Experiencing Grief.*[1] Grief is something we experience at major life transitions. We realize one chapter is concluding and a new chapter is starting. Graduating from G4 is a major life transition. You've worked hard. You've grown a lot. You're a different person than when you started.

As you read through this list, do not view it as a to-do list. That would be the equivalent of a teenager reading about puberty as something to accomplish. Instead, like the changes that happen in puberty, we name these markers so that you can put them into words as they happen and feel comfortable talking about them with others.

Begin by marking with an asterisk (*) those items that you already see emerging in your life. Allow this to remind you of God's faithfulness and give you confidence that marks not yet emerging will do so. Pray for those things that have not yet emerged, and each time one of these qualities appears, celebrate it as another fulfillment of God's promises (Philippians 1:6).

1. **Treasuring the lessons you've learned from your journey.** Pain is excellent at distracting us. When we're hurting, we fail to see how much we're learning. But you have learned a great deal on this journey. As you settle into a new, stable normal, you'll begin to realize and appreciate how much you've learned. Some of us might respond with unrest to a potential implication of that reality. We fear hearing someone say, "This was God's will for your life and what you learned made the journey worth it." You do not have to say that the lessons you learned are the reason God allowed you to experience this hardship.[2] The good lessons you've learned can simply be evidences of God's faithfulness to redeem this journey.

    ▶ **Reflection:** What key lessons have you learned on this journey? What simple truths are more meaningful and significant to you than they were before? What things did you know were true before but now you genuinely believe and embrace?

▶**Read James 1:2–4.** The marital difficulties that brought us to G4 fit into what James calls "various trials" (v. 2). How do we count it joy? Not by volunteering to do it again or pretending it was a pleasant experience, but by giving weight to the lessons we learned. These lessons will enrich our life and allow us to enrich the lives of others. Treasuring what we've learned doesn't require minimizing the pain through which we learned it. The lessons we learned and the character we developed are part, not the whole, of what God uses to bring us to the point of being "complete" (v. 4).

2. **Energy level returns to normal.** When life is hard, we are perpetually weary. When everything required effort, thought, and intentionality, the moments of rest we got didn't adequately recharge our stamina. Every decision was overwhelming because it felt like chaos could ensue. With the establishment of a new normal, you are coming out of that way of life. Rest can be rest again. When you feel more recharged than you have in a long time, rejoice. Realize this is a fruit of the work you've put into this journey and a sign of God's faithfulness.

    ▶**Read Isaiah 40:27–31.** You have likely felt disregarded by God (v. 27), and this added to your exhaustion (v. 30), but you have waited faithfully and are now experiencing God's renewal (v. 31). It is after experiences like yours that we realize how much our energy level is a gift from God. We often take it for granted, but even in our youth (v. 30) we can waste away from a life of suffering. Don't just read this passage as beautiful poetry. Read it as your testimony.

3. **Decision-making becomes easier.** Even simple decisions are not simple when it feels like your marriage is at stake. When you are uncertain about the future of your marriage, it feels impossible to anticipate the implications of your decisions. It feels inevitable that whatever decision you make could be wrong, and you'll feel guilty for having made it. It can easily begin to feel like life is a quiz where the questions have no right answers. On your G4 journey, you've been creating a different life. You've asked your spouse for the

information you need to make consequential choices. You have as much of that information as you're going to receive. Having the peace of mind that you've taken the steps to get this information allows you to make decisions free from false guilt and toward a future that is satisfying and stable. Each time you come to a decision that seems delightfully simple, realize this is a fruit of the work you've put into this journey and a sign of God's faithfulness.

▶ **Read Isaiah 46:3–4.** During the experience of significant hardship, we gain a first-person experience of God's promises, "I will carry you . . . I will bear . . . I will save" (v. 4) and realize how much this has been happening since our birth (v. 3). We experience more rest when we realize it's not just the quality of our decisions that protect our lives. You don't have to make perfect decisions to have a good life because God is actively caring for you. Part of that care was bringing you to G4, and God's care will continue when G4 is no longer needed.

4. **Appetite and sleep cycle return to normal.** Stress registers in our body. We may say we feel fine and be functioning well, but when we live under prolonged stress, it impacts our body. Two of the key indicators of this are our appetite and sleep cycle. When our life is chaotic, we either lose our appetite or eat for comfort; similarly, we either struggle to sleep or use sleep as an oasis. As you establish a new, healthier normal, pay attention to your sleep cycle and appetite. Notice when they become more balanced and regulated. As your body gets used to having appropriate rest and nutrition, it can be more of an ally in your continued recovery.

    ▶ **Read Psalm 4:6–8.** During major hardships, we ask the question of verse 6 (paraphrased), "When will life be good?" Now we bear the testimony of verses 7 and 8 (paraphrased), "God, you have given me joy, food, and rest." In this psalm, we see that good meals and good rest are blessings God wants to give and that are right for us to celebrate. Food and sleep are not just matters essential for survival; they are gifts God wants us to enjoy. Verses 7 and 8 would be good passages to memorize and use in your prayers before meals and before bed.

5. **Able to enjoy time alone**. While it is not emphasized as much in modern times, throughout church history, solitude has long been recognized as an important discipline in the life of a Christian. However, during a major marital disruption, being alone with our thoughts can be a frightening proposition. At this stage in our journey, the gift of solitude becomes a blessing again, and we are better able to savor this gift. If you have struggled with being alone, then consider reading Richard Foster's chapter on solitude in *Celebration of Discipline*. Chapter 7 contains several pages reflecting on the benefits of solitude during or after a "dark night of the soul."[3]

    ▶ **Read Passages About Jesus and Solitude: Matthew 4:1–11; 14:13, 23; 17:1–9; 26:36–46; Mark 1:35; 6:31; Luke 5:16 and 6:12.** In his full humanity, Jesus regularly sought solitude as a source of strength. Therefore, we should too. During this time of establishing a new normal, it would be wise to evaluate your practice of spiritual disciplines, including solitude. During the chaos of recent months, considerations like this seemed like a luxury. The quality of choices you have made on this journey has put you in a place where this kind of self-care and spiritual development are viable considerations. Enjoy the fruit of your labor.

6. **Begin planning for the future with optimism**. When the future of our marriage is uncertain, planning is scary and unsettling. We brace for what's next with angst instead of anticipating the future with hope. The prolonged strain conditions us to think this way. One way to think about Steps 7, 8, and 9 in your G4 journey is that they are a counterconditioning program intended to help you cultivate a life where you look forward to the future with hope. Indicators that this is happening include smiling when you make plans or using the phrase "I would like to . . ." more often. As this happens, realize this is a fruit of the work you've put into this journey and a sign of God's faithfulness.

Even with all these complex factors, God's healing grace abounds. If both partners are committed to restoring the marriage, they almost always succeed. The trauma often creates a deeper and more realistic intimacy with better boundaries in place. Greater maturity grows out of the crisis they have weathered. —Doug Rosenau[4]

▶ **Read Philippians 3:12–16.** This passage is often misapplied for suffering. Paul is not laying out a principle of forgetting the past or living in denial about painful events. In Philippians 4:9, Paul asks this church to remember how he handled his unpleasant experiences of anxiety while he was with them. In Philippians 4:12, Paul remembers being "brought low" and being hungry and in need. The principle is that the pain of our past should not become a mental block to pursuing a better future. At this stage in your G4 journey, you should begin to sense within your own heart this change in perspective.

7. **Able to use your experience to comfort others.** When our suffering is intense, we can become pain saturated. Our goal at that time was to process our own experience wisely. Earlier in your journey, it wasn't selfish to focus on your own growth and progress; it was necessary. As you acclimate to a new, healthier normal, your capacity to draw from your experience to offer care and comfort for others emerges. You can relate to their pain and have a sense of empathy to let them know God will not allow them to drown in their hardship. You do not have answers for all their questions—their relationship inevitably has features yours did not—but you have a testimony about the Shepherd of their journey and what it was like for you to walk with him on your journey.

▶ **Read 2 Corinthians 1:3–5.** It is easy to miss the time lapse implied in this passage. God comforts us. He is our Father of mercies and God of all comfort in our afflictions. Pause. God's comfort and mercies are ministered to us over time. In this case, the time you have invested in G4. God does not get impatient with us or rush us in this phase of his care. The pause is essential. If we think God has put us "on the clock" to get a return on his comfort investment in us, then we would not feel like we had much comfort to offer. Once we experience God's patience before the "so that" (v. 4), we begin to share abundantly in Christ's comfort (v. 5). God's patience toward us is part of the comfort we model toward those we seek to comfort in his name.

8. **The freedom to worship returns.** During intense suffering, worship can feel like a charade. We don't feel joyful. It can feel fake and hypocritical to celebrate the goodness of a God who feels far away. The joy implied in the word *worship* may have been notably absent as you navigated your marital disruption. Suffering reminds us that this fallen world is not currently as God intended. We feel the hopelessness that exists apart from God's intervention, guidance, and presence. This is what awakens our ability to worship. We see that God was faithful, and that God was with us. From that we can celebrate the goodness of God. As your reflex to worship returns, realize this is a fruit of the work you've put into this journey and a sign of God's faithfulness.

   ▶ **Read Psalm 23.** Remember, this psalm traces the journey. Imagine the "before" phase of this psalm. Before writing this psalm, David felt like a sheep in need of food and water. Before writing this psalm, David went through times that felt like the valley of the shadow of death. Before writing this psalm, David sat at a table with his adversaries trying not to lose his appetite. These "before" experiences were needy, fearful, and awkward. But they laid the foundation for worship. Out of these experiences, David got to know God the provider, God the protector, and God the peacemaker. Allow Psalm 23 to be your personalized template of worship. Identify the aspects of God's character that you know more personally because of your suffering.

9. **Sense of humor returns.** Proverbs 14:13 was likely your testimony over recent months: "Even in laughter the heart may ache, and the end of joy may be grief." We feel like suffering made our laughter hollow, jaded, or just polite. Humor is built on irony and proportionality. Betrayal tends to flatten or overinflate the meaning of everything to the point that humor dies. But we serve a God who used joy as his motivation to conquer death (Hebrews 12:2). Our God truly gets the last laugh (Psalm 2:4), and our laughter can

echo his victory. Without the gospel, laughter would be a form of denial. With the gospel, our pain becomes what is temporary (2 Corinthians 3:16–18) and our joy is eternal. The return of our sense of humor then becomes an expression of healthy faith rather than denial.

▶ **Read Psalm 30:5.** God does not use his victory as a reason to forbid our sorrow. This psalm validates weeping, even when it is a response to something God has conquered. In the language of Psalm 30, God's grace toward weeping that "tarries" through the night gives us the freedom to laugh again in the morning (i.e., this new, emerging season in your life). One of the lessons we draw from this is that God allows us to grow—not only in character but also in our emotions. God delights when our laughter returns and is patient when our laughter is empty. Allow the freedom this reality brings to be part of what allows your sense of humor to thaw.

> As your reflex to worship returns, realize this is a fruit of the work you've put into this journey and a sign of God's faithfulness.

10. **New relationships are built.** Disruptions in primary relationships, like marriage, make it harder to develop new ones. So much of our life feels off-limits. We avoid asking some questions because we don't want to answer the reciprocating question. At times we're unavailable, and we can't explain why. At times we're distracted, and we come across as less caring than we would otherwise be. As you acclimate to a new, healthier normal, these obstacles to developing new relationships abate. Your time in G4 has provided the opportunity to practice talking about your history. When we haven't told anyone, sharing anything feels like we'll share everything. Now that you've had a place to talk about your hardship, you can decide how much (if anything at all) you want to share with new friends. As you begin to pursue new interests, the opportunity to meet new potential friends also increases.

▶ **Reflect on the psalms you read.** In this study, you've read many psalms. Maybe you've been surprised about how many of the psalms are reflections on hard times; that is, psalms of lament rather than psalms of praise. Notice something else about these psalms: There is a great degree of variation in how specific they are about the hardships that prompted them. Sometimes the psalms give significant details about the hardship. Other times, the psalms speak in generalities about hardship. As you cultivate new friendships, you have the same freedom.

11. **Experience peace even during high-distress moments.** A new, healthier normal doesn't mean the absence of high-distress moments. It does mean we can experience these high-distress moments differently. Imagine you're carrying one hundred pounds and someone hands you ten more pounds. It's not that you can't handle ten pounds. It's that you are already at your limit. That is how additional stress is when we're living with a major stressor. We are at our stress capacity. One of the best indicators that we are embracing a new, healthier normal is our ability to be unsettled without panicking. Another way to say this is that we become better at distinguishing safe stress from unsafe stress. As this happens, realize this is a fruit of the work you've put into this journey and a sign of God's faithfulness.

   ▶ **Read Philippians 4:12.** Notice that Paul says he knows how to be "brought low." He's almost bragging about this ability because it was part of his secret of contentment (v. 11) and relying on God's strength in all things (v. 13). Paul's experiences of being brought low were intense (2 Corinthians 11:23–12:10). Too often, we only think of being brought low as moments to avoid. But we learn from Paul that these are also important times to gauge our progress. It is as if Paul is saying, "Before I learned the secret of contentment and how to rely on God's strength in all things, I often responded to level-4 stressors with level-8 angst. As I've grown, I can respond to level-4 stressors with level-4 angst and a high degree of trust that God is with me." That is the kind of growth we want to notice in ourselves as well.

12. **Appreciate your growth.** You did not just learn (point 1) and become better equipped to comfort others (point 7). You've also

grown (this point). You're a more mature person. Having a skill is different from having maturity. Maturity transcends skills. Maturity is more important than intelligence and skills. We all know people who are skilled athletically, musically, or academically but are immature. Their immaturity impairs the ability to reach the potential of their skills. That's why we're emphasizing that this journey has done more than make you smarter. While maturity is rarely a quality we enjoy acquiring, it is immensely valuable. Valuing the traits of maturity that have emerged on this journey is an important part of embracing your new, healthier normal.

> Our God truly gets the last laugh (Psalm 2:4), and our laughter can echo his victory.

▶ **Read Job 42:1–6.** At the end of the book, Job still does not know "why." He doesn't have an answer to his questions. Academically, he couldn't pass a matching quiz between events in his life and why they occurred. But he is more mature. Verse 5 summarizes Job's journey well. Job wanted answers he could hear to make sense of his suffering. Instead, Job got to see God's faithfulness in the worst times and received a peace that passes understanding (Philippians 4:7). At this stage in our journey, we may not have answers to all the questions we wanted. Job didn't either. But we will have come to the place where the answers we do have—an awareness of who God is and his faithfulness to us—are sufficient to allow us to live with hope.

CONCLUSION

Remember, this part of Step 8 isn't about something that you do. *These twelve points are not an action plan. Instead, they are a scavenger hunt.* Your primary task is to know the traits that emerge as you settle into a new, healthier normal and then be on the lookout for them. Each time you see one of these qualities, there are two ways to respond: (a) be encouraged by the fruit of your labor on this journey, and (b) praise God for his faithfulness in bringing you to this point. Enjoy the scavenger hunt!

G4 GROUP DISCUSSION: STEP 8, PART ONE

As you discuss this material in G4 group, these questions are meant to facilitate a more honest and beneficial dialogue about this material. Anyone is free to respond to whichever questions they choose.

Experienced Members

- For you, which of these twelve traits were the first to emerge?
- For you, which of these twelve traits were the last to emerge?

New Members

- These qualities are not just end-of-the-journey realities. Do you already see some of them emerging in the early stages of your journey?
- Which of these qualities—by its absence—helps you understand the impact of your suffering (Step Three) more clearly?
- How can we pray for you?

Everyone

- How did studying this list help you see that a new, healthier normal isn't a perfect, fairy-tale life?
- What qualities of maturity do you see in other members of the group that you can affirm?
- Do we need to discuss any safety-level concerns from the past week?

STEP 8
PART TWO

PREPARING TO TRANSITION FROM G4

The video for this part of Step 8 can be found at: bradhambrick.com/truebetrayal8p2.

We hope G4 has been a wonderful refuge for you, a place where you felt understood and were given the space to make important but difficult decisions. But a refuge is not a home. The long-term source of care, guidance, and fellowship should be your local church. This part of Step 8 is about helping you make that transition well.

However, don't confuse making that transition well with making that transition fast. Take the time you need as you complete your G4 journey. Part of finishing G4 well involves making sure you have the quality of relationships in your church to fill the role G4 has played in recent months. In the coming weeks, you won't come to G4 less, but you should begin to engage in church relationships more. We'll talk about four action items to help you with this transition.

1. **Be in a small group.** Your church may call these groups by a variety of names: small groups, community groups, Sunday school, missional communities, etc. Regardless of the name, these are groups that focus on general discipleship and community. This group will begin to carry the baton that G4 has carried in recent months.

   Consider these differences between G4 and small groups. It is not that one is good, and one is bad. Both are good and serve different roles that are more beneficial or less beneficial in different seasons of life.

   - G4 is a place of targeted discipleship. We have focused on one subject, responding to your spouse's sexual sin.

- Small groups are a place of general discipleship. Small groups focus on developing our whole character.
- G4 is a place of shared experience. Participants in your G4 groups are there because they felt betrayed by their spouse's actions.
- Small groups are a place of varied experiences. Members of a small group bring a greater variety of growth goals and questions to the group.
- G4 is a place of short-term care where we set aside a season of our life to overcome a life-dominating struggle of sin or suffering.
- Small groups are a place of ongoing care. Because the goal of a small group is sanctification as a whole, no one ever graduates from small group. We stay and find new areas to grow.

While it may be scary for some of us to graduate from G4, it serves an important function. *We do not want our struggle to become our identity.* Our identity is not captured in the labels *betrayed*, *forsaken*, or *rejected*. Our identity is a Christ-follower living on mission to know God and enjoy him forever. If we remain long-term in our *True Betrayal* group for our source of discipleship, we inadvertently embrace an identity rooted in our suffering.

> ▶ **Action Step:** If you are not already actively participating in a small group, take the initial step to begin visiting small groups at your church. If you are part of a small group but have reduced your engagement with that group to focus on your G4 journey, begin to reprioritize your small group participation.

2. **Learn accountability and encouragement on a broader scale.** For those of us who are hesitant to allow small groups to fill the role of G4 in our life, it is often because we have found the community in small groups to be more superficial than G4. Sometimes this is the case. G4 may be the first time you have experienced ongoing, Christian accountability and encouragement. G4 is not (or at least

should not be) special. The intentionality and engagement you experienced here, is what God wants for every church member.

▶ **Read Acts 2:42–47 and 4:32–37.** This is a picture of the quality and quantity of engagement God wants in the church. God wants his people to have one heart and one soul (4:32); meaning, our lives aren't hidden from one another and that we are invested in the same mission. God wants his people to meaningfully study the Bible together to build one another up (2:42). God wants his people sharing deep and meaningful fellowship with one another so that no one feels unknown or lonely (2:42).

> We do not want our struggle to become our identity.

Does our experience of church always live up to God's ideal? No. We believe that G4 can play an important role in helping the church grow closer to God's ideal. *G4 needs the church, and the church needs G4.* G4 needs the church so we do not create a struggle-based identity. The church needs G4 so that as people graduate from G4 and take the level of accountability and encouragement they've learned at G4 into the church, the church will become more of what God intended. In this sense, G4 and the church have a symbiotic relationship—each contributes to the thriving of the other.

How do we make our experience in a small group a broad-based-discipleship version of our experience in G4? The seven qualities below describe the kind of relationships you are seeking to build in your small group. These are the marks of discipleship relationships that last:

    a. Voluntary—Accountability is not something you have; it is something you do. You must disclose to benefit from the relationship. Hopefully, the positive experience you have had at G4 will encourage you to remain transparent and vulnerable.

    b. Trusted—The other person is someone you trust, admire their character, and believe has good judgment. You are encouraged to join a small group now so that you can build this trust. Having multiple relationships of trust in your small group should be a prerequisite for graduating from G4.

c. Mutual—Relationships that are one-sided tend to be short-lived. In a small group, you will hear the struggles of others as you share your own. You will help carry their burdens as they help carry your burdens (Galatians 6:1–2).

d. Scheduled—Accountability that is not scheduled tends to fade. This is why small groups that meet on a weekly basis are an ideal place for accountability to occur. Everyone knows when to meet and has a shared expectation for how the accountability conversations will begin.

e. Relational—We want spiritual growth to become a lifestyle not an event. This means that we invite accountability to be a part of our regular conversations, not just part of a weekly meeting. It should mean that there are times when we are doing accountability and don't realize it.

f. Comprehensive—Accountability that exclusively fixates on one subject tends to become repetitive and fade. It also tends to reduce "success" to trusting God in a single area of life.

g. Encouraging—Too often the word *accountability* carries the connotation of a "sin hunt." When that is the case, accountability is only perceived to be working when it is negative. However, accountability that lasts should celebrate growth in character as fervently as it works on slips in character. This means asking each other questions about discouragement in addition to questions about temptations.

Over the coming weeks, as you engage with your small group more, focus on cultivating these qualities in those relationships.

3. **Have a plan for future study.** We walk forward. We drift backward. At G4, you have been a part of an intentional, structured

process. If you leave that structure without a continued plan for deepening your understanding and application of Scripture to your life struggles, you won't be satisfied with the results.

This entire study has been filled with devotional Bible studies. If you have not been taking the time to read the passages and reflect on the devotions that accompany them, consider using those as a guide for daily Bible reading. This will be a way to reinforce what you've learned in this study and further solidify the biblical basis for your progress.

> We walk forward. We drift backward.

Here are two additional resources you are encouraged to read as you complete your G4 journey. Studying through them with a friend from your small group would be a great way to combine action items two and three.

- *Transformative Friendships* by Brad Hambrick. While not written in step-work format, this book brings the same level of intentionality to building friendships that this G4 curriculum has brought to your *True Betrayal* journey.
- *Saints, Sufferers, and Sinners* by Michael Emlet. This book helps you see how the gospel speaks in unique ways to your identity as a Christian (saint), the struggles you cannot control (suffering), and sin. It is a great guide to a comprehensive approach to discipleship.

4. **Write a formal transition plan.** A formal transition plan might sound like this:

   a. I will complete all nine steps of my G4 journey.
   b. I will seek the confirmation of my fellow G4 members that I am ready to graduate.
   c. I am part of a small group that meets [day, time] and [name] leads the group.
   d. I have relationships with [names] that are intentional, discipleship-focused friendships.
   e. The next area of my life that I want to grow in is [growth goal].

    f. The key habits I need to maintain to see continued progress are [list].

    g. The early warning signs that I am regressing in my progress would be [list].

Review your plan with your G4 group. Get their input on what needs to be added. As you continue to work on your final step in your G4 journey, continue to refine and develop this plan.

CONCLUSION

Step 8 is about persevering in our new identity in Christ. G4 assists you best by releasing you to your local church. G4 was a place of refuge and direction when home felt like chaos. G4 was a place you could talk openly when it felt like your words needed to be measured in other environments. But G4 should be temporary because your life is larger than your marriage difficulties.

You have a future that is so much bigger than avoiding pain. Your life is about what God has for you to pursue. Graduating from G4 is a sign that you are ready to transition your primary focus from processing your marital disruption to pursuing God's purposes for your life, which will be the focus of Step 9.

G4 GROUP DISCUSSION: STEP 8, PART TWO

As you discuss this material in G4 group, these questions are meant to facilitate a more honest and beneficial dialogue about this material. Anyone is free to respond to whichever questions they choose.

Experienced Members

- What part of your transition plan is least clear to you and needs development?
- What new growth goals are you excited to invest in once you graduate from G4?

New Members

- How does it encourage you to remember that G4 is a place where you invest a season of your life to overcome a life-dominating struggle, rather than a meeting you're expected to attend for the rest of your life?

- How does it impact you to hear "your life is larger than your marriage difficulties"?
- How can we pray for you?

Everyone

- Which trusted people outside G4 are a part of your support network? How are you cultivating those relationships?
- What other ways are you working to avoid a struggle-based identity?
- Do we need to discuss any safety-level concerns from the past week?

STEP 9
STEWARD all of my life for God's glory.

At the end of this step, I want to be able to say . . .

"God has shown me great grace; grace greater than my pain. I am learning what it means to live out of my new identity in Christ. That has pushed me to ask the question, 'How can I be a conduit of God's grace to others?' As I have sought God, examined my life, and consulted with fellow believers, I believe this [describe] is what it looks like for me to steward God's grace now."

STEP 9
PART ONE

NINE QUESTIONS TO STEWARD YOUR LIFE
FOR GOD'S GLORY

The video for this part of Step 9 can be found at: bradhambrick.com/truebetrayal9p1.

I f the law of God can be summarized in a positive command (Matthew 22:37–40), then we must end this study talking about how to run to God rather than merely how to run from the impact of betrayal. *Life is not about what we avoid but what we pursue.* How we run to God's design for our life finds a unique expression in each person's life.

For this reason, you will do most of the writing in this step because it is your life that is being stewarded for the glory of God. We will simply provide you with questions to consider. The nine questions below guide you through a life assessment as you prayerfully explore what God has for you next.

> ▶ **Read Ephesians 2:8–10.** In G4, we have traveled through the gospel (vv. 8–9) to good works (v. 10). *The nine steps are merely the gospel in slow motion.* We are not now exiting the gospel to do good works but cultivating the fruit of the gospel. Paul says that there are "good works" that "God prepared" for every believer and that these should define our daily lives ("that we should walk in them"; v. 10). This should give you hope that there are answers to the questions you will be asked in Step 9. Because of the promises of Scripture you can be confident that God has a design for your life and wants you to know what it is.

As you read through and answer these **nine questions**, remember God's patience and timing. There will be some aspects of God's design that you can engage immediately. But there will also be ways you want to serve God that will require you to mature more or be equipped before you are prepared to fulfill them. The main thing is to begin to have a vision for life that involves being God's servant and actively engaging that vision where you are currently equipped.

1. **Am I willing to commit my life to whatever God asks of me?** This is a "do not pass go" question. If your answer is no, it will bias the answers you give to each subsequent question. Do not get lost in guilt or pretend that your answer is yes. Rather, identify the obstacle. What is the cost you are unwilling to pay? Put it into words. Wrestle with what it means to trust God with this part of your life too.

   > Life is not about what we avoid but what we pursue.

   Are there specific things you believe God is asking of you? Be sure to record your thoughts on this question before reflecting on the subsequent questions.

2. **What roles have I neglected that God has placed me in?** The first part of being a good steward of one's life is to fulfill one's primary roles with excellence. When Paul says in Ephesians 5:17 that we are to "understand what the will of the Lord is," he goes on to describe God's design for major life roles (spouse, parent, child, and worker in 5:22–6:9).

3. **What are my spiritual gifts?** Stewarding your life for the glory of God involves utilizing the spiritual gifts God has given you. God gives spiritual gifts that coincide with the calling he places on each individual's life. Read Romans 12:1–8 and I Corinthians 12:1–30. If you need further assistance discerning this, talk to a pastor about taking a spiritual gifts inventory.

4. **For what group of people (age, struggle, career, ethnicity, etc.) am I burdened?** From God's earliest covenant with people, his intention was to bless us so that we might be a blessing to others (Genesis 12:2). Investing your life in those you have a burden for allows you to be others-minded and find joy in it.

5. **What am I passionate about?** At this point in the stewardship evaluation, you can begin to see Psalm 37:3–8 fulfilled in your life. What are the God-exalting desires in your life (v. 4)? What wholesome things can you give yourself to and be more energized afterward than before you started?

6. **With what talents or abilities has God blessed me?** These don't have to be spiritual gifts. Read the amazing description of abilities God gave Bezalel and how he used those abilities to serve God (Exodus 31:1–11). Think through the skills and expertise you have accumulated in your life.

7. **What are my unique life experiences?** Both pleasant and unpleasant experiences should be listed. We are sometimes tempted to think that God can only use the good or spiritual experiences of our lives. God is glad to use our successes (Matthew 5:16), but God also delights in displaying his grace by transforming our low points for his glory (2 Corinthians 1:3–5).

8. **Where do my talents and passions match up with the needs in my church and community?** We should seek to steward our lives in cooperation with our local church. God's way of blessing and maturing those we serve is through the body of Christ, the church. By identifying where your gifts, burdens, passions, and abilities fit within or expand your church's ministries, you are maximizing the impact of serving those you seek to bless.

9. **How would God have me bring these things together to glorify him?** This is not a new question but a summary question. Look back over what you have written. Talk about it with your Christian friends, family, mentor, or pastors. Dedicate a time to prayerfully ask God to give you a sense of direction. Then begin serving to steward your life for God's glory.

G4 GROUP DISCUSSION: STEP 9, PART ONE

As you discuss this material in G4 group, these questions are meant to facilitate a more honest and beneficial dialogue about this material. Anyone is free to respond to whichever questions they choose.

Experienced Members

- As you reflected on these questions, what do you believe is God's purpose for you in this next season of life?
- Which of these questions was most beneficial for you in discerning what God has for you next?

New Members

- Does talking about Step 9 create a sense of wanting to rush the journey within you?
- How does seeing the culmination of your G4 journey create hope and motivation for you?
- How can we pray for you?

Everyone

- Can you go through the nine steps and articulate how "the nine steps are merely the gospel in slow motion"?
- Based on the devotional from Ephesians 2, how has this journey helped you understand how to apply to gospel to suffering?
- Do we need to discuss any safety-level concerns from the past week?

APPENDIX A
A Word to G4 Group Leaders

T hank you for your willingness to lead a G4 group! This postscript is a microcosm of *Facilitating Church-Based Counseling Groups: A Leader's Guide for Group-Based Counseling Ministry* (New Growth, 2023), the leader's guide for G4 series books. The points below are explained and illustrated in greater detail in that resource. If you have already read *Facilitating*, this postscript is your cheat sheet reminder page. If you have not yet read *Facilitating*, then this is your "sampler's platter" to entice you to take the next step in training as a counseling group leader.

Here are a few things you need to know about leading a G4 group:

- G4 series curriculums facilitate an **open group model**—meaning anyone can join the group at any time and everyone present is likely to be at a different place on their journey.
- Because G4 is an open group model, your role is *not* to serve as a counselor for each person in the group; instead, you are a **facilitator of the group**.
- As the group facilitator, your two primary tasks are to **lead the discussion** each evening and **manage the morale** of the group.
- The **video teaching** for each segment of this journey is meant to alleviate the pressure for you to feel like a subject matter expert. For this curriculum, the video teaching can be found at **bradhambrick.com/truebetrayal**. The QR code at the beginning of each new section will take participants to the video clip for that section.
- The **expectation for each participant** of the group is to (a) faithfully attend G4, (b) watch the video clip for the section

they are working on, (c) read, reflect, and complete exercises for that section, and (d) come ready to discuss the progress or challenges they faced that week. Everyone works at their own pace, so you're not assessing the pace of their journey, but simply that they are still committed to moving forward.

- Counseling groups like G4 are for those who are **ready to change** or strongly considering their need for change. It is not your role or the role of the group to convince people to take steps they are unwilling to take. The group exists to support, not convince.

- Each **G4 curriculum is intentionally long.** No one should finish nine steps in nine weeks. While that might give you a good education about destructive relationships, it is not sufficient time to cement change over a life-dominating struggle. In reality, you may not finish one part of each step each week. G4 is less about education (mastering content) and more about transformation (accomplishing change). That takes time. G4 is not a race. No prizes are given for finishing first or fast. The reward of a restored life is the fruit of finishing well.

- As you can begin to see, G4 is a **place of support with a curriculum that provides guidance.** As you think of G4, those should be your two guiding principles: First, lead the group in a way that it becomes a place of mutual support. Second, allow the curriculum to provide counsel. The sharing time in a group is when these two components come together as members hear stories of how the curriculum was applied in each other's lives.

- When **someone needs more help than G4 can provide**, help them find a resource in your community that provides that care while continuing (if they are willing) to provide the support of your G4 group. You are not failing if someone needs more than your G4 group can provide. Do what you can do well and point people to additional resources as needed. In most cases, those additional resources will be more effective because of the support of G4. You will notice that there are not a lot of anecdotes in G4 curriculum. That is because the testimony of fellow G4 participants are the most powerful illustrations.

- To accomplish these objectives, we **recommend a schedule** for a G4 group that follows the outline below. Each segment is defined and illustrated in greater depth in *Facilitating Church-Based Counseling Groups*.
  » Welcome and orient new guests.
  » Personal updates (5–10 minutes).
  » Facilitating and sharing (30–40 minutes). These are often done simultaneously or in either order. You are free to lead your group in the way that serves it best.
    ▪ Covering a step or step segment (10–15 minutes).
    ▪ Personal step-work progress and accountability (20–25 minutes).
  » Prayer (5–10 minutes).

Serve your group with these general parameters in mind. Don't underestimate the value of having a weekly place to meet, discuss, and receive encouragement for a shared life struggle. Life-dominating struggles make us feel alone, like no one else could understand. Your group is an oasis that dispels this lie. As the leader, you hold out the hope that while we may not see the change we desire week-to-week, when we look at the lives of faithful participants month-to-month, we are encouraged by God's faithfulness. As we look at the legacy of a group year-to-year, we move from encouragement to amazement at what God accomplishes.

G4 is a long-game ministry. Stay the course, be faithful in your role, encourage participants to persevere in the process, and you will see lives transformed by the gospel in ways that sustain your soul in this weighty ministry!

APPENDIX B

How to Talk to Children When Sexual Sin Affects the Family

W hen sexual sin comes to light in a family, every member of that family is impacted. Not only is the impact *broad*, but the impact is also *unique* in how it affects each family member. The most innocent, and the ones who frequently receive the least quality or quantity of care, are the children.

Children of all ages need both *honesty* and *hope* amid the disruption that inevitably ensues. The facts, which should be age-appropriately honest, need to be delivered clearly but with as much hope as the situation allows. As parents (both offended and offending parent), our instinct is to shield our children from this hurtful reality and to try to make things less painful for them.

"Less painful" is an appropriate goal if it does not come at the cost of being truthful, creating unrealistic expectations, or avoiding legitimate questions of a child. If "less painful" compromises the child's age-appropriate ability to know the truth or ability to anticipate the future (at least to the degree that is possible), then "less painful" produces more harm than benefit.

CASE STUDY

The following case study is a fictitious example of a family of six walking through the process of a mother slowly finding out that her husband is committing adultery with a coworker. A family of six was depicted as a teaching tool to represent more ages of children and desirable responses. It is meant to help you apply the recommendations that follow by providing an example that is less personal than your current situation.

Caitlyn is three years old. She stays home with her mom most days, enjoys being outside, and loves reading stories with her dad. She has older siblings who attend school. Caleb is six and in the first grade, Kayla is eleven and just entering middle school, while Jacob is fourteen and starting high school. From the outside, all looks good for this family.

The family is active at church. The children are involved in sports, drama, and other extracurricular activities. Dad works hard to support the family financially. They look like your typical American family, the kind that you would want to have over for dinner. But behind closed doors things are quite different. Dad is critical and emotionally absent much of the time. He will do what is asked, but he rarely seems excited and does not initiate family time or individual activities with the children. He asks the standard questions about grades, school, and friends, but he seems uninterested beyond these surface-level engagements.

Mom does her best to compensate for Dad's lack of involvement by over-involvement. She tries to make sure the kids have everything they need and want. This creates tension between Mom and Dad because they can never get ahead financially. For this and other reasons, neither values time with the other.

The most recent tension appeared after Mom found some emails Dad had sent to a coworker. The emails seemed flirtatious and inappropriate. Dad quickly minimized them and proceeded to berate Mom for looking at his personal activities and not trusting him.

Over the course of the next few months, Mom continued to see emails and eventually text messages that confirmed her suspicion that Dad was having an affair. After multiple attempts at confrontation and many arguments, Dad admitted his actions. Mom was devastated, Dad was angry, *and the children were confused.*

WHAT DOES THE FAMILY DO NOW?

The scenario above is meant to serve as a framework for caring for children when a parent's sexual sin impacts their family. There are many things to keep in mind as you prepare for this type of conversation. The points below are meant to orient you to how these situations affect a child, the appropriate expectations of a child when they first learn of the sexual sin, the expectations after learning of the sexual sin, and the type of assistance a child needs to process this information.

- An event of this magnitude and the subsequent parental conflict, absence, and distraction can be severely disruptive for children, even adult children outside the home.
- If your child has not yet reached puberty or has no knowledge of or exposure to sex, your conversations about what has happened should *not* describe what happened in sexual language.
- As children age and develop, which includes their social development and sexual awareness, they may ask questions about things that have happened during this time. Answering these questions in age-appropriate ways is an important part of helping them process their grief.
- Your child's feelings may be more intense or less intense than the feelings of the offended spouse. Both parents need to accept whatever feelings surface, help the child to name those feelings, and understand how those feelings relate to the changes in their life, home, and family.
- If an experience of this magnitude happens to children who are preschool age or older, they will remember it and may need to process those memories at later developmental stages as they are able to fully comprehend more of their personal family history.
- Most children will not process their emotions about an event of this magnitude (that is, healthily assimilate these events into their life story) until they feel safe enough to do it. Once you and your spouse have reached a better place and feel as if you are moving on, may be when the children begin to process their feelings. This will feel like it drags out the healing process for the parents, but you cannot rush your children through their

process any more than the offending spouse could be rushed to repentance or the offended spouse rushed to forgiveness.

- The biggest damage that has been done is undermining the child's sense of security at home and definition of love. This is true regardless of the age of the child. The initial care and after-care for a child should focus upon providing a healthy sense of security and balanced expression of love.

- When it comes to having the "what's going on" talk, the ideal situation would be for both parents and potentially a neutral, trusted third person to talk to the children together (especially if one or both parents are likely to become emotionally disrupted during the conversation).

- The content of the "what's going on" talk should be decided before talking to the child. If an agreement cannot be reached, wait until an agreement can be reached. The delay should be as short as possible because the longer you wait, the more confusing the resulting changes become for the children.

- There may need to be more than one conversation, depending on the age differences of your children. If your children are in the same developmental range, one conversation with all family members present will suffice. If your children are at different ages and developmental stages, do not try to talk to everyone at the same time. But do make sure that what you say to everyone is as consistent in content as age-appropriateness will allow. Older children should be told if there are things their younger siblings do not know and do not need to know at the current time.

- Make sure someone in your children's lives will be their support. This is especially important for the older children and even children who are out of the house and often get overlooked in this process.

- If the sexual sin will not result in lifestyle changes (parental separation, divorce, job loss, pregnancy, etc.), seek counsel about what to disclose to your children. Your children may only need to know that you and your spouse have encountered problems because of hurtful choices by a parent and you both are trying to make things better.

- Encourage children to ask questions as they have them. It is unreasonable and unhealthy to expect children to formulate their questions at the information meeting. When you give them the freedom to ask questions, it is wise to also tell them you don't have all the answers and that there may be some things that will stay between Mom and Dad. Remember that children process at a slower pace and may ask questions well after this initial conversation. Being prepared for this prevents the emotional processing of your children from setting you back emotionally. A negative emotional response by the parents to a child's question often reinforces the common false belief that the child has some responsibility for what happened in the marriage.

- Guard yourself from feeling the need to "make up" for what is happening in your family. Neither gifts nor penance will make up for the offense or alleviate its impact. If anything, they will teach a distorted view of the gospel, repentance, forgiveness, reconciliation, and family. Patiently submitting to the reconciliation process (when possible) is the most helpful thing for your children. Only God can heal the hurt in your children, not imbalanced love.

GUIDANCE FOR CONVERSATIONS BY AGE

If the sexual sin will result in a lifestyle change—parental separation, divorce, job loss, pregnancy, etc.—you will need to have discussions with the children. We will consider each stage of development, but all the previous material should be considered relevant, unless something said about the next maturation level contradicts the earlier material. Therefore, regardless of your children's ages, please read all the sections below.

Birth Through Five Years

While you may think that children from birth to age five are unable to tell something is going on, children are very perceptive at reading their environment. If Mom is frequently crying, Dad is angry, or there is bickering and fighting, even young children can tell. They may become more "needy," experience developmental delays, or regress in already learned skills as expressions of how changes in the home environment are affecting them.

The goal for parents is to be both authentic and reassuring. (Faking calm only when you think the child is looking reveals that their parents are not being honest.) Although your spouse may have had an affair, you are still a parent. You cannot spend days crying, angry, or searching for more information without impacting your children. If restraining these behaviors is hard for you, ask for help. Take time to see a counselor or ask a friend to work through *True Betrayal* with you.

Don't have conversations with your preschooler unless a decision is made for the offending spouse to leave for an extended or indefinite period. If spouses are staying together and no one is moving out, preschool children do not need to know what has happened. Later, when they are adults or older teens, there may be a time when it's beneficial to share what God has done or what happened. But preschool children have no way of comprehending what you would tell them. The main goal at this age is to provide consistency, love, and safety—to fulfill their greatest needs. Lean on friends and trusted caregivers during this time.

If the offending parent leaves the house and the child is between two and five years old, you should give some explanation as to where the parent is going. The optimal plan would be for this conversation to be factual and done together or potentially with a neutral, trusted third person present (especially if one or both parents are likely to become emotionally disrupted during the conversation). The person leaving should be the primary speaker and communicate the following information:

> I am going to stay with (location—the child will need to know because it can cause more anxiety to say he or she is just going away) for (duration—it is important to tell the child the duration so they know an ending point. If a duration cannot be determined, then be honest and tell them you don't know how long). I know it will be hard for you to be away from me, so I will come to see you (give visitation plan).

Notice in this conversation that you did not give the preschooler the answer to the "why" question. Most will ask, but some may not. Do not try to answer the "why" question for preschoolers unless they ask because it is hard for them to spontaneously transition to abstract thinking, especially in an emotionally powerful setting.

If they ask why, the offending parent should tell them the following:

> I made some choices that I should not have made. These things really hurt Mommy/Daddy. Sometimes, if we really hurt someone, we need to give them time and space. So I am going to (location) to give Mommy/Daddy some space. [Reiterate your love for them and that you will miss them.]

There will be tears, shock, and an inability to comprehend what you are saying. Children's brains are not developed for this type of transition. They do not have the life experience to grasp what it means or know what to do when a parent is absent for punitive reasons ("punishment" is the category they have for comprehending a marriage time-out). Be patient. Prepare for tantrums and disruptions to their sleeping and eating patterns.

The experience of children (at any of the ages discussed) will look a lot like grief because they are grieving the loss of what they have known as normal. Thinking of their response as grief rather than defiance will help you comfort them.

If the parents stay together, it is important to keep a preschooler's routine as normal as possible. Enrolling in programs like Parent's Day Out or preschool for a couple of days per week may allow the offended parents time to work through what has happened.

As a parent, the offended spouse bears the role of modeling how to respond to these types of hurts. This includes encouraging the child to express their feelings and telling the offending parent what they are thinking. You are not responsible for the other parent's behavior, but you can teach your child during this difficult time how to handle conflict and express emotions healthily. It is important to think about what you are teaching your child through your modeling. Children will learn more about emotions, reconciliation, and relationships from what they see you do than what you "teach" them during this time.

Elementary-Age Children

Elementary-age children are more verbal and have more cognitive ability than preschoolers, but they should not have sexual knowledge or understanding yet. When talking with your elementary-aged child about what has happened, it is wise to say things like these:

"Mom/Dad made choices that hurt me."
"Mom and Dad are working on making our marriage better."
"Mom/Dad is working on forgiving . . ."
"Mom/Dad is working on building trust with . . ."

Children at this age will ask lots of questions. They may ask "What did you do?" "Are you getting divorced?" "Do you still love Mom/Dad?" Be honest where you can, but when the answer to their question is not age-appropriate or is undecided, it is appropriate to say, "Some of what happens between Mom and Dad is not helpful for you to know," or "We are still deciding about that."

Reassurance of your love for them is important during and after each of these conversations. It is beneficial to point them toward God and prayer. Pray with your child after these conversations, but pray in ways that express where they are at. Don't try to teach them what to think or how to respond as you talk to God. Teaching with our eyes closed isn't really praying. Listen to your child and allow your prayer to model how to express their feelings to God.

These conversations are an opportunity to talk about how even parents let them down, but God is faithful and will not let them down. If the offending spouse decides to leave the home for a time, then it will be necessary to have a conversation much like you had with your two- to five-year-old.

Middle / High School Children

Middle school and high school children are becoming sexually aware. By this age most parents have had "the talk" explaining sex. If this is the case, then being factually honest about sexual sin is appropriate. You would rather your child hear your confession about what happened than learn about it from someone else.

If the sin is adultery or an emotional affair, you should not give details about the sexual relationship. When hurt and angry, it is easy to be more vivid or derogatory than is necessary. There is no social or redemptive value in a child having that information. However, it is important to share information that allows them to understand their family story and navigate their social world.

Children in these age categories will likely be thinking about how this affects their life. Teens are still at an egocentric stage of development, so a primary fear for them often centers on how their life will be altered. One tendency for teens will be to take the role of protector for the offended spouse. This is an understandable but unhealthy role for a teenager. While it is natural for there to be a loss of trust with the offending parent, an emerging "us" (teen and offended parent) versus "them" (offending parent) makes it harder to maintain a healthy parent-child relationship in the years before the child becomes an independent adult.

> Listen to your child and allow your prayer to model how to express their feelings to God.

Another frequent dynamic is for the teen to defend or excuse the actions of the offending parent as an expression of their desire for things to get back to normal. The offended parent needs to be careful not to be defensive or condemning of their teenager's compassion. Neither should the offending parent leverage this compassion to form an alliance with that child. Both parents should affirm that this is a hard situation with few win–win choices as the parents work to determine the future of the marriage and family. Give the teen time and space to continue processing their own feelings. Ask if they have questions, and provide the freedom to appropriately share the emotions they are experiencing.

Adult Children

Sometimes children who have moved out of the house are thought to be unaffected. This is not true. Children, regardless of their age, will feel like their basis of security is shaken when their parents' marriage is traumatized or dissolved. Adult children may feel like everything they knew growing up was false. They will question whether the offending parent was really who they thought they were. Disclosure of sexual sin can be used as an excuse to turn from God and how they were raised.

It is immensely valuable for adult children to have an adult who knows them and is aware of the situation reach out to them and check on them regularly. Unless someone reaches out to them, they are forced to process things alone and without the benefit of seeing what their parents are going through. An objective opinion, not just what their mom and dad are saying, will be important for them to process these changes in their home of origin.

WHEN A CHILD FINDS OUT FIRST

What do you do if your child comes to you because they saw a parent looking at things on the internet or flirting with someone in public? In this situation, it is important for the offended spouse to assure the child of the following things:

- They did the right thing by coming to you. Continue to validate that they did the right thing in speaking up, that they are not in trouble, and that they did not get anyone else in trouble (witnesses don't cause problems; they only observe them).
- You will do your best to find out what happened. Once you do have an answer, plan a time for both parents to talk with the children.

If a child is in the position of witnessing sexual sin and then informs the betrayed parent or confronts the offending parent, it is more likely they will feel responsible for the ensuing disruption in the family because they had an active role in the sin coming to light. They will need consistent reassurance that they did not cause the disruption. Ideally, this reassurance should come from both parents as well as the adult individual identified as supporter of the children.

Notes

STEP 1, PART ONE

1. Gary and Mona Shriver, *Unfaithful: Hope and Healing After Infidelity* (David C. Cook, 2009), 41, 177.

2. Stefanie Carnes, *Mending a Shattered Heart: A Guide for Partners of Sex Addicts* (Gentle Path Press, 2011), 54, 59, 75.

3. If you live outside the United States, this Wikipedia page catalogs comparable domestic violence hotline numbers in other countries: https://en.wikipedia.org/wiki/List_of_domestic_violence_hotlines.

STEP 1, PART TWO

1. Excerpt from *False Love: 9 Steps Toward Sexual Integrity* (New Growth Press, upcoming publication, 2025).

2. Winston T. Smith, *Help! My Spouse Committed Adultery: First Steps for Dealing with Betrayal* (New Growth Press, 2020), 15.

STEP 1, PART FOUR

1. Carnes, *Mending a Shattered Heart*, 105.

2. Douglas Rosenau, *A Celebration of Sex: A Guide to Enjoying God's Gift of Sexual Intimacy* (Thomas Nelson, 2002), 347.

STEP 2, PART ONE

1. Douglas Rosenau, *A Celebration of Sex: A Guide to Enjoying God's Gift of Sexual Intimacy* (Thomas Nelson, 2002), 348.

2. Mark Laaser, *Healing the Wounds of Sexual Addiction* (Zondervan, 2004), 31.

3. Stefanie Carnes, *Mending a Shattered Heart: A Guide for Partners of Sex Addicts* (Gentle Path Press, 2011), 29.

4. Carnes, *Mending a Shattered Heart*, 31.

5. Rosenau, *A Celebration of Sex*, 349.

6. Winston T. Smith, *Help! My Spouse Committed Adultery: First Steps for Dealing with Betrayal* (New Growth Press, 2020), 6, 19.

7. Wayne Grudem, *Systematic Theology* (Zondervan, 1994), 493.

STEP 2, PART TWO

1. Carnes, *Mending a Shattered Heart*, 31.

STEP 3, PART TWO

1. Kathy Gallagher, *When His Secret Sin Breaks Your Heart: Letters to Hurting Wives* (Pure Life Ministries, 2003), 94–95.

2. Stefanie Carnes, *Mending a Shattered Heart: A Guide for Partners of Sex Addicts* (Gentle Path Press, 2011), 14.

3. The three-month distinction helps us see the difference between trauma and post-traumatic stress. To say that event is traumatic indicates that the event was severe. To say that an experience resulted in post-traumatic stress indicates that the impact of that event persisted after safety was reestablished. If you are looking for a Christian counselor who is experienced with trauma, consider the Christian Trauma Healing Network as a place to begin your search (christiantraumahealingnetwork.org).

STEP 4, PART ONE

1. Philip Yancey, *Disappointment with God: Three Questions No One Asks Aloud* (Zondervan, 1992), 235.

STEP 4, PART TWO

1. Harry Schaumburg, *False Intimacy: Understanding the Struggle of Sexual Addiction* (NavPress, 1997), 103.

2. Gary and Mona Shriver, *Unfaithful: Hope and Healing After Infidelity* (David C. Cook, 2009), 110.

STEP 4, PART THREE

1. Douglas Rosenau, *A Celebration of Sex: A Guide to Enjoying God's Gift of Sexual Intimacy* (Thomas Nelson, 2002), 347.

2. Winston Smith, *Help! My Spouse Committed Adultery: First Steps for Dealing with Betrayal* (New Growth Press, 2020), 9–11.

STEP 4, PART FOUR

1. Leslie Vernick, *How to Act Right When Your Spouse Acts Wrong* (Waterbrook Press, 2009), 38.

2. Gary and Mona Shriver, *Unfaithful*, 61, 75, 98.

STEP 5, PART ONE

1. Gary and Mona Shriver, *Unfaithful: Hope and Healing After Infidelity* (David C. Cook, 2009), 131–32.

STEP 5, PART TWO

1. If you feel particularly stuck at this point, consider my book *Angry with God: An Honest Journey through Suffering and Betrayal* (New Growth Press, 2022). It is a book about grief—specifically about grief that gets stuck in the anger phase making us feel that God is against us.

STEP 6, PART ONE

1. If you are curious about Paul writing more than two letters to the Corinthians, see "Paul Actually Wrote Four Letters to the Corinthians," *Zondervan Academic* (blog), July 6, 2020, https://zondervanacademic.com/blog/four-letters-corinthians.

STEP 6, PART TWO

1. Diane Langberg, *Counseling Survivors of Sexual Abuse* (Xulon Press, 2003), 31, 57.

STEP 6, PART THREE

1. C. S. Lewis, *The Four Loves* (HarperOne, Reissue Edition, 2017), 169.

2. Miroslav Volf, *The End of Memory: Remembering Rightly in a Violent World* (Eerdmans, 2006), 80, 103, 108–9, and 192.

STEP 7, PART ONE

1. If forgiveness is still a sticking point for you and you want more guidance than Step 7 provides, consider reading my book *Making Sense of Forgiveness: Moving from Hurt toward Hope* (New Growth Press, 2021).

2. Mike Summers, *Help! My Spouse Has Been Unfaithful* (Shepherd Press, 2014), 30.

3. Winston Smith, *Help! My Spouse Committed Adultery: First Steps for Dealing with Betrayal* (New Growth Press, 2020), 18.

STEP 7, PART TWO

1. This material is modified and adapted from Brad Hambrick, *Making Sense of Forgiveness*, chapter 13, "Identifying Wise Trust on a Spectrum" (New Growth Press, 2021). Used by publisher permission.

STEP 7, PART THREE

1. Smith, *Help! My Spouse Committed Adultery*, 16.

2. Gary and Mona Shriver, *Unfaithful: Hope and Healing After Infidelity* (David C. Cook, 2009), 103.

STEP 7, PART FOUR

1. If you are unfamiliar with what a church discipline process looks like, this link provides a tutorial for church leaders on implementing the Matthew 18 process: bradhambrick.com/churchdiscipline/. Your reason for reviewing it would be to become more familiar with the steps ahead if your church pursued a disciplinary response with your spouse.

STEP 8, PART ONE

1. H. Norman Wright, *Experiencing Grief* (B&H, 2004), 79–80.

2. If this is a sticking point for you, I encourage you to read the article "Making Peace with Romans 8:28" available at http://bradhambrick.com/romans828/.

3. Richard Foster, *Celebration of Discipline: The Path to Spiritual Growth* (Harper, 2000).

4. Douglas Rosenau, *A Celebration of Sex: A Guide to Enjoying God's Gift of Sexual Intimacy* (Thomas Nelson, 2002), 351.

OVERCOMING ADDICTION

Brad Hambrick

If you are willing to admit that alcohol and/or drugs are disrupting your life, *Overcoming Addiction* will guide you toward healing. Counselor Brad Hambrick provides a 9-step framework to help you reclaim your life and experience the freedom God wants for you.

NAVIGATING DESTRUCTIVE RELATIONSHIPS

Brad Hambrick

All relationships disappoint us from time to time. But some relationships are destructive, especially those marked by addiction, abuse, and/or life-dominating problems. *Navigating Destructive Relationships*, a support group curriculum, provides you with a safe and stable place where you can name what's going on and turn toward God.

MOBILIZING CHURCH-BASED COUNSELING

Brad Hambrick

Mobilizing Church-Based Counseling, the first book in the Church-Based Counseling series, provides a framework for guiding churches through the process of building a volunteer-led counseling ministry.

FACILITATING COUNSELING GROUPS

Brad Hambrick and John Chapman

Facilitating Counseling Groups, the second book in the Church-Based Counseling series, provides training for lay leaders to guide a group-based church counseling ministry (G4 model) that addresses common life struggles.

TRANSFORMATIVE FRIENDSHIPS

Brad Hambrick

Transformative Friendships, the third book in the Church-Based Counseling series, provides a solid relational foundation for church members outside a structured counseling ministry by utilizing seven simple questions to build deep, intentional relationships that enrich the lives of individuals and the church as a whole.

NEW GROWTH PRESS   newgrowthpress.com